Edgar

THE PLAYWRIGHT

Susan Painter

METHUEN DRAMA

First published in Great Britain in 1996
by Methuen Drama
an imprint of Reed International Books Ltd
Michelin House, 81 Fulham Road, London SW3 6RB
and Auckland, Melbourne, Singapore and Toronto
and distributed in the United States of America
by Heinemann, a division of Reed Elsevier Inc.
361 Hanover Street, Portsmouth, New Hampshire NH 03801 3959

Copyright © 1996 by Susan Painter

The author has asserted her moral rights

A CIP catalogue record for this book is available
at the British Library

ISBN 0 413 69960 9

Typeset by Wilmaset Ltd, Birkenhead, Wirral
Printed in Great Britain by
Cox & Wyman Ltd, Reading, Berkshire

Contents

To Jamie

Illustrations

Chronology

1948   Born (26 February) in Birmingham, into a theatrical family.

1952   Saw his first stage play, *Beauty and the Beast* by Nicholas Stuart Grey, at the Birmingham Repertory Theatre.

1958   Wrote 'The Life and Times of William Shakespeare'.

1961–65   At Oundle school. Played Miss Prism in *The Importance of Being Earnest*. Designed *Henry IV, Part One* and *The Fire Raisers*. Directed *The Caretaker* and *Mother Courage and her Children*. Read Oscar Wilde, edited the poetry magazine, and was active in CND.

1966   Taught at Hallfield preparatory school for one term.

1966–69   Studied drama at Manchester University. Wrote and directed 'The Author' for student drama group. Directed *Salome*. Chaired Socialist Society. Edited student newspaper, the *Independent*. Built his talent as a public speaker. BA in Drama, 1969.

1969–72   Journalist on *Bradford Telegraph and Argus*. Assistant reporter in the John Poulson investigation. Met Chris Parr (Fellow in Theatre at Bradford University). *Two Kinds of Angel*, 1970, commissioned by Parr, first professionally performed and published play. Wrote and had performed eighteen plays including four agitprop plays for the General Will company set up by Bradford students. Acted (in Bradford and Edinburgh): God in Howard Brenton's *Scott of the Antarctic*, Captain Bligh in Richard Crane's 'Mutiny on the Bounty', Flashman in Richard Crane's 'Tom

Brown', a rocker in Richard Crane's 'Oil', the title role in *Toad of Toad Hall*, and George in John Grillo's 'George and Moira Entertain a Member of the Opposite Sex to Dinner'. Political position: 'soft Trotskyite'. Close to International Socialists.

1972   Became full-time writer. Collaborated on 'England's Ireland' with Tony Bicât, Howard Brenton, Brian Clark, Francis Fuchs, David Hare and Snoo Wilson.

1972–74   Fellowship in Creative Writing at Leeds Polytechnic.

1973   First television play (for Granada), 'The Eagle has Landed'.

1974–75   Resident playwright at Birmingham Repertory Theatre.

1974–78   Taught undergraduate course in playwriting at Birmingham University. Among his students were Louise Page and Terry Johnson.

1975   Co-founded Theatre Writers' Union.

1976   Anti-fascist play *Destiny* (directed by Ron Daniels, for the Royal Shakespeare Company [RSC] at The Other Place, Stratford-upon-Avon).

1977   *Destiny* transferred to the Aldwych Theatre (the main London home of the RSC at that time), winning the John Whiting Award. Became speaker for the Anti-Nazi League. Wrote a detailed analysis, 'Racism, Fascism and the Politics of the National Front' for *Race and Class*. First original radio play, *Ecclesiastes*.

1977–78   *Wreckers* for 7:84; *Our Own People* for Pirate Jenny; *Teendreams* (with Susan Todd) for Monstrous Regiment. Adapted *The Jail Diary of Albie Sachs* (directed by Howard Davies, for the RSC at the Warehouse Theatre, London) and *Mary Barnes* (directed by Peter Farago, for the Birmingham Repertory Theatre Studio, and transferring to the Royal Court Theatre in 1979).

1978–79   Wrote a pair of articles for the Socialist Workers Party's *Socialist Review* (1978) which were reprinted as one in *Theatre Quarterly* (1979): 'Ten Years of Political Theatre, 1968–1978'; the *TQ* article has become the most frequently cited piece on the subject. Spent a year in America on Bicentennial Fellowship. Rethought his political position.

1979   Married Eve Brook, then lecturer, later Birmingham City Councillor.

1980   Adapted *The Life and Adventures of Nicholas Nickleby* (directed by Trevor Nunn and John Caird, assisted by Leon Rubin, for the RSC at the Aldwych Theatre). Society of West End Theatres and New York Tony awards.

1981   Joined the Labour Party.

1983   *Maydays* (directed by Ron Daniels, for the RSC at the Barbican Theatre). *Plays and Players* Best Play award.

1984–88 Literary adviser to the RSC.

1984   Active in move to amalgamate Theatre Writers' Union and Writers' Guild of Great Britain. Awarded honorary MA degree by Bradford University.

1985   *Entertaining Strangers*, a community play for Dorchester (commissioned and directed by Ann Jellicoe). Wrote 'The Free or the Good', a piece emphasising the distinction between the authoritarian and libertarian elements of Thatcherism.

1986   First film, 'Lady Jane' (directed by Trevor Nunn, for Paramount Pictures).

1987   Revised *Entertaining Strangers* for the National Theatre (directed by Peter Hall at the Cottesloe Theatre). *That Summer* for Hampstead Theatre (directed by Michael Attenborough).

1988   Published a collection of political and theatre journalism, *The Second Time as Farce*.

1989   Honorary Associate Artist of the RSC. Founded Britain's first MA course in Playwriting Studies at

Birmingham University. *Heartlanders* (with Stephen Bill and Anne Devlin), a celebratory play for Birmingham (directed by Chris Parr for the Birmingham Repertory Theatre). *Vote for Them* (with Neil Grant) for BBC Television.

1990   Initiated a series of annual conferences at Birmingham University. *The Shape of the Table* (directed by Jenny Killick, for the Royal National Theatre) was the first of a number of plays directly concerned with Eastern Europe.

1991   Awarded honorary Fellowship at Birmingham Polytechnic. Elected Chair of Theatre Writers' Union. 'A Movie Starring Me' for BBC Radio. Adapted *The Strange Case of Dr Jekyll and Mr Hyde* (directed by Peter Wood, for the RSC). Wrote film script 'Parallel Bars' and essay 'From Metroland to the Medicis: The Cultural Politics of the City State'.

1992   'Buying a Landslide' (directed by Simon Curtis, for BBC Television). Wrote text for the British Council exhibition titled Contemporary Dramatists. Appointed Honorary Professor in the School of Performance Studies at Birmingham University.

1993   Awarded honorary degree of DUniv by Surrey University.

1994   'Citizen Locke' (directed by Agnieszka Piotrowska, for Channel Four). *Pentecost* (directed by Michael Attenborough, for the RSC at The Other Place, Stratford-upon-Avon).

1995   *Pentecost* transferred to the Young Vic Theatre, London.

Note: This list makes selective use of the *File on Edgar* brief chronology.

The Plays of David Edgar

This list indicates first productions. Plays with titles in italics have been published.

One-Act Plays

Two Kinds of Angel: Bradford University, July 1970.

'A Truer Shade of Blue': Bradford University, August 1970.

'Still Life: Man in Bed': Pool Theatre, Edinburgh, May 1971.

'Acid': Bradford University, July 1971.

'The National Interest': Bradford University, then General Will Theatre Company, August 1971.

'Conversation in Paradise': Edinburgh University, October 1971.

'Tedderella': Pool Theatre, Edinburgh, December 1971.

'The Rupert Show': General Will Theatre Company, January 1972.

'State of Emergency': General Will Theatre Company, August 1972.

'Road to Hanoi' (scene in 'Point 101'): Paradise Foundry Theatre Company, October 1972.

'A Fart for Europe' (with Howard Brenton): Royal Court Theatre Upstairs, London, January 1973.

'Chamberlains' (section of 'Up Spaghetti Junction'): Birmingham Repertory Theatre, February 1973.

'Gangsters': Soho Poly, London, February 1973.

Baby Love: Leeds Playhouse, March 1973.

'Liberated Zone': Bingley College of Education, June 1973.

'The Eagle Has Landed': Liverpool University, November 1973.

The National Theatre: Open Space, London, October 1975.

Ball Boys (part of *Blood Sports*): Royal Shakespeare Company at Newcastle, March 1977.

Revue

'The Perils of Bardfrod' (with Richard Crane): Theatre in the Mill, Bradford University, November 1976.

Full-length Plays

'Bloody Rosa': Manchester University, at the Edinburgh Fringe Festival, August 1971.

'The End': Bradford University, March 1972.

'Excuses Excuses': Belgrade Theatre Studio, Coventry, May 1972.

'Rent, or Caught in the Act': General Will Theatre Company, May 1972.

'England's Ireland' (with Tony Bicât, Howard Brenton, Brian Clark, Francis Fuchs, David Hare and Snoo Wilson): Shoot Theatre Company, Mickery Theatre, Amsterdam, September 1972, then on tour.

'Not with a Bang but a Whimper': Leeds Polytechnic, November 1972.

'Death Story': Birmingham Repertory Theatre Studio, November 1972.

'The Case of the Workers' Plane': Bristol New Vic, June 1973; (as 'Concorde Cabaret'): Avon Touring Company, January 1975.

'Operation Iskra': Paradise Foundry Theatre Company, September 1973.

Dick Deterred: Bush Theatre, London, February 1974.

'The Dunkirk Spirit': General Will Theatre Company, January 1974.

'The All-Singing All-Talking Golden Oldie Rock Revival Ho Chi Minh Peace Love and Revolution Show': Bingley College of Education, March 1974.

'Man Only Dines': Leeds Polytechnic, June 1974.

O Fair Jerusalem: Birmingham Repertory Theatre Studio, May 1975.

'Summer Sports': Birmingham Arts Lab, July 1975; (as *Blood Sports*): Bush Theatre, London, June 1976.

'Events Following the Closure of a Motorcycle Factory': Birmingham Repertory Theatre Studio, February 1976.

Saigon Rose: Traverse Theatre, Edinburgh, July 1976.

Destiny: Royal Shakespeare Company at The Other Place, Stratford-upon-Avon, September 1976, transferring to the Aldwych Theatre, London, May 1977.

Wreckers: 7:84 Theatre Company, England, Barnfield Theatre, Exeter, February 1977, then on tour.

Our Own People: Pirate Jenny Theatre Company, November 1977.

The Jail Diary of Albie Sachs (adaptation of the book with the same title by Albie Sachs): Royal Shakespeare Company at the Warehouse Theatre, London, June 1978.

Mary Barnes (adaptation of *Mary Barnes: Two Accounts of a Journey Through Madness* by Mary Barnes and Joseph Berke): Birmingham Repertory Theatre Studio, August 1978, transferring to the Royal Court Theatre, London, January 1979.

Teendreams (with Susan Todd): Monstrous Regiment, January 1979; (in revised version): Bristol University Drama Department, March 1987.

The Life and Adventures of Nicholas Nickleby (adaptation of the novel by Charles Dickens): Royal Shakespeare Company at the Aldwych Theatre, London, previewed June 1980, opened July

1980, revived November 1980 and April 1981, transferring to Plymouth Theatre, New York, October 1981.

Maydays: Royal Shakespeare Company at the Barbican Theatre, London, October 1983.

Entertaining Strangers: A Play for Dorchester: Colway Theatre Trust at St Mary's Church, Dorchester, November 1985.

Entertaining Strangers (new version): National Theatre at the Cottesloe Theatre, London, October 1987.

That Summer: Hampstead Theatre, London, July 1987.

Heartlanders (with Stephen Bill and Anne Devlin): Birmingham Repertory Theatre, October 1989.

The Shape of the Table: Royal National Theatre at the Cottesloe Theatre, London, November 1990.

The Strange Case of Dr Jekyll and Mr Hyde (adaptation of the novella by Robert Louis Stevenson): Royal Shakespeare Company at the Barbican Theatre, London, November 1991.

Pentecost: Royal Shakespeare Company at The Other Place, Stratford-upon-Avon, October 1994.

Television Plays

'The Eagle Has Landed' (version of stage play): Granada Television, April 1973.

'Sanctuary' (adaptation of 'Gangsters'): Scottish Television, December 1973.

'I Know What I Meant': Granada Television, July 1974.

'Baby Love' (version of stage play): BBC Play for Today, November 1974.

'Concorde Cabaret' (version of stage play): Harlech Television, October 1975.

'Censors' (with Robert Muller and Hugh Whitemore): Eleventh Hour, BBC, June 1975.

The Midas Connection: Eleventh Hour, BBC, August 1975.

'Destiny' (version of stage play): BBC Play for Today, January 1978.

'The Jail Diary of Albie Sachs' (version of stage play): Channel Four, November 1982.

'Nicholas Nickleby' (version of stage play): Channel Four, November 1982.

Vote for Them (three part play, with Neil Grant): BBC2, June 1989.

'Buying a Landslide': BBC2, September 1992.

'Citizen Locke': Channel Four, April 1994.

Radio Plays

Schools Radio: 'The Owners': March 1974; 'Bad Buy': April 1975; 'Hero or Villain': March 1976; 'Do Something – Somebody': May 1977.

Ecclesiastes: BBC Radio Four, April 1977.

'Destiny' (version of stage play): BBC Radio Four, January 1979.

'Saigon Rose' (version of stage play): BBC Radio Three, April 1979.

'The Jail Diary of Albie Sachs' (adaptation by Madeline Sotheby of stage play): BBC Radio Three, June 1979.

'Maydays' (adaptation by Christer Brosjö of stage play): Swedish Radio, May 1987.

'A Movie Starring Me': BBC Radio Four, November 1991.

'The Shape of the Table' (adaptation by Hilary Norrish of stage play): BBC World Service, October 1992.

'That Summer' (version of stage play): BBC World Service, August 1993.

'Mary Barnes' (version of stage play): BBC Radio Four, June 1995.

Cinema

'Lady Jane': Paramount Pictures, 1986.

Acknowledgements

I am most grateful to David Edgar for allowing me access to unpublished scripts and patiently answering my numerous questions in several lengthy interviews. Michael Attenborough, Michael Billington, Simon Callow, Ron Daniels, Ann Jellicoe, Rachel Kavanaugh, Ian McDiarmid, John McGrath, Chris Parr and Lily Susan Todd were generous in finding time for interviews. I want to thank Peter Wood who granted me the privilege of rehearsal attendance with regard to his RSC production of *The Strange Case of Dr Jekyll and Mr Hyde*. The BBC gave permission to quote from the following radio interviews: Robert Cushman, *Talking Theatre*, first broadcast on BBC Radio Four, 27 January 1988; and *Kaleidoscope*, first broadcast on BBC Radio Four, 2 September 1992, and the television interview on *The Late Show*, first broadcast on BBC2, 9 November 1994. Many friends gave support and encouragement: in particular, I would like to thank David Allen, Peter Billingham, Bill Bray, Burt Caesar, Claire Cousins, Robert Gordon, Jane Harrison, Miri Lawrence, Irmgard Maassen, Catherine MacKinnon, Derek Paget, Lucy Rothstein and Jinnie Schiele. My greatest debt is to James Redmond.

Introduction:
secretary for the times

> The best review I've ever had was when Michael Billington said that, like Balzac, David Edgar seems to be a secretary for our times. And that defined, rather more precisely than I'd ever defined before, what I'd like to be. I'd like to be a secretary for the times through which I'm living.   David Edgar, 1981[1]

On 14 June 1980 the two parts of *The Life and Adventures of Nicholas Nickleby* were presented together for the first time. The fifteen-minute ovation that followed was to be typical of the ecstatic reception of an event that filled eight and a half hours, had thirty-nine performers and 123 speaking parts. The production won the most prestigious awards in London and New York and re-emphasised the Royal Shakespeare Company's distinguished reputation. *Nickleby* was and is to date David Edgar's biggest popular success. Its extraordinary nightly ovations signalled that the audience accepted the play in the terms that it was offered; it was a theatrical discourse concerned directly with the condition of England in 1980. Its true political dimension was that of the first term of the Thatcher government.

Nickleby is the most famous example of a general truth about Edgar's entire span of plays: their theatrical effectiveness actively encourages positive political debate. Edgar has emphasised the purpose of history in his writing: 'I've always wanted to set the present in history. The important thing is to understand the present from the past.'[2] The renowned historian E.H. Carr defines history as 'a continuous process of interaction between the historian and his facts, an unending dialogue between the present and the past';[3] Edgar's plays extend that dialogue to the audience. In this way, characters are clearly drawn as products of particular historical

1

forces, and the challenge to the audience is to reshape the distorted situations that are dramatised. An especially interesting example is the character Dennis Turner in *Destiny*, whose choices for supporting the neo-fascist cause are coherently shown to be the product of an historical process that was set in motion by the British imperialist past. Turner is set within a situation where the terror of 1930s fascist Germany is shown to be about to repeat itself in 1970s Britain. The play is not, however, a tragedy in the Aristotelian sense because it does not invite the audience to have a strong emotional reaction to events beyond human control or understanding. The central message of the play is that there is no such thing as destiny. Edgar encourages the audience to understand the draw of the emotional appeal of fascism; he does so through a well-informed political analysis of the causes of fascism, and through a story. It is the contemporary present that Edgar is always concerned with and his central theatrical technique is to tell a story about our times.

This book argues that David Edgar is uniquely placed to adopt Balzac's intriguing self-definition as secretary for the times. The *Comédie humaine* series of novels established Balzac as a contemporary social historian in the medium of prose fiction; he functioned as 'secretary of his epoch'.[4] It would be a mistake to regard the role as neutral. When Michael Billington applied it to Edgar in his notice of the 1976 documentary 'Events following the Closure of a Motorcycle Factory', he wrote: 'Balzac once described himself as the secretary of French society and David Edgar seems to be aiming to fill the post over here.'[5] In interview in 1994 Billington recalled the tendentious nature of 'Events': 'What David's play was particularly doing was drawing attention to an industrial scandal. The workers themselves, in response to the closure of their factory, had formed a co-operative of their own to keep the business going, rather as the shipbuilders were to do on the Clyde.'[6] He was adamant that the term 'secretary' is ambiguous:

> What Balzac meant was that he had to fulfil the role of the documentary recorder of his time, to act as the recording angel of that society. It seemed to me a useful definition of what a writer could be: someone who sees what is going on, records it and also takes the moral temperature of the times. To me, the word secretary has a dual meaning. It means the person who

objectively observes what is going on and puts it down, but also someone who interprets the moral values and the systems behind that (which is precisely what Balzac did).

The function of secretary is not only to record but to record and evaluate. It is worth remembering that Émile Zola, advocate of naturalism and strong supporter of objectivity in writing, understood that in any writer's work the world is necessarily perceived through the particular temperament of the writer.[7] David Edgar perceives the world through a political sensibility.

Edgar's particular conviction about drama-documentary is applicable to his view of drama as a whole; it is that the medium of dramatic fiction 'can uniquely illumine certain aspects of public life; and the dramatic power of drama-documentary lies in its capacity to show us not that certain events occurred (the headlines can do that) or even, perhaps why they occurred (for such information we can go to the weekly magazines or the history books), but *how* they occurred: how recognisable human beings rule, fight, judge, negotiate, suppress and overthrow'.[8] At the beginning of his career he wrote propagandist plays from a vigorous Marxist viewpoint. The times were ripe for this. He was a playwright of public life, writing in the wake of the 1968 student revolutionary events and the abolition of theatre censorship; and in the context of the potential for revolution associated with the industrial militancy of the early 1970s. His theatre was his contribution to the socialist movement at a time when there was a new Conservative administration under Edward Heath. Edgar has said of his work at this time: 'I was certainly very consciously anti-art ... The only function of art was to propagandise.'[9] It was the reception of *Destiny* that gave Edgar 'a political life above and beyond political theatre':

> In the early 1970s, the two were indistinguishable: my theatre work (largely in touring agitprop) *was* my political activity. In the late 1970s, it was liberating to discover that politics and theatre could operate not simultaneously but in parallel; that I could treat of British neo-fascism in one way in the theatre, and in quite another way in articles for the anti-racist and anti-fascist movement.[10]

The political journalism and public speaking are complementary to (but independent of) the plays. For example, the essay 'Racism,

3

Fascism and the Politics of the National Front' complements *Destiny*; 'The Free or the Good' (on aspects of Thatcherism) complements *Maydays* and 'Never Too Old' (on the positive legacy of the 1960s) complements *Mary Barnes*. This book refers readers to Edgar's political journalism wherever it is unquestionably relevant to the plays I have chosen to discuss. Among his generation of playwrights, Edgar is unique in that his non-dramatic writing is prolific; a glance at the substantial bibliography will confirm its diverse and extensive range. A separate study could be made of this area of Edgar's work; indeed, his discussions of political movements and philosophies are cited in books of political analysis that do not give his plays a mention.[11]

The separation of political activity from theatre work has allowed Edgar to become more multivocal. The plays have become richer and more complex, dealing in the ambiguity and contradiction of the late twentieth century, where political ideologies have provided no panaceas. Metanarratives such as the Marxist narrative of determinist historical progression are in disrepute. Nationalisms have re-emerged as the quest for European integration becomes in some countries a descent into disintegration. These are, as Edgar puts it, 'mean, greedy and increasingly frightening times; times inhabited and, indeed, in many ways defined by the most painful and often genuinely horrifying contradictions between human behaviour as we would will it – and sometimes glimpse it – and the actuality of much human action as it is.'[12] The later plays are part of a resistance to the 'mean' times; they are as tendentious as the early work but in different ways, for new times. As the century draws to its close, Edgar's theatre is a source of public investigation on a wider level. He has broadened his scope from scrutiny of British history and public events to focus especially on Eastern Europe; and he has renewed the interest in American politics that is evident in *Dick Deterred* and *Maydays*. This befits his wider political purpose of investigation into, on the one hand, the collapse of the Eastern bloc and, on the other, the rise of the new right. These wider investigations throw light on the British situation. Despite a central theme of disillusion and a dialectical theatre practice, the core of conscious socialist conviction, the upholding of particular values and vision, still holds.

Edgar's essays on his own theatre practice and that of his

contemporaries are valuable reference points; in particular, it would certainly be inadequate to write a book on theatre in the 1970s without citing the seminal piece, 'Ten Years of Political Theatre, 1968–1978'. More recently, Edgar has lectured and written on the effect on culture of the right-wing Conservative government (which came into power in 1979 and in 1992 began its fourth consecutive term). The cultural growth at the start of Edgar's career, and the consequent flourishing of Fringe theatre companies, have been ruthlessly cut back. In 1988 Edgar's 'Thoughts for the Third Term' assessed Margaret Thatcher's cultural policies as 'essentially, inherently and inescapably reactionary, restrictive and indeed censorious'.[13] The Arts Council document *A Great British Success Story* (1985) had pushed the arts firmly into the market-place; and cultural institutions such as the Royal Shakespeare Company succumbed to the relevant strategies (in the commercial sector). Edgar's lecture 'State of Play' (1993)[14] charted a decline of new work from 1985 to 1990 in the repertoire of the main houses of regional and London repertory theatres. The 1980s also saw the Royal Shakespeare Company and the (Royal) National Theatre[15] finding space for fewer new plays; even the Royal Court Theatre, which had hitherto been consistently famous for its productions of new work, decreased its overall number of such productions; and the large stages of these companies were reserved for bland and safe productions of tried and tested plays. As for the small-scale and touring sector, diminution or denial of Arts Council funding has led to the closure of a number of companies (including the renowned Foco Novo, Joint Stock and 7:84 England).[16]

The overall picture has been one of a governmental pressure towards arts privatisation. In its angling for commercial sponsorship, theatre adopted a business vocabulary; commercial sponsors withdrew sponsorship from plays they saw as offensive, effectively renewing censorship; playgoers became 'customers' and theatre administrators proliferated. Edgar concludes that 'the decline in innovatory stage drama was the intended result of consciously provoked changes in the cultural economy'.[17] Nevertheless, he insists that resistance is flourishing. He points to an increase in women writers, the resilience of the 1970s polemical playwrights, an emergence of a movement of playwriterly self-help in the 1980s, and an increase of new work in the early 1990s. Edgar sees

5

a danger in the 1980s-nurtured emphasis on spectacle: 'a theatre which has forgotten that before they are sensational, spectacular or skilful, plays in the theatre have meaning is a theatre that aspires to the condition of the circus'.[18] Of all the media, because of its 'capacity to engage in a live conversation with its audience',[19] theatre can most consistently address the urgent subjects of the limits and consequences of particular types of social and political organisation. It is a persuasive argument.

Edgar has demonstrated a continuing process of initiative championing the cause of his profession. He co-founded the Theatre Writers' Union in 1975 and was elected its Chair in 1991. Catherine Itzin notes that, 'The rapid growth of the Theatre Writers' Union and its radical activities epitomised the political principles operating in the theatre in the seventies.'[20] Importantly, playwrights ceased to be isolated figures in their garrets; they are now recognised as workers with the right to wages, rehearsal attendance, and involvement with casting, directing and publicity decisions. Edgar extends the anti-garret principle through his chairing of Britain's first postgraduate course in Playwriting Studies. He founded the MA course at Birmingham University in 1989 and, after its first five years, asserted that: 'Ultimately the course is based on the conviction that there are techniques, devices and principles that govern dramatic structure, and that while new techniques are added to the canon through time (there is no flashback in Shakespeare), and some techniques go in and out of fashion, plays from Aeschylus to Ayckbourn share a great deal more than divides them.'[21] This conviction is an anti-romantic approach to a work process, celebrating collectivity rather than the isolated imagination, craft rather than spectacle. Part of Edgar's role as educationalist has been to organise a major theatre conference at Birmingham University each year since 1990. These conferences have gathered together theatre people from many countries to discuss (thus far) themes of regional theatre, new writing, the relationship of text to performance, the connection between theatre and nationalism, the crisis of content in British theatre, and music and drama in contemporary Britain. The questions asked and the issues raised in these conferences have aired and advanced important debates. All aspects of Edgar's work, his part in establishing the Theatre Writers' Union, the theatre conferences, the MA course, his political and theatre journalism

6

and, above all, the plays themselves, show a dedication to progression, an active encouragement of constructive political thought. It is that energy that is celebrated in this book.

Edgar has written plays of public life through a period of defeat for the left – national and international – and the death of state bureaucracy in Eastern Europe. The prolific output of plays is listed on pages xv to xix; in a discussion of this length I have had to be selective. My aim has been to include the plays from 1970 to 1994 that best give a sense of Edgar's position as secretary for the times, his response to the leading social and political events that he has lived through. From the start it made sense to single out the importance of *Destiny* (on which there is an entire chapter). The concluding chapter analyses *Pentecost*, the most powerful dramatic investigation of the millennial crisis. I have grouped other plays in coherent categories. Because Edgar has written far more extensively for theatre than for television, radio and cinema, I have chosen to concentrate on the stage plays. I see the theatre work as the major achievement but, in keeping with my overall definition of Edgar's role as recorder and evaluator of the age, I have chosen to analyse two recent television plays: 'Parallel Bars' (about Eastern Europe) and 'Buying a Landslide' (about America); the purpose is to broaden out a commentary on Edgar's recent political landscapes for theatre. I also use the television version of *Maydays* in a discussion of the stage play's ideas. While it would have interested me, for example, to analyse the conventions of the radio plays (and particularly to make an analysis of 'A Movie Starring Me', a structurally exciting piece that builds on a usage of Chekhov); or to tackle 'Lady Jane' as the solitary film for cinema; or to assess the parodies 'Tedderella' and *Dick Deterred*; or to make a detailed analysis of the early unpublished propaganda pieces; or to discuss the short published plays; I have nevertheless kept in mind that this book is an introduction to a continuing career with an emphasis on theatre. As such, it needed to be brought as near as possible to the present (1995), to give a particular, roughly chronological perspective on the playwright (in reference to the title), and to concentrate on major published texts.

Chapter One examines the early theatre of agitation and propaganda with the General Will company; the exploration is of a type of theatre that came out of a particular revolutionary

7

movement, its limitations, and Edgar's abandonment of it. Chapter Two analyses *Destiny* as a turning-point in Edgar's career. This play caught the spirit of the times with an exactness that is rare in contemporary theatre history. The keenness of its political analysis is all the more remarkable today; there is no doubt that *Destiny's* time has come again in the mid-1990s when there is a gaining momentum of neo-fascist terror throughout Europe. The play marked the start of Edgar's long association with the Royal Shakespeare Company; surprisingly, and successfully, it adopted the form of social realism. Chapter Three deals with the adaptations of autobiography (*The Jail Diary of Albie Sachs* and *Mary Barnes*) and fiction (the novel *The Life and Adventures of Nicholas Nickleby* and the novella *The Strange Case of Dr Jekyll and Mr Hyde*). I take up the much vaunted issue of hostility to stage adaptations, arguing that these particular examples are (as Edgar asserts) 'real' plays bearing contemporary social and political relevance.

Chapter Four examines Edgar's principal subject of disillusion with the left, centring on *Teendreams*, *Maydays*, and *That Summer* and considering the debate about theatre of public life on our main subsidised stages. *Teendreams* is a product of collaboration; it was written with Susan Todd for the socialist–feminist company Monstrous Regiment and it exposes some of the contradictions of socialist feminism. *That Summer* is (unusually for Edgar) a domestic play about the bringing together of working-class miners and intellectual urban socialists during the 1984–1985 miners' strike. It tells of a consequent rekindling of socialist vision. I accord more space to *Maydays* for several reasons. The theme of disillusion is charted most exactly in this epic which is Edgar's most ambitious, authoritative, referential and personal play. In its extraordinary scope it covers three different generations and three parts of the world. It is about Thatcherism and (paradoxically) it reaches that subject of right-wing Conservatism through an analysis of the far left. Stylistically, it is very rich. Later plays which analyse East European and American politics can be seen to refer back to it. In all three plays there is reaffirmation of a spirit of resistance. Unlike some of his colleagues (in particular, John McGrath), Edgar confronts disillusion; in contrast to some others (for example, David Hare), his plays reaffirm a socialist vision. Moreover, the production of *Maydays* at the Barbican Theatre opened a debate about the type of contemporary play that our subsidised sector grants room on its large stages. This debate is certainly as relevant in the mid-1990s as it was in 1983; indeed, *Maydays* saw out the 1980s as the only large-scale contemporary public play on the Barbican stage.

Chapter Five scrutinises the work in community theatre. I examine the Dorchester context of *Entertaining Strangers* and argue that the revised version for the National Theatre is an exciting experiment in form with an exact political purpose. Although I do not accord *Heartlanders* a full examination – it is co-written and does not compare with *Entertaining Strangers* in stature – it nevertheless seems to me crucial to point to the existence of city community plays (which potentially serve the function of uniting the citizens who take part in them) and to note Edgar's involvement with the Birmingham example. Chapter Six analyses Edgar's most recent political landscapes of Eastern Europe (*The Shape of the Table* and 'Parallel Bars') and America ('Buying a Landslide'), emphasising his continuing skill at dramatising contemporary politics in plays that, while they go beyond an insular examination of British affairs, still retain a bearing on this country. Chapter Seven focuses on *Pentecost*, a state-of-Europe play that, in its complexity and richness, marks a considerable advance for Edgar.

David Edgar has made a unique contribution to the socialist theatre movement in Britain post-1968. Edgar is a public figure in a way that his contemporaries are not. Through his energy and initiative in co-founding and now chairing the Theatre Writers' Union; in his founding and chairing the MA course in Playwriting Studies at Birmingham University; in his organisation of annual theatre conferences; and in his lectures and essays on aspects of contemporary theatre, he actively influences the professional theatre, often bringing together playwrights in the spirit of communality that he fosters in his plays. His association with the Royal Shakespeare Company has ensured that his politically committed plays enter the main subsidised arena, opening debates with relatively diverse audiences. His political journalism, which is meticulously researched and strongly analytical, complements the plays; he is well-informed about the subjects he deals with. His active involvement with the day-to-day working of politics – the student revolutionary activity in the late 1960s, trade unionism, the anti-fascist movement, the Labour Party – ensures that he knows from the inside how public meetings work. This familiarity is crucial for a playwright of public life who writes scenes centring on pivotal meetings that demonstrate how political process changes countries. Moreover, his experimentation with form, structure, genre and language has covered a very wide range, a diversity and scope that are unequalled among his contemporaries.

In his dramatisation of political ideas and themes Edgar has ranged from agitprop to epic to realism to adaptation to carnivalesque, striving for an appropriateness of form to content and the spirit of the times. He has written variety performance 'turns', pastiche music hall and melodrama, political pantomime, social comedy, Shakespearian parody and satire. It is broadly the case that his work operates within an idea of history. He has been influenced by Brecht and Shakespeare rather more than by Ibsen and Chekhov, yet he uses the personal, psychological and realistic where these emphases enhance the public analysis. A love of words is a typical feature of the plays: a delight in testing all possible uses of language results in detailed experimentation with style and parody; various British dialects, typical American idiomatic expression, Soviet communist jargon; as well as song, multiple uses of verse, formal public speeches, quick-fire one-liners and wit bounce through the work. A sense of Edgar's skill with words can be found by reading Oneeye's 'revenge of the ugly' speech in *Ball Boys*. The hyperbolic peroration of protest against beautiful people goes like this:

AND ONE DAY. ONE DAY. WE'LL RISE. And, up and down the land, the boiled and warted wreak a horrible revenge. Then shall unlovely losers liquidate the latest faces, then shall the balding depilate the hirsute, and the weaklings, raving in wild mobs, kick sand in every eye; then ageing tailors run amok in dark boutiques and obese housewives butcher slimmers of the month. Then shall plump, acned groupies rise and slay the Osmond Brothers; starlets juggle with the severed limbs of stars, and stars will dance round smoking pyres of superstars; and secret wankers, formed in violent gangs, shall do destruction on the objects of their masturbation fantasies . . . And all the maimed, deformed and corpulent; the ugly, hare-lipped and incontinent; shall rise and seek, destroy, and will inherit all the earth.

10

The comic effect of this speech rests on its contribution to the characterisation of Oneeye, an absurdly erudite orphan ball boy at Wimbledon. Here is a very different style of speech from *Dick Deterred*:

> RICHARD: Now is the winter of our discontent
> Made glorious summer by this Texan bum
> And all the crowds that didn't duck the draft
> Vacating are the bosoms of Saigon.
> Our brows now bound with wreaths of compromise,
> Our bruised armies are demobilized,
> Our napalm bombs are changed to Paris meetings,
> Our My Lai massacres to diplomatic measures.
> But I, that am not shaped for aught but tricks,
> Nor made to court an amorous CBS,
> I, that am rudely stamped, and want capacity
> To strut before a wanton East Coast liberal;
> I, that was spurned by the electorate,
> Cheated in 1960 by dissembling fortune,
> Held as a has-been, spent before my time
> Out of this world before my star was set.
> And seen so lamely and unfashionable
> That now they chuckle when I halt by them:
> Why I, now partner in a Wall Street legal firm,
> Have no delight in handling Pepsi-Cola
> And mourn the days I strutted in the sun
> Before I lost the California governorship
> And told the gloating press, with quiv'ring jaw,
> They'd not have Dick to kick around no more...

This is of course a parody of the opening soliloquy of *Richard III* to fit the Watergate scandal. Not only is it strongly apposite to parallel Richard Nixon with Shakespeare's villain, but also the political satire is much enlivened by the congruity. The play is a good example of Edgar's many successful attempts to fit new material to traditional forms.

While Edgar steadily continues to write new plays, adding to his impressively long list of works, his early plays are revived with regularity. In recent years there have been productions of *The National Theatre* (a 1975 play about a strip club as metaphor for the nation), *Baby Love* (a 1973 play that investigates the social

11

reality of a babysnatcher's predicament), *Blood Sports* (a 1975 satire of Britain as a divided nation, warning that the real blood sports will involve acts of revenge) and *Saigon Rose* (a 1976 play using a metaphor of sexually transmitted disease to satirise the American colonisation of Scotland), as well as revivals of the major plays, *Teendreams*, *Destiny*, *Mary Barnes*, *The Life and Adventures of Nicholas Nickleby* and *Entertaining Strangers*. These plays have sustained the passage of time because Edgar has the ability to make ideas good theatre. It is David Edgar's equal commitment to politics and theatre that securely underpins his plays.

1

Theatre of Agitation and Propaganda: early work

> There was a very conscious, a very strong feeling: what can I do? What contribution can I make?   David Edgar, 1979[1]

In 1968 David Edgar was in his final year as an undergraduate at Manchester University. He had chosen to read drama with the specific vocational intention of a career in theatre and he embraced wholeheartedly the revolutionary spirit of the times. He edited the student newspaper; he chaired the socialist society; he developed a talent for public oratory; he marched against the Vietnam War; he campaigned against examinations. His own experience was representative of student radicalism at an exciting time of youth revolt: 'bliss was it in that dawn to be alive, but to be in full-time higher education was very heaven'.[2] When he left university he became a journalist on the *Bradford Telegraph and Argus*, and during this three year stint he investigated the John Poulson scandal.[3] The student political activity and the discipline of research necessary for his social and political writing were strongly formative of Edgar's practice as a playwright. He has written and had produced some fifty plays for the stage, as well as a substantial number of pieces for television and radio and one film for cinema. Almost all of this prolific output has been based on extensive research into subjects of public life.

The confidence in the first place to attempt a theatrical career had been gained from an encouraging and influential family environment in Birmingham. The context for Edgar's fascination with performance was defined by a television producer father, an actress then radio announcer mother, a theatre administrator aunt who went on to supervise the design of the new Birmingham Repertory Theatre, a comedy actress maternal grandmother and a broadcaster paternal grandfather. He was regularly taken to the theatre from a very early age; he started writing plays when he was five, and at ten he wrote the comprehensive-sounding piece 'The Life and Times of William Shakespeare'. He had seen almost all of Shakespeare's plays by the time he was fifteen and his father had introduced him to what he describes as 'the tatty end of showbiz': he remembers seeing Ken Dodd in a pier show at Great Yarmouth when he was a child. He spent a lot of time 'standing in the wings of things'[4] and at first he wanted to be an actor (after he played Miss Prism in high heels in an Oundle School production of *The Importance of Being Earnest* his mother is reputed to have told him 'It's not going to be acting, dear'). He directed an all-male *Mother Courage* at school, made attempts to design plays, and continued to write. The plays he wrote at Oundle were all huge epics and were never performed; they included a life of St Stephen and a play called 'Polynices' (influenced by Anouilh's *Antigone*).[5] At Manchester directing and designing were experimented with and eliminated from the career prospects. He chose to be a writer.

The years in Bradford solidified that choice in a particular way. Edgar's association with the University of Bradford Drama Group launched his playwriting career. In 1969 Chris Parr, a director who had worked extensively with new writers, was invited to be Fellow in Theatre at Bradford. The aim was to introduce into the scientific and technological training ground of the university opportunities for practical work in the arts. Parr was given no brief. He could have used the fellowship to build a professional group within the university but instead he devised a far-sighted and admirable scheme whereby new writers would be paid to write for the already established student Drama Group and a new show would be done once a month. These writers included Michael Almaz, Howard Brenton, Richard Crane, John Grillo and Jeff Nuttall. The arrangement importantly contributed to a flourishing theatre scene in Bradford where several experimental tendencies of the newly burgeoning Fringe were gathered together.

One such tendency was towards performance art. Albert Hunt ran a drama group at the College of Art; John Fox (founder of Welfare State International company) was librarian and lecturer there.[6] Hunt and Fox collaborated on some large-scale theatre events such as the staging of 'The Russian Revolution in the Streets of Bradford'. The anarchic John Bull Puncture Repair Kit group was also based in Bradford. Another tendency was towards the socialist propagandist theatre known as agitprop. Agitational propaganda theatre (to give it the full name) derives from the post-revolutionary Soviet programme of the 1920s which had the immediate purpose of teaching the illiterate masses a particular political viewpoint. 1970s agitprop theatre in Britain sought to build up working-class audiences, to educate them in Marxist economic principles (the 'prop') and to arouse their support for the socialist movement by raising consciousness of their oppression (the 'agit'). David Edgar was to make a key contribution to the agitprop form.[7]

Edgar reported university affairs and reviewed university plays for the *Telegraph and Argus*. Chris Parr grew to recognise 'the large owlish figure standing at the back on a first night';[8] Edgar became close to the politically active students as well as those involved in theatre, and he wrote a play for Parr about South Africa that was 'overtaken by events' and left unperformed.[9] On the evidence that 'David had something special', Parr commissioned a play to take to the Edinburgh Festival. This was *Two Kinds of Angel* (1970) which became Edgar's first published and professionally performed piece. It is a short one act two-hander for women based on research into the lives of Rosa Luxemburg and Marilyn Monroe. The flatmates Rosa and Norma are opposites in disposition (reflected in their namesake heroines). Rosa tries to find security in her political activism, Norma in her sexuality:

> NORMA. I love to stifle, to enclose a man.
>
> ROSA. It's untidy. And counter-productive to a close relation-ship of human beings.
>
> NORMA. Who wants clarity when they can have love?
>
> ROSA. Who wants to spend their time lying in fields of daisies when they can change the world?

During the course of the play fantasy sequences about their respective heroines punctuate the growing discord between the women. Norma's rejection by a man leads her to ask Rosa for sex and love. Rejected again, she kills Rosa.

As a first play *Two Kinds of Angel* is a mixture of the predictable and the innovative. Although it ends in expected violence and is, as

15

Edgar comments, 'a highly melodramatic piece ... relying on a series of fairly obvious effects' it does 'jump about in space and time' as it shifts to the fantasy sequences and back to the contemporary present.[10] It is remarkable too for its lack of autobiographical content and its serious roles for women actors. In its research basis, its dramatisation of a clash between thought (Rosa) and feeling (Norma), and its reference to student politics, it embryonically dramatises some of Edgar's major preoccupations: the play looks forward to further adaptations of biography (*The Jail Diary of Albie Sachs*, *Mary Barnes*), scenes of late 1960s and early 1970s student politics (*Teendreams*, *Maydays*), and characters who struggle with the relationship between reason and feeling (Martin Glass in *Maydays* is the obvious example). However, the 'sex and violence' action is more imitative of Howard Brenton's early work (for Portable Theatre and Bradford) than genuine Edgar. Although the play was rapidly professionally produced in London, Edgar was searching for a new politically committed form: 'I was trying to find ways to write about socialism, about the working class, from my own background ... What I could offer was a reasonably analytical mind and a talent for research, therefore I would write documentaries ... There was a very conscious, a very strong feeling: what can I do? What contribution can I make?'[11]

Among the very different kinds of play Edgar wrote for Bradford was a huge piece of environmental theatre, a documentary about the Peace Movement; this established his skill in making ideas theatrical on a large scale. Chris Parr had organised a series of epic spectaculars for specific environments: one for a local ice rink (Brenton's *Scott of the Antarctic*), one for Bradford Cathedral (Richard Crane's 'David, King of the Jews') and one for a Methodist hall (Brenton's *Wesley*). Edgar played God in *Scott of the Antarctic* (he wore dark spectacles and a long white beard and sat in a wheelchair; the piece is alternatively titled *What God Didn't See*) and contributed his own play to the series. 'The End' (1972) was performed in the Great Hall of the university, a giant space used for examinations and sports, into which a computer console was installed. The play involves the audience in a computer Cold War game whereby, at various points in the action, individual spectators are invited to play (respectively) the Soviet Union, America and China (and other countries as required) by making decisions in response to incidents flashed up on the

16

computer screens all around the environment. According to the sum total of these choices at the end of the play, a state of war or peace is arrived at and there are two alternative endings, one much more frightening than the other. By inviting the audience to actively participate in its choice of fate, the implications of civil disobedience could be experienced. This is but one part of the interlinked events. On the stage are sequences on board the control room of a Polaris submarine. On the floor is 'The Marchers' Play' (the main action) about CND and the Committee of 100, with the audience in a horseshoe shape around it. The cast of 'The Marchers' Play' take on multiple roles, portraying among others the public figures of Hugh Gaitskell, Bertrand Russell and John F. Kennedy. The story is energetically told through familiar entertainment techniques such as song and strong visual image. One stanza of a song typifies the ironical method of getting the point across:

> On the third day of Christmas
> MacMillan sent to me
> Emaciation
> Vomiting and nausea
> And a lovely dose of Strontium Nine-Tee

The demonstration of factual evidence is hard-hitting, direct and polemical.

The documentary form was pioneered by Erwin Piscator in his epic theatre experiments in 1920s Germany. Piscator established what he labelled 'the political theatre', with a specifically revolutionary socialist content. He was keen to use the new technology of radio and film and he laid the entire groundwork for a theatre of fact. Piscator coined the term 'epic theatre' subsequently taken up by Brecht.[12] Clive Barker has concisely detailed the characteristics of playmaking and form used by Piscator's collective:

> Since no one playwright was capable of comprehending the full political and economic complexity of the late capitalist world, a dramaturgical collective was set up to construct texts. This collective included politicos and economists as well as dramaturgs and directors. Piscator's other great contribution was to establish the *epic* form, against the prevailing *dramatic* form of the bourgeois theatre, as the basic necessity for a political theatre. In

17

order to deal with political issues, let alone take part in political action, the theatre must break free from domestic settings and conflicting representative characters and must be able to use montage and juxtaposed scenes; to utilise a wide range of locales and to fragment character. It must also be able to break the proscenium frame and to address the audience directly.[13]

David Edgar's work for the General Will company would pay attention to all these criteria. The insurmountable difference of situation was that in Piscator's Germany the political context involved a clear choice between Communism and Fascism. As Edgar was increasingly to discover, such unambiguous choice was by no means a clear feature of the early 1970s British political situation. The reasons for Edgar's ultimate abandonment of agitprop have their seed in this lack of parallel context.

The General Will was a small professional agitprop touring company arising out of Edgar's work at Bradford. In 1971 Edgar wrote 'The National Interest', a documentary on the first year of the Conservative government. Two actors who wanted to set up an agitprop company were in that Bradford play and it became the first touring show. It was to be the first of three aggressively propagandist state-of-the-nation pieces that Edgar wrote for and with the company. The General Will was one of a large number of travelling theatre groups founded out of the radical zeal of the post-1968 period. The late 1960s cultural revolution in performance, principally through rock music, meant that there was greater potential for the working class to be reached through theatre.[14] Theatre censorship was abolished in Britain in 1968. The Arts Council enhanced public subsidy up until 1975. Between 1968 and 1975 there flourished many performance groups, and as Chris Parr perceptively pointed out: 'I remember at the time being very conscious that on the theatre level they were very like pop groups. They started like pop groups, coming out of nowhere, and they finished up like pop groups, often acrimoniously.' The specifically socialist theatre groups responded to the 1970–74 period of industrial militancy which spanned the Heath government; the social crisis gave the opportunity for interventionist theatre about economic conditions. Edgar commented: 'Agitprop was a response to the times . . . the historical conditions of 1970–74 were unique in post-war history – suddenly after thirty years the working-class

18

movement awoke with such speed and strode back onto the stage of history, like a broom sweeping people in its path ... the surprise, the joy, enthusiasm, mistakes of that period are in a sense very specific. And that was the soil in which agitprop grew.'[15]

This renewed combativeness was a surprise to the late 1960s counter-culturalists who, in New Left fashion, had rejected the model of working-class revolution provided by Marx. Howard Brenton, for example, had been very much influenced by the New Left French situationists with their theory of the capitalist world as 'the society of the spectacle': 'There is a screen called public life which is reported on the telly and in the newspapers. This version of public life is a spectacle, it operates within its own laws. It's a vast, intricate confidence game.'[16] Brenton's early plays for the Portable Theatre company sought to smash through the capitalist 'spectacle' with a violent anarchical energy that had nothing to do with class organisation. As Edgar put it, for the many counter-culturalists of the late 1960s, 'Revolutionary politics was seen as being much less about the organisation of the working class at the point of production, and much more about the disruption of bourgeois ideology at the point of consumption. The centre of the revolution had shifted from the factory-floor to the supermarket.'[17] The early 1970s unrest held out the hope of a contrary political understanding based on Marx's prediction of working-class revolution in the face of exploitation and oppression. David Edgar was exactly the right person at the right time to become a participant in this political and cultural situation. His political literacy and skill at finding techniques to theatricalise economic theory were the starting-points for the General Will. He has described the transition of techniques from the Bradford work: 'The techniques ['The End'] used of fairly rapid, brisk, multi-doubling, and the cartoon-storytelling style were clearly features that carried over into the General Will. And I think that the most finished technique that came out of Bradford was for anecdotal storytelling – sliding very quickly from different images which would tell a consistent story through any number of different settings or images. So if one bit of it was best done in Chicago-gangster-style and the next bit was dressed up completely differently, then one developed a style of managing that and of using it to make simple points, quickly and clearly.'[18]

19

'The National Interest' toured for a year. The play takes the audience through 1970–71 in a series of quickly shifting, cleverly linked variety 'turns': stand-up comic routines, song, dance and double acts. Parody is unflagging; facets of pantomime, nursery rhyme, gangster movie and television advertisement are burlesqued. Edgar was soon to write full-length burlesques ('Tedderella' in 1971 and *Dick Deterred* in 1974) and the considerable talent for parody has been developed throughout his career. The most fully developed section of parody in 'The National Interest' is the gangster section. The 1970 Industrial Relations Act is dramatised through the conflict of 'de Tory gang' and 'de Labour gang', and at one point parodic pantomime verse is juxtaposed with gangster argot to attention-grabbing effect:

> *Enter* LYNNE, *on her points, with a wand.*
>
> LYNNE. Fear not, brave Tories, for your fairy guardian's here,
> From darkest depths of despond bringing cheer.
> Though now with troubles grave you are surrounded,
> Your evil spirits will ere long all be confounded.
> I'll put a spell on Labour, cause a split
> To land their future prospects in the shit!
> But how to see that dispute and dissent is rife?
> I know! I've got it! I'll create In Place Of Strife!
>
> *Exit* LYNNE. JOHN *gets up, enthusiastic.*
>
> JOHN. Dis is what we've been praying for, boys! A split in de
> Labour gang! De union gang on de one side and de Wilson
> mob on de udder. Now we can move in and make de big
> killing. I always said de fairies were on de side of de
> Tories.

Another 'turn' is that of the Dreaded Dolebeast. An actor plays a hideously aggressive beast doing the high jump to demonstrate rising unemployment levels, a strong and energetic image to illustrate an economic fact. Audience involvement is a strong feature of the show: the Dolebeast attacks the audience; the Chicago gangsters frisk them; and they are arrested after they have been tricked into singing a song in support of strikes. The visual device used to explain the Industrial Relations Act was derived from a recurring scene in the Ealing comedy films in which a group

20

of gangsters plan a robbery using a doll's house. In 'The National Interest' the model factory has little figures of workers which are moved about by the Tory gangsters to give a parodic explanation of the government's purpose in their legislation in the fields of both immigration and industrial relations. Almost twenty years later Edgar's much more sophisticated central image in *The Shape of the Table* (1990) is a development of his experimentation in his agitprop plays with techniques which use visual demonstration to theatricalise the argument.

'State of Emergency', a second Tory government play, followed in 1972. This was a chronology play about the 1971–72 industrial unrest, covering the Upper Clyde Shipbuilders' work-in, the miners' strike, the rail dispute, and the jailing of five dockers under the Industrial Relations Act. This play involved, in the Living Newspaper tradition,[19] a process of sifting through a pile of cuttings and discussion by the company before Edgar wrote the individual scenes. The approach was thus very close to the Piscator collective method of constructing texts. It ran for eighteen months during which time Edgar wrote new scenes every three or four months and cut scenes that events had rendered redundant. 'The Dunkirk Spirit' (1974) was the third and last in the series about the government; it traced the economic history of Britain since the war.

The essential question to ask about these bitingly satirical plays written for the General Will is: how useful were they politically? During this period, Edgar was writing other types of political plays for other groups and for theatre venues; the General Will developed one strand of his work for touring in mainly non-theatre venues. Other writers were providing material for the company too. A turning-point for Edgar was in 1972 when he left the *Telegraph and Argus* to become a full-time professional playwright. He was still committed to political journalism but now the plays were the day job. The 'baptism of fire' was Edgar's collaboration on 'England's Ireland' with Tony Bicât, Howard Brenton, Brian Clark, Francis Fuchs, David Hare and Snoo Wilson.[20] This play about the Irish 'troubles' made a forceful attack on public attitudes; Richard Boon notes that 'the dramatising of historical background challenges audience ignorance, a horrifying torture scene its apathy; contemporary (non-partisan) government policy is condemned, but no more than the

21

racist laughter provoked by an Irish joke'.[21] It was a Brentonesque 'disruption of the spectacle' play, nihilistic and savage, which was planned to go around large theatres; it was refused space by those theatres once they became aware of its politically subversive subject, and this effective censorship meant that it had only some single night performances and a run at the Roundhouse. Edgar's collaboration with the writers he most admired firmly established him as part of a generation of professional British playwrights with shared principles and purposes: 'a belief in collaborative production processes, an aspiration to an audience wider than the usual metropolitan coterie, an open attitude to form, a concern with the public world and its relation to the private world, and a commitment to radical social change'.[22] Would these purposes best be served by the agitprop form?

Agitprop's strengths are also its limitations. If this simple, unsophisticated theatre is offered in complex, contradictory times; if it has the wrong audiences and venues; if notions of 'class' change, then the entire enterprise fails. One problem with the General Will was that the company did not in the main build up working-class audiences. They played a mixture of arts venues (for example, the Birmingham Repertory Theatre Studio and the Royal Court Theatre Upstairs) and colleges, and only occasionally did they play working-class gigs (such as canteens and working-men's clubs). At a particular gig in Stoke-on-Trent, Edgar was struck by the harsh fact that 'although it was a working-men's club, actually the audience was the same audience we would have got in an arts centre. They had just happened to have come to it there. One of the things that came to me was that we had developed an audience. Although we spoke to an audience as if it were a proletarian audience and tended to assume all of our audiences were in industrial trades unions, it became clear that this was a sort of delusion.'[23] The audience was in reality a socialist movement audience; that is, they were people sympathetic to the working-class struggle, 'members of revolutionary parties, and non-aligned supporters of various left-wing organisations, causes and campaigns'.[24] They were in the main an audience of the faithful meeting performers dedicated to the faith. Agitprop in the early 1970s, in Edgar's experience with the General Will, was on the whole theatre of celebration for audiences who did not need the agitation and were already committed to the propaganda.

Another related point was that Edgar yearned for political complexity, and on one level provided it in the intense two-hour show 'The Dunkirk Spirit', which covered 'a massive amount of extremely complex material' where contemporary events were seen in the context of an overview of British capitalism since the war.[25] If agitprop is to be complete and accurate as political statement, it is necessary to provide such an overview but the audience's attention was not held. With this play Edgar felt that he 'personally broke the form' which started in the streets and originally had a short performance span. Paradoxically, this was the play that Edgar was most pleased to have written for the General Will but 'it ended up being savaged for different environments: miners' bits were done for miners; hard-line economics bits for hard-line economists. The connections had been lost.'[26] Although the fantasy play that Edgar did not write 'had no people in it at all, in which everybody was either an aeroplane or a graph of labour migration from the north west during the 1960s – an entirely economistic kind of play',[27] the General Will play that was most useful politically was 'Rent, or Caught in the Act' (1972).

'Rent' had both people and a strong storyline about a family, the Harddonebys, and their lawyers Devious, Devious, Devious and Downright Dishonest. It explained an Act of Parliament, the Housing Finance Act, to targeted audiences: these were tenants' groups, to whom the company showed the possibility of squatting and rent strikes. 'Rent' became part of the Child Poverty Action Group campaign against the Act. Melodrama and music hall were used as structural principles; in the following extract from the end of Act One, several conventions from melodrama (tableau, villain laugh, the fainting heroine, moral absolutism embodied in characters of pure good and pure evil) combine with teaching purpose:

DEVIOUS *hits* FATHER's *stick aside and strides about the flat.*

FATHER. You villain, sir!

DEVIOUS. E'en so, sir, I'll not deny it. Tis done! I have decided. Your rent will double now, old man, from eleven pounds to twenty-two!

LYDIA. Oh, Tom! (*Faints.*)

DEVIOUS. And with the best allowance government allows,
you'll still pay fourteen pounds a week! Ha! Ha! Ha!

FATHER (*sinks into chair*). No one must tell my wife. Twill
break her heart.

DEVIOUS. Ha! Ha! Ha!

Exit. Tableau.

Clearly 'Rent' was accessible in style but complex (or subtle) it
was not. Edgar wanted to find a form capable of introducing
psychology and emotion.

Edgar was to draw certain conclusions about agitprop after the
demise of the General Will company. By 1975 the company
wanted to be more entertaining and Edgar, in his precise,
researched political cerebralism, was no longer the writer for
them. The conflict that finally, spectacularly, split the group
reflected a central political truth: class divisions are not the only
divisions between people. In the middle of a performance of 'The
Dunkirk Spirit' one of the actors went on strike; this was Noël
Greig, who joined Gay Sweatshop in 1977. Philip Osment
comments:

> His 'strike' occurred at a time when the General Will was
> composed mainly of heterosexual men. Its work reflected strictly
> applied Marxist attitudes and appraised the world in an objective
> 'male' fashion which left little room for the feminist and radical
> gay politics which were opening up new debates in the town
> [Bradford]. These debates were not only around sexuality. GLF
> [the Gay Liberation Front] was making its presence felt in local
> politics generally, particularly in anti-fascist work. Most
> significantly, of all the radical groups in Bradford the lesbian and
> gay movement had large working-class support because its
> membership was made up of local working-class people ...
> Noël's strike was, in effect, a seventies-style 'zap' and resulted
> in the lesbian and gay community taking over the company.[28]

Socialist theatre had to make connections between different areas
of oppression; a simple class analysis was not sufficient. The times
were far more intricate than the 1920s and 1930s in Piscator's
Germany. Race, class and sexual divisions and oppressions had
each to be taken into account and understood. Noël Greig had (with

24

friends) set up the alternative theatre group Brighton Combination in the late 1960s and remembers 'working on a play about the Cuban Revolution and then catching the train up to London to go to one of the GLF meetings at the LSE and not being able to link up the two experiences'.[29]

Edgar has argued that the agitprop that was a response to particular militant times and historical conditions was redundant by the mid 1970s because 'the world about us was getting more complicated'.[30] In a period of 'class retreat', after the Heath government had been brought down by a mass movement of industrial conflicts, when it was irrevocably clear that the working class was not moving towards a classic revolutionary position, he felt that agitprop had outlived its usefulness (or, certainly, temporarily so).[31] Direct propaganda had no hope of working in the face of grave defeats of the left; socialist theatre of a propagandist type can only work as part of a mass revolutionary movement of advanced workers or in a post-revolutionary society (where it becomes celebratory theatre). Edgar realised the contradictions everywhere. The consensus of socialist playmakers was fracturing as was the homogenous culture. There were radical constituencies – those of women, gays, lesbians, blacks, to name the most obvious – across class boundaries. The traditional class model of radicalism would not do and Edgar was convinced that a plural vision was necessary:

> The problem is the connection with other struggles: with the fight of the Irish working class, black workers and the women's movement. The problem is political, but it is also psychological. It is the breaking down of barriers of consciousness. It is resolving the contradictions of car workers striking to smash the IRA.[32]

Could a socialist theatre preserve sympathy for dockers who marched for Enoch Powell's racist ideas? Or for an industrial struggle that derided feminist demands? It was obvious to Edgar:

> By the end of 1975 the 68 generation had lost its innocence, and the section of that generation that had gone into the theatre began to appreciate that anybody seriously attempting to represent the times that followed was inevitably going to be dealing with complexity, contradiction and even just plain doubt.[33]

25

The political truth could no longer be portrayed in a simple form because it was not unambiguous. This reappraisal of his political position in relation to the times is characteristic of Edgar's critical intelligence; he has the ability to be publicly 'self-critical, in the sense of being critical of the movement of which [he is] a part'.[34]

What new form would Edgar seek? The General Will work had treated economic history with vivacity and boldness, excluding psychology and the individual's private journey through an experience: 'because it was an era of primarily economic struggle, our major purpose was to present a Marxist economic perspective of what was going on – of the crisis of capitalism, why it was in crisis, of the economic tactics of the ruling class to solve that crisis, and the response of the working class'.[35] Now the plays would involve the relationship of individual behaviour to the public situation of contemporary Britain. Edgar argued retrospectively that agitprop 'can only present models of the world, and even then (frankly) not very sophisticated ones'.[36] Edgar's early 1970s agitprop work assumes a shared objective understanding of political reality from a Marxist worldview, a certainty of perspective that argues 'this is how it is, how history will progress'. Similarly, it takes for granted a certainty of characterisation: the archetypal hero (the worker) and the archetypal villain (the boss who exploits him). These certainties do not allow for psychological exploration, because what counts is the conviction of the viewpoint: we must hate all bosses because they exploit; we must see individuals from a class perspective.

The specific issue of 'correct' form has been argued over wherever socialist plays have been produced. This was so in Meyerhold's Soviet society, Piscator's Germany, and the amateur Workers' Theatre Movement in Britain in the 1930s.[37] The argument has often gone like this: why reject naturalism? Because it is too subjective and individual in its explanations of people's behaviour. Why choose agitprop? Because it is a form capable of showing the objective political, economic and social determinations of people's class behaviour. These distinctions are on an important level dishonest. Edgar has argued that it is just as partial and elitist for a play to show a determinist analysis of history as it is for a television soap to pretend 'that life is a continuous, endlessly repeated series of ... domestic conflicts and reconciliations, as predictable and unchanging as the cogs and wheels of a

clock'.[38] The audience will either agree or disagree with .
analysis of history demonstrated in agitprop, but (as Richard Seyd
of the Red Ladder company wrote): 'if people don't think that
capitalism is an absurd and damaging way of organising society,
then very little that one does is going to change their minds.'[39]

David Edgar was now striving for a theatre of public life that
would be as complex as the familiar theatre of domestic life. He
wanted to write about subjects such as fascism and the women's
movement for which agitprop was not appropriate 'because they
are the areas in which the subtle combination of the personal and
political, the emotional and the intellectual, takes place'.[40] The
new form that he envisaged would depict the dynamic between
people's subjective perceptions of their social situation, and the
objective underlying political reality at certain historical moments.
The audience could then come to conclusions and there was the
possibility that they would take on board the discrepancy between
the subjective and the objective, coming to consciousness of their
situation. Edgar's immediate achievement was a form that
combined agitprop with social realism. This was realised in the
anti-fascist play *Destiny*.

2

Destiny

> *Destiny* had more effect, by virtue of being done at the Aldwych, than anything else I've written. Partly because it's better than a lot of what I've written, but partly because it became an event. And I would argue that its performance at the Aldwych had more effect than its production on television, despite the fact that it was seen by four million people on television and by twenty-two thousand at the Aldwych.   David Edgar, 1979[1]

David Edgar's bold argument about the political effect of his full-length anti-fascist play for the Royal Shakespeare Company called into question two main strategies of socialist theatre in Britain since 1968. John McGrath's commitment to a popular theatre form and his emphasis on non-bourgeois context; Trevor Griffiths's insistence on the strategic penetration of television: these emphases were now seen from a new perspective. In his seminal essay 'Ten Years of Political Theatre, 1968–1978', Edgar examined the tactics of theatre practitioners in their attempt to contribute to the socialist movement, and backed up with examples this opinion: 'It seems to me demonstrably if paradoxically true that the most potent, rich, and in many ways politically acute theatrical statements of the past ten years have been made in custom-built buildings patronised almost exclusively by the middle class.'[2]

It has to be emphasised that this conviction meant neither that Edgar wanted all socialist theatre to be confined to establishment buildings nor that he was thus to confine himself. Following the success of *Destiny* he immediately worked with two touring companies (7:84 England with *Wreckers* and Pirate Jenny with *Our Own People*) before returning to the RSC with *The Jail Diary of Albie Sachs*. *Jail Diary* was followed by *Teendreams* with the touring company Monstrous Regiment. However, there is no doubt that he has found his most certain voice in writing for audiences

28

within our large theatre institutions. This affiliation has disappointed John McGrath and it is worth analysing the differences between the two colleagues in order to lead into a discussion of *Destiny*.

McGrath's model for revolutionary theatre has relied on appropriating working-class 'popular' cultural forms, using these as a structural framework within which to introduce didactic socialist content. In the early 1970s he saw 'The National Interest' in Bradford. He found it entertaining but simplistic: 'propaganda without experience of life ... not political theatre ... politics mouthed in the theatre.' As he understood it, the General Will's approach was wrong for a working-class audience.[3] In Edgar's experience, however, the General Will audiences had related to images not from working-class popular culture but from 'populist' culture (films and television), such as the Tory cabinet portrayed as Chicago gangsters in 'The National Interest'. This distinction between popular and populist is one that Edgar has very clearly stressed. His maintained position is directly converse to McGrath's: the popular tradition has atrophied, popular forms such as music hall and melodrama are no longer part of people's cultural experience, therefore it is a mistake to say that 'we will relate to ordinary people by taking on their forms as a kind of passport into their consciousness'.[4] McGrath's stance relies on a class model for revolution that, as we have seen, Edgar had found grounds for rejecting. Edgar summed up:

> I think that the forms that have survived the televisual onslaught
> – including poor old panto – have been so extensively corrupted
> with that very televisual culture that they no longer have any
> usable relationship with autochthonous folk forms at all ...
> Everywhere there is rupture, and even in the countryside the folk
> song, the morris dance and the mummers' play are not
> remembered but reclaimed, an act of social archaeology. And let
> us not delude ourselves either that even in the most militant pit
> villages – where if there was a living industrial tradition you'd
> expect to find it – the ballad, the brass band or even the lodge
> library or billiard room are central elements in people's lives
> today.[5]

Edgar acknowledged McGrath's considerable success with 7:84 Scotland's use of the ceilidh form in *The Cheviot, the Stag and the*

Black Black Oil, attributing this success to the play's localism: 'it drew on a rural folk form and, indeed, was directed at audiences in the rural highlands of Scotland.'[6]

In 1992 Edgar was adamant that the early 1970s project of creating a mass working-class audience had not worked:

> Despite considerable energy there wasn't a voluntaristic solution to that. There wasn't 'Just try a bit harder and it will'. What I did see however was that the theatre was being able to articulate a number of other movements. I suppose if I was to attempt to outflank John by a sort of act of impish conciliation I'd say that actually I think his achievement has been to do for Scotland, and to do for a certain proletarian tradition within Scottish Nationalism in particular, what the upsurge of women's theatre did for women, and what the upsurge of black theatre did for black people, and what my participation in the anti-racist movement in a play like *Destiny* did for that movement.[7]

Ultimately it could be argued that what is most interesting (paradoxically) about this whole debate – and McGrath has vigorously kept up his side of it – is that the divisions between these two socialist practitioners result in importantly complementary work.[8] The great achievement of *The Cheviot* in 1973 on tour in Scotland and using the ceilidh popular form, was to give a voice to the people of the Scottish Highlands. The great achievement of *Destiny* produced by the RSC in 1976 at The Other Place in Stratford and transferring to the Aldwych in 1977, was not only that an agitprop play had penetrated the establishment but that it had penetrated it in such a cunning way (within the guise of social realism) that its propaganda was more politically effective than that of 'The National Interest' had ever been.

Destiny was directed by Ron Daniels. Had it not been for his intervention, the play would not have been produced by the RSC and, more than likely, would not have been produced at all. Edgar had longed for a big stage for a number of reasons: personal career ambition, the chance for theatrical spectacle, and primarily because public subjects need big casts and 'did not take place in rooms but in *areas*, which it is nice to have the space to represent. Because streets are larger than houses, and battlefields are larger than bedrooms.'[9] Nottingham Playhouse had commissioned the piece through David Hare as dramaturg. The first draft, written in 1973, would have played at five hours and had fifty characters. Hare commented: 'I know you don't think construction is very important, but this time you have Gone Too Far.'[10] That draft contained the Court of Inquiry section that was to become the play *Our Own People*. Edgar cut and rewrote to half the length. But across the nation they turned it down. Birmingham Repertory Theatre, Nottingham Playhouse, Sheffield Crucible, the National under Peter Hall, the Royal Court, and the RSC itself, rejected what was to prove one of the most persuasive socialist plays of the decade.

In 1976 Ron Daniels was one of the most exciting young RSC directors. He had directed (as a freelance) the David Rudkin play *Afore Night Come* in the first The Other Place season, and was to become Artistic Director of that studio shortly after the production of *Destiny*. As an RSC director his background was untypical. He was born in Brazil where he had founded and built the Theatre Workshop in São Paolo. He had worked for several years in English theatre; this included work as actor and director with Peter Cheeseman's company at Stoke and experience of working on documentaries, including one about Ford at Dagenham. In an interview in July 1991 he recalled the production of *Destiny* with impassioned enthusiasm as a landmark for the RSC and for political theatre. What he was looking for was a new play that conveyed 'the spirit of the times, the excitement of the times, the dialectic of the times, but which wasn't in an agitprop fashion. I remember reading *Destiny* with a tremendous feeling of excitement and actually feeling that here is somebody who has a finger on the pulse, even though the text at that time was huge – very, very long. The subject matter was explosive.' His work in theatre reflecting the life of the community meant that *Destiny* was 'totally familiar territory'. He was passionate about plays 'to awaken consciousness, make people more aware of the lives they led, their hidden pressures in common, the things that make us what we are. *Destiny* in many ways brought those things into complete focus.'[11]

Daniels negotiated a meeting with Edgar in a London pub, where the playwright showed him, in minute handwriting, Major Rolfe's speech at the end of Act Two. Daniels's recognition that this was a play that 'had to be done' in Stratford was made there and then. A by-election in the West Midlands (in West Bromwich) had secured

31

a large number of votes for the National Front: an anti-fascist play needed to be seen in that part of Britain. Most importantly, too, Daniels understood that the writing was 'not political in an agitprop way but profoundly political, looking at people's predicaments and particular circumstances and making extremely good theatre'. Within forty-eight hours, Trevor Nunn, Artistic Director of the RSC, had confirmed to Ron Daniels that he had a slot at The Other Place for Edgar's play. Nunn later admitted 'We were lucky to get [it], we didn't deserve it' (after the initial rejection).[12] Edgar tried to reject the RSC, but overcame his anxiety about The Other Place (ironically the small venue he had been trying to escape) when he was persuaded that the play might transfer to the Warehouse, the new RSC space about to open in London.

By this circuitous route, *Destiny* found precisely the most propitious company to produce it. Daniels had been sensitive to what was to be the most hotly debated feature of the play:

> It did speak as *Look Back in Anger* had done in 1956 of a very particular time. More than just capturing the spirit of the times, it actually spoke a language, had a theatrical immediacy that people in 1976 really understood – which was no longer the simplified rhetoric of agitprop but where the world was perceived as more complicated than that, where socialist panaceas were not sufficient to portray complex realities. There was a sudden qualitative difference. David had done an enormous amount of fine work and the RSC had obviously done new plays before, and Trevor had been interested in new work before, and all my work at that time was to do with new writing, but suddenly there was this particular play that was different, was one step further – not a turning-point because we weren't going in the wrong direction, but suddenly everything made much more sense, everything cohered, everything came together at that particular time.

Destiny's moral intricacy was profoundly disturbing, and yet its truths caught a mood of confusion and change. When, in the early 1970s, Edgar originally had the idea for the play: 'For the first time in my life there was a feeling that the institutions and assumptions of British public life were under absolute threat.'[13] What Edgar showed in the play was a group of people all acting because of their care about the destiny of Britain.

32

One such character is Major Rolfe, the *petit-bourgeois* ex-Army officer whose speech at the end of Act Two had fired Ron Daniels's interest. Rolfe is cradling a crumpled Union Jack 'as he would a baby': symbolically the nation is his child. The monologue is delivered out front and it is full of emotional rhetoric. Rolfe's son has been killed in Northern Ireland. In his grief, Rolfe reaches a warped understanding. He shocks us by his realisation that he has more respect for the killer of his son than for the government who have reneged on the conditions of Empire. The speech is in prose but the imagery, rhythms and alliteration give it a heightened quality. The sun imagery of the play as a whole is continued and the punning echoes a famous speech from *Richard II*. The monologue crystallises the despair that leads to Rolfe's fascist sympathies, and is at the heart of Edgar's approach to the subject: we will be allowed into the emotions that lead to an embracing of Fascism. There is despondency in the face of betrayal: 'The Generals. The Ministers. Assured us that the sun would never set. The Generals, could not prevent my son, in his high morning, his sun going down' and there is resolution:

> *The tears stop.* ROLFE *raises the flag, holding it in a high salute.*
>
> We need an iron dawn.
>
> *He stands there, holding up the flag. Lights fade to darkness.*

Ron Daniels has spoken of the Shakespearian quality of the play, in the sense of its embracing both public and private worlds, the historical and the individual perspectives. In this sense, the RSC was most suited to produce *Destiny* and it was Edgar who defined this more closely: 'really it is an epic in non-epic surroundings. It is a difficult thing to achieve, but using Shakespearian actors is useful, because they understand the rhetoric in the play. To a certain extent, it's about rhetoric.'[14]

As an epic play, *Destiny* merges social realism and agitprop. Edgar has discussed this hybrid:

> It's an agitprop structure, still, in a funny kind of way – each scene makes its own point ... If it has a major fault of which I'm aware it's that the complexity of the characters and the

complexity of the language is to a certain extent imposed on the structure, which is perhaps slightly too skeletal, slightly too meccano-like.[15]

The play is an example of 'faction': fictitious characters are placed in real-life factual situations. The audience must be aware of the actual political circumstances of 1970s Britain in order to appreciate fully the final scene which is an imaginative product of all that occurs in the play, and a prediction of the future. Social realism has consistently been defined by Edgar in terms of Lukács's definition: 'type' characters are shown in a 'total' social–historical context.[16] The overt propaganda that involves simple allegorical characters each of whom represents an objective moral position is replaced by the subtler technique of equipping the audience with information to raise consciousness. To this end, the play seeks to inhabit the spectrum of political positions through realistic characters' subjective reactions to situations. The verbal language in *Destiny* is varied in form: sometimes colloquial, sometimes highly wrought and rhetorical with strong patterns of imagery (as in Rolfe's monologue); there is a certain use of non-realistic conventions such as verse and direct address. There are patterns also of visual imagery: the symbolic signs of Union Jack flag and the Indian Mutiny painting recur to emphasise political meaning. The whole feeling is of a dramatist delighting in experimentation, freed from the straitjacket of the simple propaganda play. Nevertheless, it is the agitprop structure that primarily makes us aware of social causation and shocks through dramatic irony. We are carefully encouraged to see the characters' behaviour in terms of their public life rather than their individual psychology and, through this, to see events as alterable.

The play is about the effects of the death of Empire on 1970s England. The first scene acts as historical prologue, set in a British Army barracks on Independence Day in India in 1947. The four characters in the first scene are relocated and flashed forward in time more than twenty years to Taddley, a fictitious West Midlands town where a by-election is imminent. They are introduced in separate scenes in Act One and each announces his homecoming in doggerel tropes. The actor playing the old-style Tory Colonel Chandler announces Chandler's death. Major Rolfe describes the nation he perceives as 'a flaccid spongers' state'. He has lost the

Tory nomination to Crosby, Chandler's nephew, and is bitter about the betrayal 'on all counts' of the *petit-bourgeoisie*:

> Their property no longer secure. Their social status, now irrelevant. And in the place of what's important to them, national destiny and hope ... it's not true that we've lost an Empire, haven't found a role. We have a role. As Europe's whipping boy. The one who's far worse off than you are. Kind of − awful warning system of the West. And to play that role, we must become more shoddy, threadbare, second-rate. Not even charming, quite unloveable. And for those − the people that I come from, that despair is a betrayal.

Khera, a Sikh from the Punjab, also has a perception of his position: as a constituent of a workers' underclass in a prejudiced England, where he rejects his background 'so he can be a proper Englishman' and 'Keep faith in human virtue, while attempting to condone/The mother country's horror at her children coming home'. By the time we see Khera's relocation (at the very end of Act One), we have witnessed the horror of the most shocking scene in the play: the Hitler birthday party of 20 April 1968, the day that Enoch Powell made his 'rivers of blood' speech. The national mood of despair, racism and change is set, and these 'type' characters will be seen in that 'total' context. But it is the fourth character, Sergeant Turner, on whom the audience is allowed to focus most clearly.

The lower-middle-class Turner is self-employed. His perception is of a world where old virtues, values and certainties have changed. His small antiques business is lost when a large property developer grabs the shop. The Jewish agent for the Metropolitan Investment Trust issues a threat of violence if Turner refuses to leave, and that violence will come from the West Indians who will be persuaded to wreck the shop. The Jew Monty teaches the lesson of capitalist enterprise:

> TURNER. But why destroy my livelihood.
>
> MONTY (*harsh, quick, nearly angry*). Because my love, destroying you will make someone somewhere some money. All it is. Cupidity. What you got, but just not enough. Cos we, we make our money out of money. We covet on a global

scale. We got cupidity beyond your wildest dreams of avarice. And you, the little man, the honest trader, know your basic handicap? You're suffering a gross deficiency of greed.

Turner's absorption of this lesson only comes at the very end of the play. By then, he has become a parliamentary candidate for the far right party, Nation Forward. He has gained 23% of the votes in the by-election that the Conservative wins. His faith in fascism has been won through ignorance. When Cleaver of Nation Forward reveals the anti-Semitic nature of the conspiracy theory, he can point to something specific from Turner's own experience, reminding him that a Jew took his shop.[17] The terrible irony of the final scene is that Rolfe (the big industrialist who represents the firm that ousted Turner) is seen negotiating with the party, contemplating a financial backing of it. Edgar stated: 'It is the most direct polemical point the play makes – that the *petit-bourgeois* masses commit themselves to Fascism and only later discover that Fascism is in fact operating in the interests of the very big businessmen that it claims to oppose. It's a very clear example. In fact, it worked rather well. I was always amazed that the audience remembered the name, the Metropolitan Investment Trust.'[18]

Within this overall defining structure of irony, the basic drive of the play is 'first act Tory, second act fascist, third act Labour'.[19] Within each act, each scene makes a point and is separable from the whole, so that the play is at once episodic (built of small propagandist scenes) and also has the very clear cause and effect of continuing narrative with conflict, turning points and recognitions. It is vital that the audience should not lose a social-political perspective. Act One establishes this perspective by interrupting chronology so that we learn from the sequence of six scenes. This interruption of linear time works as follows: Scene One (1947); Scenes Two, Three and Four (the contemporary present, 1976); Scene Five (1970); Scene Six (20 April 1968 until the last three speeches which propel us forward again to 1976). Edgar has talked of 'thematic linking'. One scene poses a question which is answered by the following scene: 'What I wanted the audience to do was actually view the play in terms of its theme, in terms of the social forces involved, not necessarily to be bothered with strict chronology.'[20] Throughout Act One we are, in this way, made to look at a particular view of history. Thus, when Khera is shown at work in the foundry right at the end of the act, his current social position has been defined by his position in India in 1947 (Scene One) and is threatened by the forces of Fascism which gathered impetus following the Powell speech on 20 April 1968. Powell's attempt to create and exploit racial hatred will fuel the Nation Forward party and the philosophy of that party will affect Khera's life in England. During the course of the play he represents the cause of the Sikh workers discriminated against at the foundry; he negotiates with the Labour MP; there is a strike; the Nation Forward party breaks the picket line; he does not secure the illegal immigrant Patel's stay in the country; the Labour MP betrays him (and all Sikhs fighting in the union) and he draws conclusions about the effects of Empire.

The play argues a specific view of Fascism drawn from what Edgar describes as the 'extraordinarily prescient' writings of Trotsky on the rise of Fascism in the 1930s. In Edgar's article for the Institute of Race Relations' Journal *Race and Class*, 'Racism, Fascism and the Politics of the National Front', he sets out this specific definition, which is then presented in *Destiny*:

> Fascism is the mobilisation of a counter-revolutionary mass
> movement during a period of capitalist crisis in which the
> conventional forces of the state are seen to be incapable of
> resolving the contradictions of the system. The participants in
> this mass movement tend to be drawn from those sectors of
> society – notably the lower-middle class, unorganised workers,
> the peasantry and backward sections of the ruling class – which
> are facing a relative and progressive worsening of their
> economic and social position, but who nonetheless see no future
> in an alliance with the organised proletariat. The role of Fascism,
> both in power and on the road to it, is the destruction of the
> independent organisations of the working class, sometimes in
> collusion with and always in the broad interests of the
> employing classes.[21]

The play offers this analysis in order to defeat it in contemporary Britain. Within this broad aim, Edgar had other goals. He eschewed simplicity. It had to be faced that 'it is extremely difficult for little white old ladies in streets that have gone black'.[22] It did also have to be faced that people who join the National Front are not monsters. He wanted to get across to the left that those people attracted to the far right had understandable fears, although their response to those fears was barbarous and dangerous. He wanted to impress on the liberal middle-class audience the argument that those on the left were well aware of before the play started: that 'the National Front was not a mildly unpleasant anti-immigration pressure group but a fascist organisation with a conscious strategy to win hearts and minds to the idea of authoritarian dictatorship', which (as indeed some reviewers suggested) seemed to be 'evidence of the wildest left-wing paranoia in 1976'.[23] Finally, the Act Three defeats for the left were meant to cry out for certain tactics: 'the last act is a piece of propaganda for a more aggressive and militant way of countering fascists, reflecting the debate that was taking place within the Labour Party in the late seventies: basically, between a more aggressive, militant, on-the-streets approach and the approach of the Labour candidate [in the play] which is a much more moderate one which the play argued collapses into racism. It's actually really quite propagandist in that respect.'[24]

As Edgar put it, the play is 'more propagandist than it looks'.[25] The two most propagandist scenes in the very complicated structure of the play are the meeting scene in Act Two and the last scene of the entire play. Act Two Scene Two is politically and theatrically one of the best scenes Edgar has ever written. Act Two itself centres on the fascists: their ideas, factions, in-fighting and purges; the growth of support for the movement; and Turner's comic schooling as their candidate. The scenes at the Baron Castings works and the Labour Club demonstrate the growth of the Asian workers' politicised struggle against discrimination and emphasise the need to counteract racism. Rolfe's emotional speech at the end of the act heralds the interest of an industrialist in the party.

What the Taddley Patriotic League meeting scene so effectively does is to collect together representatives of class, section and group in English society, all discontent and, in class terms, enemies, facing each other across the various boundaries of their difference, and all being persuaded into the philosophy of Fascism by Maxwell, General Secretary of Nation Forward:

> Of course, we disagree on many issues. But much, much more unites us than divides us. It's an old saying, but you can change your class and your creed. But you can't change the blood in

38

your veins ... we have a common enemy ... There are people, still, who laugh at the idea of a conspiracy. A world-wide conspiracy. But there's one, small group of men and women who don't laugh. There is one, small, growing party which knows what is happening and is determined to reverse it. That is Nation Forward. And I hope, with all sincerity, that you will wish to join this party, join with us, and make our country great again.

The scene very clearly shows a specific political process, how people are led into a particular understanding, how people make political decisions, and why in the first place they are dissatisfied. It dramatises Edgar's belief that 'What seems to be attractive about Fascism is the sheer demagogic appeal it has and its capacity to dupe so many kinds of people with genuine frustrations. It numbs people to the class struggle or rather it racialises the class struggle and that is its biggest threat.'[26]

Edgar hoped that the audience would recognise the format of meetings; and, just as in domestic drama they recognise the intimate embarrassments of a bedroom scene, so in this play of public life they are encouraged to perceive the somewhat bungled protocol of an essential meeting. The horror of Maxwell's efficiency is built into a strongly comic framework where Turner's incompetence with the Union Jack, the failure of the microphone, the collection for the hire of the hall, and the feeble jokes to cover embarrassment, give a general impression of playing at politics. Turner is especially amateurish, with his slip of referring to Maxwell as 'leader' rather than General Secretary and his emphasis on transmitted disease. Yet through the awkward silences and the jokes penetrates the aesthetic and economic hatred of immigrants. This hatred unites (for example) Mrs Howard (the upper-middle-class Conservative) and Attwood (the working-class trade unionist from Baron Castings). It is Attwood who is unequivocal: 'I'll be quite frank about the blacks, I hate 'em.' The grievances aired at the meeting, from inability to sell property in a black area, to the dangers of parasitic worms, to inflation, are summed up in a song. The Kipling poem set to music and sung by the working-class Tony encapsulates the ugliness of nationalist fervour:

It was not suddenly bred
It will not swiftly abate

39

Through the chill years ahead
When time shall count from the date
That the English began to hate.

It is from this scene onwards that Turner will be exploited by the party as their candidate. Maxwell's election message voice-over covers the transition to the next scene, demonstrating how emotion is gathered into slick campaigning slogans: 'Our nation is under threat ... Most of all, treacherous politicians have conspired to flood our country with the refuse of the slums Africa and Asia. Vote for a change. Vote Nation Forward. Vote Dennis Turner.'

For Ron Daniels, the texture of this scene characterises one of the key strengths of David Edgar's work. As a director he could focus on the pragmatic human details of it, yet it is a crucial ideological scene; he memorably described this approach as Edgar's attempt 'to reach the cosmos through particularity'. Similarly, Ian McDiarmid, who played Turner in the original production, discussed the way in which the audience had to be allowed to find the situation ridiculous and technically incompetent.[27] By this recognisable comic particularity the political lesson of the scene is framed. The audience may be repressing similar emotions; they could be manipulated in the same direction by a Maxwell. The technique is to chill by identification not to bludgeon by denunciation.

The final scene of the entire play represents a situation that is a direct product of the meeting scene. Kershaw, the industrialist who sides with Rolfe, spells out the counter-revolutionary nature of the fascist movement. What is needed, he says, is 'Fighting the Reds, wherever they appear.' The businessmen argue with Cleaver that the police will not be effective in doing this, neither will the army, who 'can't destroy'. Race will be the ideological glue: 'To stick the nation to itself', to combat 'A community of tolerance, compassion, moderation. Tolerance of crime, permissiveness. Compassion for the multi-coloured misfits of the world. And moderation, military reserve, low profile in the face of insurrection.' By dramatising the involvement of capitalists with the Fascist party, Edgar was making a prediction that depends on the audience's knowledge of events in 1930s Germany:

I proceeded on from the argument that said we have in Britain now in the seventies the constituents which are equivalent to the

40

constituents that were there in thirties Germany to sufficient degree for this to be a worry. I then went on – because, as everyone knows, the fascists in Germany in the thirties were backed by big business, and fascism to a certain extent became big business's mailed fist – I then went on to speculate how British businessmen would support such a move.[28]

Exactly 'how' they would support the party is different in each of the three published texts of the play. In the 1976 text, financial backing is offered both personally and on behalf of the companies concerned:

> ROLFE. We felt, by bankers' order. Neater. Transfer, straight.
>   From Tory coffers into yours.

Here, Edgar makes it clear that the businessmen have betrayed the Conservative Party:

> CLEAVER. They know?
>
> ROLFE. The Party? Yes. They called us Judases. We pointed
>   out, in this case, we're the paymasters.

In the revised text (1978), Rolfe is more circumspect:

> ROLFE. We felt, by bankers' order. Quietly. No more, yet, than
>   insurance. Down payment, on a possible tomorrow.

In the re-revised text (volume one of the collected *Plays*, 1987), Kershaw is adamant: 'There's no question of a deal.' There is no money 'yet. Not yet at all.' The approach is personal, not on behalf of the companies:

> CLEAVER. Is this – approach, just you?
>
> KERSHAW. Oh, yes. Just us. Hardly United Vehicles. Not now.
>
> ROLFE. Hardly the Metropolitan Investment Trust. Not now.
>   Not yet.

This last revision was made for the 1985 revival of the play. The point was that, midway through the 1980s, the prediction about the backing of the fascist party no longer applied because Thatcherism had 'articulated and redressed ... the sense of national humiliation' that, in the 1970s, neo-Fascism had exploited.[29]

These revisions indicate Edgar's scrupulousness in writing for the exact configuration of the times. The final moments of the play in the 1987 volume chillingly stress the conditions that may pertain at a future date. These would indeed be the conditions of 1930s Germany when the stark choice was between Fascism and Communism. Cleaver tries to persuade Turner that the financial backing will come 'In the long term. When their precious law and order falls apart, the cities burn, the centre cannot hold ... When it's the ultra-left or us ...'. Turner has by now learnt that his fascist campaigning has been in the interests of the Metropolitan Investment Trust, ironically the company that betrayed him. He has stared at the painting of the Indian Mutiny, the implications of that massacre obviously filtering through to him. In his moment of recognition he clamours to be told what can stop the movement:

CLEAVER. What on earth can stop us now?

A long pause. Then TURNER, *to* CLEAVER.

TURNER. So tell me. Tell me. *Tell me.*

The light changes so that Cleaver and Turner are in silhouette. They are placed in a continuum of history as 'a voice is heard; gentle, quiet, insistent. It is the voice of Adolf Hitler':

ADOLF HITLER. Only one thing could have stopped our
Movement: if our adversaries had understood its principle,
and had smashed, with the utmost brutality, the nucleus of our
new Movement.

Slight pause.

Hitler. Nuremberg. Third of September, 1933.

Blackout.

The shock of the final documentary facts is harder and more forceful than the ending of the 1976 text, where Hitler comes on stage and reads the statement 'gently and almost apologetically'.

The propagandist point is coherently made: history is not a matter of 'destiny': it is alterable; if we understand the principles of neo-Fascism in contemporary Britain, it can be smashed.

The way in which this final scene and the earlier meeting scene work is to provide the social–historical context for type characters. Edgar was anxious to emphasise the social and political typicality of his characters in order to eliminate psychological explanations of their choices. He depersonalised the characters on the right by refusing to present aspects of their familial or domestic or sexual lives, arguing:

> The character Turner is absolutely described in terms of his movement through the public world. He turns to the extreme right because he loses his business, because of an event that occurs at work. The three central characters on the right: Turner, we know nothing about his personal life at all and all we know is his structuring through public events, his military service, his business; and the two fascists, Cleaver and Maxwell, again we know nothing of them personally at all and so they're absolutely, one could argue to excess, representing political perspectives; Rolfe had his own very specific move through life that was about his own relationships with his army service, and with the changes in the world around him and a sense of personal betrayal which culminated in the wasted death of his son, so that probably was more personal in one sense.[30]

Of course, actors presenting realistic individuals on stage obey certain conventions that are in accordance with observed actuality; for example, they are not masked and talk in natural speech tones. There is an argument that stresses that a political presentation should always nail its colours to the mast by depersonalising through definite anti-realistic techniques. It should, however, be considered a strength of the play that there is a measure of realism.

The play is aimed at a particular audience; as Ron Daniels has defined them, 'the Turners of the world', the lower-middle class, for the most part non-unionised people who do not work in large collectives, with political attitudes that veer to the centre. They are not the radical converted of the General Will audiences. The familiar realism reassures the audience, rather than making them feel uncomfortable, so that they are more responsive to the propagandist argument. They are allowed a measure of identification in order to

43

understand the emotional draw that Fascism uses: as Ian McDiarmid has pointed out, Turner's progress from Tory supporter to fascist parliamentary candidate invites the question 'Would I do it?' Turner's journey is interrupted by all the other strands of the play: he is not the only focus of attention and, indeed, he does not speak, despite being on stage twice, from the end of Act Two to the end of Act Three. He is always seen as a figure constructed by a network of social and political forces, and he is reconstructed by his fascist electoral schooling. Nevertheless, McDiarmid centred on a psychological motivation for the role; he understood Turner as a character motivated by a feeling of dispossession:

> He was dispossessed from India onwards and that is a feeling one understands and it was a strong feeling. The play was about what can happen to someone who's dispossessed, who has a void in himself, who doesn't feel fulfilled in any particular direction, who's disappointed by what's on offer, so goes to an area which looks as if it may supply him with what he thinks he needs. People looking for an identity, feeling they don't have a personal identity, can grasp hold too easily perhaps of a dogmatic line and consequently be imprisoned by it and transformed by it and made, perhaps, more animal by it. That's ultimately why I found it such a rewarding play to be in and part to play. It posed difficult questions and didn't provide easy answers. One could have written a perfectly straightforward play about the horrors of the National Front, but David wrote a much more complex play than that.

The way was left open for the audience to understand Turner's predicament through an identifiable emotion. Edgar knew that this was vital: 'It's a play which ... is intended for a middle-class audience, it's about the middle class, the class I come from and know best. The fears and panics and despairs of the middle class are what it's all about.'[31]

In contrast to Turner's growth as a character, there are characters in the play, often seen in pairs to state a dialectic, who are more obviously limited types representing political positions. An important contradiction within the fascist party opposes Maxwell and Cleaver. Maxwell takes the 'National' out of 'National Socialism', a heresy that invites the anti-Semitic Cleaver's 'little purge' in Act Two. The subtlety of in-fighting among the fascists, together with Cleaver's personal statement about his uncle who lives in Southall – 'this harmless old fellow is quite genuinely terrified that after he's dead, some time in the future, an Indian temple may be built over his grave' – and the Conservative candidate's judgement of the fascists' 'monstrous chauvinism', are all working towards the audience's understanding of complexity. The density of detail means that, in a row with her husband, the Labour candidate's wife has arguments and examples about the difficulties of integrating people from different cultural back-grounds; Khera can make clear the Irish parallel to his predicament as the legacy of Empire: 'Even the poor, white British, think that they, not just their masters, are born to rule. And us, the blacks, the Irish, all of us – a lesser breed, without the Rule of Law'; and Tony and Paul are working-class friends who make opposed political choices. In the Act Three police station scene Tony and Paul are ironically arrested for being on opposite sides of the picket line skirmish. The contradictions in their thinking are very strongly made clear in a simple lesson scene:

PAUL. All history's the struggle of the classes.

TONY. No. All history's the struggle of the races.

Tony voices the central lie of the neo-fascists: 'No, no, Paul. It never happened. Auschwitz, n' all. Just factories. The holocaust, just photos forged. Invented by the Jews.' Paul gives the audience the point of the scene in an out-front address:

PAUL. And, you know, it was like looking in a mirror, looking at him, me old mate, Tony. All correct, the same, identical. Just one thing wrong. Left's right. Class–race. As different as can be. The opposite. The bleeding wrong way round...

It is Paul in Act Three who carries the thrust of socialist conviction after the Labour candidate Clifton sells out to racism. Clifton's child has been threatened, a motive that Edgar expunged from the television version. Edgar also dropped the domestic scene: 'It's very interesting that one of the reviews of *Destiny* said that the Labour MP was a better character than the Tory MP, because we saw him at home. And I thought: mistake, David.'[32] We can understand Clifton's compromise but we should not

45

condone it. There has also to be a voice for a socialist vision, otherwise the play would lack positive focus and resemble the impartial reportage of naturalism. This would be a severe risk for a play depicting the pull of fascist ideology. In the 1976 text such a character is lacking and the play seems far too one-sided in giving the devil his due. In that text, Paul has a rather clichéd riposte to Clifton's accusations concerning his (Paul's) self-righteousness: 'sooner or later you're going to have to make up your mind, which side you're on. Cos you're standing on a little pack of ice, that's floating in a sharky sea, and there's too many people on it, Bob, and the bugger's melting away.' In the later texts Paul is instead, very tellingly, given a speech that re-uses and redefines the sun imagery of Rolfe's Act Two direct-address monologue. The effect is rhetorical and intensely moving, working to the climactic lines which echo in rhythm and reshape the actual words of the final lines of Rolfe's speech:

> PAUL (*quietly, gently, a genuine need to explain*). You know, there's a funny moment, comes to you, you see your real friends. Came to me, a meeting of the Barons strikers. Oh, yuh, sure, all clenched fists and synthetic Maoist fervour.
>
> Just, amid all that, some people learning. Talking, for the first time, 'bout just how to do it, working out, quite slowly, tortuously, quite frustrating, you know, for us old pros, to sit there and listen to it all.
>
> But it is listening to people grow. Learning that it's possible for them to make their future. Bit like the morning. Sun comes up, so slow, can't see it changing. But it's growing lighter. Think of that.
>
> Their fault. No turning back. The need, to be our own. To change, the real world.

The sun image, originally Crosby's reference to the Empire over which 'the sun will never set' (Act One Scene Two) is taken up in the Remembrance Sunday service (Act One Scene Four), used by Drumont to indicate the growth of fascist strength (Act One Scene Six), punned on by Rolfe (Act Two Scene Eight) and finally redefined by Paul. Another strong image pattern recurring throughout *Destiny* is associated with the 'rivers of blood' metaphor. Edgar's use of imagery, poetic prose, verse and rhetoric throughout balances the journalistic factual base. The vast amount of research and interviews that went into the preparation for *Destiny* have a very positive result in the informed detail of the play. What Edgar had also learnt since the documentaries of the General Will days was a poetic ability and, indeed, an emotional quality which, however much he strove to eliminate the personal, is very definitely present in *Destiny* and adds to its force as a politically convincing play. For, if *Destiny* is extraordinarily truthful in its scenes of violence, picket lines, Hitler birthday party ugliness, Labour Party compromise and depiction of national despair, it is also extraordinarily moving. Ron Daniels corroborated: 'David comes from the world of newspapers, observed fact, connections made with the real world. He succeeds in creating a poetic world which I find deeply touching.'

Bernard Crick reviewed *Destiny* with the highest praise precisely because of the psychological detail which he had missed in socialist propaganda plays:

> Here was a project I have often imagined but never hoped to see: a strong and committed left-winger able to understand and to dramatise empathetically the psychology and doctrine of fascism; and, indeed, its working-class as well as its elitist appeal ... [Edgar's] clinical empathy is extraordinary. He does something so rare in the political theatre: he sends out the audience informed, disturbed, and thinking, not full of a surrogate glow of an evening's political passion.[33]

Edgar had refused to write villains. To any argument that might deplore the play's lack of denunciation in this respect, Ian McDiarmid had an answer: he is sure that the real political danger is in 'not seeing people who might become members of the National Front or adopt these kind of views as being human. The things they say are far from human sometimes, and the things they do are quite often beyond our comprehension of what it is to be human; nevertheless, they are. It's important to understand that. They're not another species. We're all part of the same world. As one understands that, one understands the problem. David examined the problem.'

Edgar worked closely with Ron Daniels and the company in rehearsal, providing perceptive and precise commentary and a fund of relevant books and tapes, as well as instructing McDiarmid in

47

the Birmingham accent he adopted as Turner. The happy collaboration of director, writer and company was evidently a contributory factor in the success of the play which was, as McDiarmid put it, 'on the edge of things about to happen at the RSC'. The Warehouse was to open in July 1977 with its new plays policy and its new work was strongly socialist. The acting company for *Destiny* were suitable for it: 'they had done that sort of work together; they were of a generation and sensibility', and included Bob Peck, Michael Pennington, Paul Moriarty and Cherie Lunghi.[34] *Destiny* was premièred in the 1976 The Other Place season that also included Trevor Nunn's celebrated *Macbeth* (with Judi Dench and Ian McKellen) and Bond's *Bingo*. Its very positive reception meant transfer to the Aldwych where, in May 1977, it finally got the big stage Edgar had desired. It ran in rep with *King Lear*. A new play of urgent political relevance, about political parties in contemporary Britain, was sharing a space with a world-famous play. Throughout the run, the theatre building was bedecked with patriotic bunting for the Queen's Silver Jubilee and Edgar has relished the irony that the audience entered that bedecked building in order to see either a play about a mad king or his own play about fascists taking over the country.[35]

On the last night of the London run, the National Party (a split-off from the National Front) demonstrated outside the Aldwych. Neo-fascists waved Union Jacks; their booing could be heard inside the auditorium, someone was hit and the police were called. An extremely articulate, highly researched, politically sophistic-ated play for an RSC audience had provoked a reaction on the streets. Indeed, *Destiny*'s political importance was in the various reactions it provoked. In 1992 Edgar could still say that 'It intervened in the public debate that play, more than anything else I've written before or since' and he had confirmed why this was so over a decade earlier:

> There is absolutely no question that the play of mine which has had the most effect on the way people think about things is a play which was presented at the Aldwych Theatre in the West End of London – *Destiny*. And it was not just because it was a better play, it was because by making that statement in the very eye of the capital, that statement had an effect beyond the people who actually saw it. It was discussed in the political columns of

the newspapers as well as the arts pages. I wasn't asked to talk about the docks when I wrote *Wreckers*. I hadn't been asked to talk about housing when I'd written *Rent*. I wasn't asked to talk about the Industrial Relations Act when I'd written *The National Interest*. I wasn't asked to talk about the politics of health when I'd written a play called *O Fair Jerusalem*. But I wrote a play called *Destiny* which went on in the West End and within twenty-four hours the editors of three left-wing newspapers had rung me up asking me to write articles. Now that may be depressing news about the editors of left-wing newspapers – that they, too, are not immune to the attraction of the bright lights – but that's what it's like.[36]

Edgar was immediately invited to Anti-Nazi League meetings as a speaker and he directly contributed, in about fifty talks, to the fight against Fascism in the 1970s. He wrote for *Searchlight*, the anti-fascist research journal, and for *Race and Class*, the Institute of Race Relations' journal. In these articles and talks he could be vehemently polemical, thus separating the journalist and playwright sides of himself: '*Destiny* deliberately eschews tub-thumping at the same time as I was going round the country tub-thumping.'[37]

Destiny was broadcast as a BBC Play for Today in 1978. It was revived on stage at the Library Theatre, Manchester and the Theatre Royal, Bristol in the late 1970s. At the Half Moon in 1985 there was again a disruption by Fascist demonstrations. This time the play was seen in the heart of London's East End with its constant serious skirmishes between Asians and fascists. Restrictions on immigration have continued. During the 1980s the nationalist parties did not go from strength to strength as Edgar had predicted in *Destiny*, but the 1990s saw the far right re-emerging all over Europe; in Britain, the Anti-Nazi League has been re-formed; and the Anti-Racist Alliance has emerged. In March 1993 *Destiny* was revived by Birmingham Library Theatre Company. It had not been updated and it was billed as 'a classic play about racist politics in the West Midlands'. The play deserves a major new production by a leading company in a revised version for 1990s Europe. Its time has come again.

Destiny had penetrated the consciousness of its audiences precisely because it caught the spirit of the times with the necessary moral conflict and intricacy. It directly contributed to the anti-Fascist movement, demonstrating the power of the stage as political forum. It won the Arts Council's John Whiting Award for the best new play with contemporary relevance. Its production showed the determination of a young RSC director to put burning political issues onto the stage of the most distinguished British company. As Colin Chambers has pointed out, the play was 'certainly the most immediately political of any of the plays presented by the RSC in the 1970s'.[38] *Destiny* heralded Edgar's association with that company. In the 1980s he was to collaborate with Howard Davies on productions of *Henry VIII* and Trevor Griffiths's *The Party*, become the company's dramaturg, work again with Ron Daniels (on *Maydays*) and, most famously, to adapt a Dickens novel with that company. The adaptation of *The Life and Adventures of Nicholas Nickleby* was a resounding popular success. David Edgar has, to date, made four adaptations for the stage. There was a question everyone was to ask: was adaptation the correct territory for a socialist playwright?

3

Adaptations:
The Jail Diary of Albie Sachs, Mary Barnes, The Life and Adventures of Nicholas Nickleby and *The Strange Case of Dr Jekyll and Mr Hyde*

I dislike all theatrical adaptations of classic novels, except *Les Liaisons Dangereuses*. I reserve the right to stay away indefinitely from all cut-up versions of Dickens, Austen, Fielding, Thackeray, Hardy, Tolstoy, Dostoevsky, Flaubert, Balzac and any of the all-time greats. My most exquisite reason? They reduce great fiction to bare-bones melodrama, eliminate irony, authorial vision and the transforming effect of time, and – most serious of all – are gradually supplanting new work on the British stage. To hell with them!   Michael Billington, 1991[1]

I know that the directors of *Nicholas Nickleby* gave real directions, the designers produced real designs, and the actors delivered real performances. I like to think – well, no, actually I *do* think – that I wrote a real play.   David Edgar, 1983[2]

There is a contemporary theory which condemns all adaptation for the theatre as a safe and soft option for those playwrights whose fountain of imagination has dried up. The implied lament is partly for the death of what might have been: the 'creative' new piece that embraces the unique position of the dramatist in response to his or her times. Moreover, this theory holds that there is a further threat that the perceived cultural miscegenation

51

between non-dramatic source (which in the late twentieth century is most popularly that of nineteenth-century prose fiction) and theatrical adaptation may effect a stage explosion of such inferior hybrid monsters. David Edgar has written four adaptations, using as source material two autobiographies (*The Jail Diary of Albie Sachs* and *Mary Barnes*) and two nineteenth century novels (*The Life and Adventures of Nicholas Nickleby* and *The Strange Case of Dr Jekyll and Mr Hyde*). He has no need of apology because his work has refuted the attacks on adaptation in general. These four plays reinvent their source texts with skill and theatrical confidence, interrogating the relevant contexts (authorial, cultural, historical, political) in relation to our contemporary reality. Here it is apposite to cite Eric Bentley, who has argued that 'The Germans have a term, *Zeitstück*, for a play that tries to cope with a problem of the day. A leading playwright, I believe, might be expected to cope with *the* leading problem of the day. It will, of course, be of the highest interest *what* he considers that problem to be.'[3] In his adaptations, Edgar offers us an analysis of 'the leading problem(s) of the day' that is consistent with his practice as political commentator for the stage.

That practice is necessarily a product of what Edgar described at his 1992 'Beyond Words' Birmingham University conference as 'hyphenation'. He defines himself not generically as 'writer' but as 'writer–person, writer–political being, writer–actor in the world'. As a research writer he is always involved with collection and assembly (rather than pure imagination) in order to demonstrate meaning: 'The universe is complex and comprehensible. It is the writer's duty to comprehend it.'[4] In his essay 'Adapting *Nickleby*', Edgar has rejected as 'too pat' the idea that an adaptation could be seen to be a play researched from a single source[5] and yet there is something not unreasonable about the suggestion. On another level, with reference to current theory of performance analysis, each performance text is not a simple 'realisation' of the written text but a separate signifying system to be 'read' by an audience familiar with the cultural codes of the piece; thus each performance text is surely a 'making suitable', or adaptation, for stage performance of a written dramatic text. In this way, it could be persuasively argued that adaptation is endemic to all performance but, in any event, in the specific radical practice of twentieth-century political makers of theatre we find a positive tradition of adaptation of the classics for purposes of social and historical reassessment. Piscator, Brecht and Meyerhold repossessed the classics in order to demonstrate in the very act of so doing the alterability of the social world and its hierarchies. Meyerhold famously thus renewed *The Government Inspector*; Piscator championed revitalisation of the classics and famously adapted the novel *The Adventures of the Good Soldier Schweik*; Brecht time and again reworked old material to his own purpose.[6] As Eric Bentley points out, 'After 1933 the radical German authors couldn't be performed any more. But this did not mean that the theatres were flooded with Nazi plays ... the Nazi regime cherished the classics.'[7]

The issue is one of point of view. When Edgar adapted *Mary Barnes*, for example, he did so in order to bring the late 1970s audience to a particular complex consciousness of a 1960s psychiatric experiment and indeed 1960s counter-culture as a whole. By drawing attention to two specific time-frames, he could objectively present on stage a seminal and strongly emotional autobiographical record and could thereby prompt audience awareness in such a way that the non-mediated reading of the source could not achieve. This relates to another point by Eric Bentley: 'The artist has learned his craft but is never content to be a craftsman.'[8] This chapter will argue that Edgar's craft in adaptation (and he regards himself as an architect in his care for assembly and construction) defines him as a political artist. For although the *Guardian* critic Michael Billington has dubbed adaptation *le vice anglais*, he has also repeatedly expressed his commitment to theatre as an oppositional, protesting medium.[9] The irony is that it is not only perfectly possible to combine the two functions of adaptor and social critic but that to do so has indeed been a strategy central to socialist theatre. The strategy is that of intertextual commentary to assist analysis of history in relation to the present. A related point is surely that the individual's voice (and in the case of Edgar's adaptations, the voice is that of Mary Barnes or Joseph Berke or Albie Sachs or Charles Dickens or Robert Louis Stevenson) becomes a collective voice in the subsequent theatre collaborations, further rejecting the individualist position of our Conservative age. Nowhere is this more true than in the 'collective possession'[10] by the RSC players of the text of *Nicholas Nickleby*.

In 1978 David Edgar's two adaptations of autobiographical records were premièred. *The Jail Diary of Albie Sachs* was given its first production in London by the RSC at the Warehouse. *Mary Barnes* was first produced at the Birmingham Repertory Theatre Studio. Edgar's choices to 'sculpt' *Jail Diary* ('taking what was already there – the book – as a fairly precise little block of stone, and chipping neatly away at it') and to 'hang things' on *Mary Barnes* ('a kind of trampoline, or linear row of pegs, on which various things would hang which would rush off down different avenues') developed his technical skills as a writer in very precise ways to do with structure, language and characterisation.[11] This reflects the ease with which Edgar had always tackled work based on source material, and it is worth briefly reflecting on the continuum in evidence here. He had worked with short scenes of various types of parody very extensively in the General Will days, and then at full-length in 'Tedderella' and *Dick Deterred*, where he had devastatingly pinpointed extremely apt literary resonances with contemporary political events in Europe and America, and could rely on audience knowledge respectively of *Cinderella* and pantomime conventions, and *Richard III*. Similarly in several non-parodic plays he has assumed an audience's knowledge of Shakespeare and Chekhov in order to introduce ideas and parallels. He has elaborated on this aspect in a comment on 'A Movie Starring Me', the 1991 radio play: 'I use *The Seagull* in 'A Movie Starring Me' as I use *As You Like It* to a lesser extent in *Vote for Them* (where the parliament is a Utopian experiment as the move into the forest is in *As You Like It*). The comparison is with *The National Theatre*, my satirical strip-club play,which is a version of *Three Sisters*. What I'm saying with *The Seagull* [in 'A Movie'] is people internalise fictions and play them out in their lives.' Such intertextual juxtaposition illuminates theme throughout the canon, whether this is play-within-the-play (as with the Crummles' *Romeo and Juliet* in *Nickleby*), version of the modern classic (as in 'A Movie Starring Me') or full-blown adaptation (where prose narrative source and play text are constantly cleverly rubbing against each other). In the adaptations the meaning is produced by the counterpoint between source and play.

Edgar's use of autobiography as source was an extension of and departure from the accustomed reaching out to factual and literary material. These were narratives recording real events and heroic life experiences of contemporary individuals. If 'the classic realist formulation is to present recognisable reality within a context that makes clear its place in history' (in accordance with Lukács's realism as Edgar understands it),[12] then here was a splendid opportunity to reassess the recent context of the 1960s through the prism of the late 1970s. It is interesting to note that both *Jail Diary* and *Mary Barnes* were out of print when Edgar chose to dramatise them; he could not in either case count on his audience's knowledge of the original. This was a situation in marked contrast to that of *Nickleby* and *Jekyll*, where audiences were almost certain to know the novels or some version of them in advance. Indeed, in *Jekyll*'s case there is to be counted into the equation the mythic status of Stevenson's novella, the power of which is such that, even to the unlettered, the very title has automatic connotations.

The Jail Diary of Albie Sachs

In *Jail Diary* the purpose is to provide a tension between heroic and anti-heroic perceptions and self-perceptions of Albie. Edgar wanted to write positively about 'individual revolutionary heroism' while showing, in a benign spirit, the political naïveté of the white South African lawyer.[13] Sachs's own account of his detention in solitary confinement for anti-apartheid activity could not explore his 'internal ambivalence about his own heroism in resisting the authorities';[14] Edgar selects events from the autobiographical diary and uses other sources as well as his imagination to shape this theme. Sachs himself in the original diary supplied the idea for the famous scene at the end of Act One, where there is a two-minute silence, forcing the audience to empathise with Albie's confinement in his cell.[15]

The Ninety-Day Law was introduced by the then Minister of Justice B. J. Vorster in 1963. Sachs's 168-day detention without trial started on 1 October 1963 and is seen in the play in the context of the infant police state where there was a new pecking order among the security forces themselves. These ironies give the play its interest as an historical piece but its chilling force is found in the recognition that (as Edgar argued) it is not 'a history play for England. I think it's a story that addressed itself, acutely, to this country's present. *Jail Diary* is a book about a person who discovers, painfully, that his rhetoric is real. It's about the ending of an age of political innocence, and the move into a different kind of world, in which the choices really matter, and therefore hurt a great deal more. And there are now many people in this country – good, radical people – who are finding that they too are speaking in a colder climate to a starker world.'[16] The play on an important level addressed itself to 'good, radical people' in the RSC audience at the Warehouse in 1978, British socialists who had travelled from the rhetorical bliss of 1968 to the failures of the left after the mid-1970s, whose revolutionary vision had been clouded by disappointments at home and painful recognitions about the reality of 'socialist' states abroad.

Jail Diary is a testing play for the left. The two opposing philosophies of right and left are spelt out and 'we can test the strength of our own commitment to our values and principles by looking at someone in an extreme situation'.[17] The predominantly white British audience should experience the boredom and despair of solitary confinement and empathise with the individual, while placing Albie as a 'paradigmatic' figure in a representative social context of early 1960s Afrikanerdom;[18] moreover, they should discover an uneasy challenge to their own feelings about an increasingly racist Britain and their own privilege within the hierarchy. This last point is stressed in the opening address, a monologue that casts the audience as participants in a political meeting. Albie details the ironical benefits of Vorster's new law: 'it tells us what it's like'; now that the law is used against them, whites will have to choose their side, oppressors or oppressed. In jail the black prisoners are tortured; we hear the guards laughing at their pain and the screams of a child enduring a caning while Albie is free to play intellectual word-games. He may be a Jewish Communist and a dissident but he is nevertheless hierarchically superior to his fellow prisoners. In the monologue at the opening of Act Two he recognises his privilege and questions the principles of non-violence which he has come to see as effected by cowardice. The irony is that he survives because he draws on 'his own *individuality*', conditioned by his middle-class way of life to structure the day and measure the small treats: 'all the things that were disastrous in terms of being a revolutionary activist, in that situation became virtues.'[19] The further irony is that he engages

56

charmingly with Nazis such as the comic walking Bible concordance Snyman, his Afrikaner jailor. Albie's need to be 'nice', to seek approval and communication, leads him to help the enemy instead of himself, and nowhere more tellingly than when Albie steadies Snyman when the old man almost falls, so missing an escape route. Albie must learn to separate love of person and hatred of deed: he hates 'the whip but not the men who wield it'.

Freeman consistently and sadistically prods at the ironies of the gaps between Albie's conscience and actions, and between socialist aspiration and reality. Freeman is British, a Special Branch officer who has served in Kenya with the British Army. His British accent signals a particular goad to the sensitivity of British socialists; he is the man on the right who undermines by attacking the very real doubts and fears of the socialist struggling with contradiction and trying to maintain a vision of the goodness of human nature. Through Freeman, Edgar gives a complex perspective on Albie's political naïveté:

FREEMAN. Any complaints? About the way they treat you?

ALBIE. Well, they're not beating me up or anything like that.

FREEMAN. Good.

ALBIE. But I do think, now you ask, I think it is extremely cruel and uncivilised to subject a person to prolonged isolation. Also the facilities are rather primitive.

FREEMAN (*quietly*). Primitive. Uncivilised. You want to build a state like Ghana or the Congo and you say that South Africa is primitive and uncivilised.

Slight pause.

Or, for that matter, Hungary.

Slight pause.

The reference to Hungary brings home to Europe the grim actuality of existing 'socialist' states and taunts the 'good, radical people' in the audience. Freeman contemptuously sneers at Albie about his self-doubt: 'Equality and justice. Late night chats with Nazis ... You hate the whip but not the man who wields it, Albie'; 'Why be

57

a hero, Albie? Haven't you read the sacred texts? It's not the individual, it's the masses. Not the man that matters, it's the movement.'

And yet, by the end of the play, there is a clear identification of Albie as hero. The final scene 'which is set some time after the main story, to throw the events of the story into relief, to help the audience think historically about them',[20] involves Danny, the black whistler from the first prison, who convinces Albie that the people 'won't forget' the things he did for them. The Albie Sachs they will remember has heroic status, and the play's last line, from Albie, affirms the analysis: 'You're right. That is the one. They must remember.' Albie has endured sleep deprivation on his third arrest, and he has journeyed from innocence to experience: 'Intellectually, of course, it's still all there, but all the feelings, all the passions, all that wild-eyed innocence, been shorn away. What's left is the belief, a little core, as hard as steel, quite pure, but rather cold.' He has lost his 'niceness' and the implication is that he has learnt to lose his sympathy for the people who wield the whip. He has learnt that violent retaliation is necessary.

The agents of South Africa's security forces tried to kill Albie Sachs on 7 April 1988 in Maputo, the capital of Mozambique. In London, where Sachs was hospitalised, David Edgar arranged a benefit performance of *Jail Diary*. Sachs had seen a revival of the original RSC production; and the play had been televised, broadcast on radio, and revived in two other productions. The benefit at the Young Vic was cast from all five British productions, with the four actors who had played Albie taking part in it. These were Peter McEnery, Simon Callow, Martin Jacobs and Matthew Marsh. Edgar recalls it as one of the best theatre nights of his life 'because we were doing unambiguous good and it was a celebration of all that's best about the theatre'. Albie Sachs, his mother, and the woman (Dorothy Adams) on whom the character of Danny was based, were in the audience. They all came on stage after the show, as did David Edgar. The event is recorded in Sachs's *The Soft Vengeance of a Freedom Fighter*, and he emphasises the solidarity of the occasion:

> The clapping swells to a high point that is held for a long time; this has been an unusual evening in the theatre, we all want to feel it has been memorable and special, and that through the

actors and the producer and the playwright we are expressing our repudiation of those responsible for planting the bomb and our human solidarity with each other ... this is a specially wonderful night for us all, a night of mutual emotional recognition and support, and for me, a night of soft and joyous vengeance.[21]

The play had more than completed its task of demonstrating individual revolutionary heroism: it had had the originally desired mirror effect of illustrating British resistance against right-wing regimes. Albie Sachs had become one of the martyrs of the socialist movement.[22]

Mary Barnes

Mary Barnes is based on an account by Mary Barnes and Joseph Berke (an American psychiatrist) of Mary Barnes's 'voyage through madness'. Its setting is Kingsley Hall, the alternative community inaugurated by the 'anti-psychiatrist' R. D. Laing in 1965. Through the methods of irony and what Edgar has called 'dynamic ambiguity', the audience was urged to assess the contradictions of a particular counter-cultural experiment and, in broader terms, the 1960s contribution to changing the world.[23] Although on one level the play is 'about' Laingianism and alternative therapy, its larger purpose is to use Laing's project as a springboard from which to bounce an exploration of the counter-culture. In the late 1970s the backlash against 1960s experimentalism was just beginning to mould opinion and it was time to take stock. By choosing to adapt *Mary Barnes*, Edgar was confronting his own attitude, the trajectory of which had altered after the early 1970s. Whereas by 1974 his Trotskyist perspective had brought about the rationalisation that 'if the late sixties had done anything it had been to act as a spark for the early seventies upsurge of industrial militancy', by 1976 it was quite obvious to him that 'the reading had been wrong'. He, along with many others, started to take the 1960s legacies more seriously and '*Mary Barnes* was part of [his] attempt to grapple and wrestle with that'.

Edgar had also to confront his own scepticism towards some of R. D. Laing's ideas. Laing's progressive reasoning about madness had led famously to his argument that 'the "mad" are in fact considerably more sensitive to their environment than the "sane"".[24] In *Sanity, Madness and the Family*, co-authored by Laing with Aaron Esterson in 1964, the condition of schizophrenia itself is questioned. The diagnosis of Mary Barnes as schizophrenic and her subsequent recovery at Kingsley Hall can be contextualised in the light of this statement by Laing and Esterson:

> We do not accept 'schizophrenia' as being a biochemical, neurophysiological, psychological fact, and we regard it as palpable error, in the present state of the evidence, to take it to be a fact. Nor do we assume its existence. Nor do we adopt it as a hypothesis. We propose no model of it.
>
> This is the position from which we start. Our question is: are the experience and behaviour that psychiatrists take as symptoms and signs of schizophrenia more socially intelligible than has come to be supposed?[25]

Laing did not push this reasoning to socialist ends and indeed felt that Edgar's play distorted the 'message' by identifying it 'with a socialist ideology'. He also criticised the 'period' quality of the piece, arguing that the 'issue' (the efficacy of alternative healing, presumably) is 'contemporary'.[26] Clearly, Laing had missed the point of the play. For his own part, Edgar retained a scepticism: 'It was very clear to me that Laingianism could have a right-wing reading, a very individualist anti-collectivist reading, and the play explores the contradiction between the individualism and collectivism of the endeavour.' The importance of Laing for Edgar lies not so much in the reasoning about madness but in Laing's perceptions that 'individual relations can operate as a paradigm of social relations, that the personal is both metaphorically and literally political'.[27] The people resident in Kingsley Hall lived (and live, as characters in the play) their lives in that perception, and the politics of orthodox psychiatry are seen in contrast to be oppressive.

Edgar carefully structures the play through a method of counterpoint whereby the audience are invited to judge the satisfactoriness of the experiment in healing. One minute he delves into the psychiatrists' diverse points of view in order to amuse and irritate the audience, exposing the arguments about their collective; then, antithetically, he shows through the huge emotional pull of Mary's story that, despite the contentions, the set-up did succeed in healing her without the use of drugs or shock treatment. The play is extremely theatrically powerful for this very reason: it fully engages both cerebrally and emotionally with the audience. The emotional rawness shocks and horrifies on a very deep level and through the behaviour of Mary Barnes, Edgar for the first time in his work provides a cathartic 'letting go'. That release is contained by the cerebral debates surrounding it and a further shock is sustained when we are pulled back to the rational intellect. We are reminded constantly that this is indeed a period piece: 1960s music, reference to social, political and cultural phenomena, and referential jokes clearly index the context.

The two dinner scenes (Act One Scene Eight and Act Two Scene Three) are the cerebral centre of the play. The cast and entire production team had initially debated the political emphasis, and Simon Callow has stressed the contradictory views that emerged:

> There was a sense among some people in the cast that the sixties were on trial. It was the beginning of the big reaction against the sixties, the feeling that permissiveness had turned sour, that the social dream had been naïve and possibly counter-productive. The feminist thing was beginning to be much harder-edged, the notion of 'love, peace, let it all hang out, man' was under attack and Ann [Mitchell, who played Brenda] particularly had a feeling that the sixties were being unduly dismissed, that tremendous breakthroughs had occurred and the play should show a serious attempt had been made. Other people in the cast thought they were all hilariously misguided and wrongheaded.[28]

A hint of parody emerges in the first dinner scene. The psychiatrists state various examples of the oppressive politics of orthodox psychiatry. These bullying tactics are seen convincingly as a metaphor of social oppression and a particularly keen example is offered by Eddie: 'Last century, the Southern States, the medical profession had to classify a new disease. Occurred exclusively among black slaves. They called it drapetomania. It was manifested in the slave's desire to run away.' The irony is that when the East End working-class neighbours react against the 'nutters, perverts, layabouts' of Kingsley Hall by posting excrement through the letterbox, Douglas calls the police. There is an authoritarian principle in their midst despite all efforts to rid themselves of rules and hierarchies, and they need the very part of society they most consciously reject, in order to protect themselves. An audience would be right at this point to question the practicalities of Kingsley Hall as a collective and unified endeavour but the narrative must be followed through to see the full implications.

The play thoroughly confronts the paradox set up by the fearful reactions of the working-class population of the area around Kingsley Hall, and it is through Keith, their representative, that we finally assess how much gain there has been for those people. In the epilogue scene at the end, set in an abandoned Kingsley Hall in the present, Keith and Angie look back to the 1960s collective. Keith is fully conscious of the inefficacy of drugs to cure pain partly through the example of his sister who 'gets through the day clogged up on valium, cos she's so petrified of what she'd feel if she woke up'. Moreover, he has retained an understanding of Mary Barnes (and, by implication, her heroic process of reintegration) but his awareness is not yet extended into action. It is up to the audience to decide just how positive Keith's insight is. Part of their reading will rest on the theme of division between the psychiatrists. Douglas and Hugo have a bitter row in the Act Two dinner scene. Douglas insists on rules, partly as a result of Mary's lack of control. He breaks the code of metaphor on which the community is structured: 'I am suggesting that we are pretending not to be doctors and we are doctors and we can in the context of a non-coercive environment, without drugs or shocks, admit to so being.'

Edgar was very interested in the way in which the psychiatrists 'were living in their own confusion of metaphors' and the theme is constantly reinforced in the very fabric of their understanding of diagnosis (which rests on David Cooper's aphoristic point that 'a delusion [is] a real idea which a psychiatrist deludes himself into taking literally').[29] An example of this comes in Act One Scene Five:

DOUGLAS. Of course she thinks she's a foetus.

HUGO. No. She *is* a foetus. That's what she's experiencing.

The question is, if 'mad' people live in metaphors and if the healers in this community also do, who is 'mad' and who is 'sane'?

An extended example of this existence within metaphor comes in Act Two. All the characters, not just Mary, treat Act Two as the Passion. The dinner itself is the Last Supper and Douglas is Judas. When Mary takes on the suffering of the world we have the most powerful moment in the play, not least because that scene symbolises the metaphor-finding of the whole community. But an examination of this moment takes us from the cerebral discourse side of the play to the very heart of the emotional rawness.

The story of Mary's recovery turns on the very moving interaction with Eddie and these intimate scenes are the most potent in the play. Simon Callow played Eddie in the original production and had spent some time with Joseph Berke on whom the character is based. He talked of the 'love story' at the centre of the play, the compulsive emotional need in both characters: 'Joe and Mary were kind of mirrors of each other, and that fascinated me very much, that the helper and the helped are locked into this relationship where both could behave as badly and both are redeemed.' Patti Love played Mary with complete empathy, utterly immersing herself in the emotional reality of the situation, and the central relationship stirred an archetypal longing in the audience: 'It was as if everybody found a need inside them to do what Mary had done, and a craving for someone to take them through it.'[30] The 42-year-old Mary 'goes down', returns to foetal state and grows through childhood. Eddie is father and mother to her, feeding her with milk from a baby's bottle, playing crocodiles with her, teaching her that anger is allowable: they play on the floor like children, fight with each other and form a total co-dependency. Throughout these scenes, Edgar experiments with the minimum of verbal language, in direct contrast to the discussion scenes. The result is often tender and always touching as expression is found through the simplest of vocal sound, gesture and interaction, all the time serving to stress Eddie's and Mary's emotional needs. An example of such a moment is in Act One Scene Seven when they are playing crocodiles:

EDDIE *bites* MARY. MARY *bites* EDDIE. *Both growling,* MARY *is squealing with delight.* EDDIE *grabs a chair, still kneeling, growling through the bars.* MARY *does the same with another chair. Enter* BRENDA.

The happiness of this moment is shattered almost immediately, and a source of the disturbing power of the Mary/Eddie scenes is that emphasis on switch of mood, so that the audience is made to feel the terror of deprivation when Eddie has to leave Mary.

Eddie defends Mary when she creates havoc in the community, and he shows his greatest love for her when she tests him, 'naked, covered from head to foot in her own shit.' This is the crucifixion moment, metaphor of her suffering and rebirth. Eddie is the redeemer, giving her exactly what is needed, a ritual, another metaphor in action:

> EDDIE *comes back in with half an onion and a pot of honey and a spoon. He thrusts the onion at* MARY.
>
> EDDIE. OK, monster, put that in your mouth.
>
> MARY *puts the onion in her mouth.*
>
> OK, now, creature. Spit it out.
>
> MARY *spits it out.* EDDIE *spoons a spoonful of honey.*
>
> Now that is badness coming out. And this –
>
> *He puts the spoon in Mary's mouth.*
>
> Is goodness going in.
>
> MARY *stands there, the spoon in her mouth.*
>
> That's better? Good. Now, monster, creature from the black lagoon ...
>
> MARY *a slight smile behind the spoon.*
>
> We better clean you up.

The 'gist' line of the scene is delivered by Brenda: 'She that takes upon herself, the shit of the whole world.'

The audience reaction to this scene was recalled by Simon Callow: 'People were absolutely shaken, shattered. It was hard for me not to be moved to tears myself by the scene, by the gesture it represented. Patti really went as far as I think any actress could ever go in making herself absolutely desperate, pushing, testing, the truth of Joe's love for her.' Patti Love's Method performance emerged from her own need to go through the therapeutic experiences of Mary Barnes. She had originally suggested the adaptation of Barnes and Berke's account, and Edgar affirmed: 'In a subliminal way I clearly did write to her very particular strengths.' Although the cathartic extremes of the story of healing are set in contrast with the emotional distance of the surrounding ironies it is irrefutable that, by the penultimate scene, Mary has come through: she has found expression through painting, fulfilment in Catholicism (accepted by Eddie as 'real and right and true for her'), and she has helped her brother Simon and attempted to help Angie away from punitive psychiatric treatment. Her example vindicates the entire experiment, and there is no question that the 'unsacred' family has pulled her through. Brenda's moment of doubt: 'I just, just sometimes, wonder if it's possible', is triumphantly answered, and it is through the example of Angie's recovery that we ultimately test the Kingsley Hall project. She is a young radical who is reclaimed by her bourgeois family from the community. In the final scene with Keith she reports on her electric shock treatment. It has allowed her to 'forget the things that hurt' her. She has been conditioned to accept her life, her family and the oppressive social organisation she once fought to escape. She cannot remember Mary Barnes or the revolutionary slogan 'Hey, hey, LBJ'; she is effectively depoliticised. It is left to the audience to make up their minds whether this effective amnesia cure is preferable to an alternative attempt to help individuals like Angie by eradicating the ways of living that lead to mental instability. Mary's messy route to recovery has conversely gone against the grain of convention, persuasively indicating that alternative treatments cannot be ignored and, by extension, her example shows that the 1960s progressive movements should not be ignored when it comes to social healing.

According to Simon Callow, the play at the Birmingham Repertory Theatre Studio became 'a kind of Happening', a piece of Holy Theatre, partly because there was no proscenium barrier between audience and actors and partly because there was a continuity from the intensity of rehearsals to performance. The transfer to the Royal Court with its metropolitan audience and proscenium staging ensured a 'cooler event', but the audiences flocked to it nevertheless.[31] This most moving of all Edgar's plays deserves to be filmed and both Callow and Edgar regret that the original production was not recorded. What is self-evident is that the collaborative nature of the venture mirrored the collective experiment under scrutiny: the production team discussed the original book, read a selection of Laing texts, argued over the 1960s context; suggestions (particularly by Callow) were made to the playwright; Patti Love met Mary Barnes and developed an intense relationship with her; Joseph Berke talked to the group; and Edgar discussed the subtext of the piece with the director, Peter Farago. By choosing to adapt the account of an individual journey, Edgar had given collective force to the subject. He had illustrated the imperatives of the slogan 'the personal is political' which he cogently analyses in his essay 'The Morals Dilemma':

> Socialism is at base about challenging and eliminating unequal power relations by and on behalf of the powerless. It is completely appropriate that it should extend that project from the macrocosm to the microcosm, from the unequal relations of classes to the unequal relations of individuals ... if the left is seriously to address society's present and its own recent past, then personal behaviour cannot remain off political limits. After all, the connection between the two was *our* slogan, *our* insight, *our* perception.[32]

There is no doubt that the choice to adapt both *Mary Barnes* and *Jail Diary* was politically appropriate to the times typified by the late 1970s. The argument about political relevance is no less watertight in relation to the two novel adaptations.

The Life and Adventures of Nicholas Nickleby

The RSC *Nickleby* adaptation was exceptional in England in that there was a very long gestation period in which the entire company found inspiration from the Dickens novel. George Orwell's 1939 essay on Charles Dickens was read and re-read by the *Nickleby* team during the six-month adaptation process. Because the play (which turned out to be in two long parts) firmly expresses an attitude towards Dickens's social and political understanding, it is pertinent to quote Orwell: 'All art is propaganda. Neither Dickens himself nor the majority of Victorian novelists would have thought of denying this ... Dickens is one of those writers who are felt to be worth stealing. He has been stolen by Marxists, by Catholics, and, above all, by Conservatives. The question is, What is there to steal? Why does anyone care about Dickens? Why do *I* care about Dickens?'[33] To Roger Rees, who played Nicholas, Dickens had given social awareness,[34] and this particular gift is received by many young readers of the novels. It is certainly the case that the play in two parts premièred in entirety in June 1980 is socially extended on a scale so vast that thirty-nine performers played 123 speaking parts and various non-speaking roles ranging from the aristocracy to 'beggars, criminals, the poor and the mad ... the lowest of the low of London's poor'. Nicholas's adventures take him through acquaintance with all levels of English class society in the second decade of the nineteenth century when the action of the novel takes place. Yet the most important fact about David Edgar's adaptation is that its locality was the Aldwych Theatre and its time setting, the present. Its true political dimension was that of the first term of the Thatcher government.

While a strong respect for the original text and a sympathy for the novelist's social critique ('a man who is *generously angry*,' Orwell says)[35] thoroughly inform the play, they do not constitute its *raison d'être*. Michael Billington, in a review of what was to prove one of the most successful RSC productions in all the company's repertoire, asked provocatively 'if the whole thing wasn't a waste of the RSC's amazing resources' and concluded that 'the RSC has come up with a perverse and needless triumph: a great deal of skill and imagination has been expended on the creation of something that gains only marginally, if at all, from being seen rather than read. Undeniably this *Nicholas Nickleby* has been done well. My question is: should it have been done at all?' His reasoning was that there were 'large-cast plays more urgently in need of the RSC's attention' and that the Dickens book is perfectly accessible.[36]

These considerations are irrelevant to the success of this particular enterprise because the Edgar–RSC adaptation provided a late twentieth-century perspective on, variously, Dickens himself, the moral expectations of the audience, the relation of our times to the early Victorian period, and the 'cultural heritage' putative version that could have emerged if the novel had been merely 'put on its feet'. As Edgar stated:

I think it's a matter of how conscious you are ... It's very
difficult in the current literary climate not to wish to acknowledge the nature of the negotiation that has taken place.
Shakespeare doesn't substantially write very differently between
writing drawn from Holinshed and drawn from myth and drawn
from other plays. The nature of the engagement with the
material is not radically different, whereas you can't prevent the
audience knowing *Nicholas Nickleby* was a novel and it seems to
me absolutely clear that you must acknowledge within the
theatrical text itself that it is a novel. We were saying, no, this is
not the play Dickens would have written had he written *Nicholas
Nickleby* as a play.

The self-conscious aspect of the adaptation was that 'the event
took place in four time-frames': 1810–20 when the novel was set;
1838 when it was written; in the intervening period when other
adaptations were made; and in 1980, the time of performance.
These reference points were ultimately subsumed in the 1980 time-
frame, the present perspective from which all else is necessarily
seen.

The technique through which this self-consciousness became
possible was that of narration. From the very beginning of Part One
the actors drew attention to the story by conspicuously telling the
story and showing attitudes to it. They had had 'collective
possession' of the story since the first rehearsal when they had sat
in a huge circle to share it.[37] In a reflection of this initial exercise
there were deliveries of narration by the entire company, each
taking at least one line so that the story was passed on and shared
with the audience. A related strategy was for an actor to comment
in the third person on his or her character, relaying Dickens's point
of view on the character (in words from the 1838 novel).
Throughout, the actors watched the action unfold when they
were not directly in role, so that the 1980 immediacy was
maintained; and certain important alterations to the story indicated
the shift from previous adaptations. In short, although the
production was based very much on social reality (and in his
essay 'Adapting *Nickleby*' Edgar describes the research conducted
by the cast into various aspects of early nineteenth-century social
conditions), the techniques used were anti-illusionist and theatrical.[38] Edgar had of course used out-front address from the
General Will days onwards, and there were models of such address

in the Brechtian-influenced work of the Fringe. He commented: '*Nickleby* is always billed as the first show of the eighties but what it was indeed was the last show of the sixties, because what it did do was bring in all sorts of techniques that had been developed since the sixties and did them on a very big scale.' The 'zoom lens' effect of commentary and then focus is often full of ironical interest and suits the typically cool and distanced style of English actors. Harriet Walter has particularly appositely described Roger Rees's style of playing 'with a wink to the audience'.[39]

The democratic quality of the work was very much to the fore of the public's attention. Edgar stressed at the time that it was 'the most democratic work process' he had ever encountered: 'It's not a personal statement; it's Dickens having been passed through a filter of 45 people and written down by me.'[40] We could talk of *Nickleby*'s 'hyphenated' quality: Trevor Nunn was at times a director–designer and a director–writer; the actors were actor–narrators, and they initially improvised sections that subsequently became crucial to the play; John Napier, the designer, influenced the writing of the second half with his constructivist set; Trevor Nunn and John Caird contributed to the structural resolutions of Part Two; there is a Shakespeare–Edgar version of *Romeo and Juliet* as a play-within-the-play; and, of course, the whole is a Dickens–Edgar–RSC version of *Nickleby*. The multiple roles played by most of the actors accentuated the ensemble nature of the performance and the crowd scenes were participated in by the entire cast.

The vastness of the democratic endeavour was not without its problems and power struggles, various examples of which have been charted by Leon Rubin. Edgar has written illuminatingly and positively about the 'egalitarian myth' which informed early 1970s fringe theatre and had by the late 1970s infiltrated the RSC:

> *Nickleby* was perhaps the most dramatic example of the power of the egalitarian myth in full flight. Here you had a company of around 45 people, varying in age from 20 to 70, in experience widely, and in talent hugely. In cold reality, the contribution of the 'leading actors' (and indeed their power) was vastly greater than those who played the small parts, and the contribution (and power) of the directors was in essence as great as it ever was or is. So, superficially, the fact that we began working on the play

sitting in a huge egalitarian circle, that everyone was encouraged to feel that they made an equal contribution, could be seen as a sentimental hypocrisy. But it was of course nothing of the kind: the egalitarianism of the making of *Nicholas Nickleby* was a fiction, but it was a necessary fiction; it was a myth, not in the sense that it was untrue, but in the sense that its literal truth (or otherwise) was by no means its most important characteristic.[41]

The encouragement of this 'egalitarian myth' created an ensemble atmosphere opposed to 'stars' whereby everybody could make contributions over and above their nominated role.

On 14 June 1980 Parts One and Two were put together, in front of an audience, for the first time. Each part had previously played separately, with cuts and rewrites in constant flow until the very last possible moment. The loose baggy monsters of plays (eventually totalling eight and a half hours of viewing time) were received rapturously by the audience who gave a fifteen-minute ovation. *Nickleby* continued to receive fifteen-minute ovations night after night. It was and is to date David Edgar's biggest popular success. It recovered the RSC from the financial doldrums of that time, won prestigious awards both in this country and America (where it transferred to Broadway), was televised in both countries, and is frequently revived.

As Sally Beauman notes, 'It solidified the RSC's growing reputation as one of the great theatre companies of the Western world' and 'recharged the company at a moment of psychological importance for it just before the move to the Barbican.'[42] Bernard Levin, in an analysis of the initial lukewarm critical response, hit upon one of the reasons for the audience ecstasy. He called *Nickleby* a 'morality play'.[43] The audience, as in the entire tradition of morality plays since their medieval origins, discovered a clear moral absolutism despite the cast's insistence on the complexity of the characters. In particular, the 'good' of Nicholas's compassion in his dealings with Smike, and the 'evil' of Ralph's greed and corruption by money were oppositions that tested their own moral behaviour and invited the traditional boos and cheers of melodrama. Moreover, the sheer spectacle of the event, with the catwalk around the front of the dress circle and the gangway into the stalls (a kind of *hanamichi*), linked the action firmly with the audience who were also chatted up by the actors

70

before the show. After the very cool approach of the 1960s and 1970s (where audiences could expect to be offended, ignored, or offered a Beckettesque minimum of set, lack of action, and a patchwork of pauses, silences and monosyllables), here was a production that exuded rich warmth, energy and emotion. The audience was treated to the self(RSC)-referential Crummles theatricals and a rewritten *Romeo and Juliet* ending; a ballad recitation; dance; songs, incidental music and an opera pastiche by the virtuoso composer Stephen Oliver; a gaggle of comic eccentrics; moments of *commedia lazzi*; and the extremely moving death scene where Smike harks back to his great theatrical success as the Apothecary in *Romeo and Juliet*: above all, this was a story well told. As Edgar chronicles in his essay 'Thoughts for the Third Term', the RSC were making a conscious bid for 'popular' theatre.[44]

This was expensive 'popular' theatre, however, and the people it played to were a section, not a cross-section, of society. It has for this very reason been suggested that Edgar's acceptance of the RSC invitation represented a safe political 'selling out'.[45] Yet, the play is emphatically not part of the heritage industry and, contrary to Bernard Levin's sentimental conclusions, it is equally emphatically not 'Dickensian' in that heritage sense. The narrative is centred on money, its uses and abuses, and at its core is the story of Smike, Nicholas's cousin, the schizophrenic outcast so movingly played by David Threlfall. The structure, whereby Smike meets with emotional support at the end of each act, encourages audience compassion intrinsically in contrast to the social injustice, exploitation and oppression seen in such abundance elsewhere. Nicholas fulfils the emotional request embodied in Smike's simple statement, 'You are my home.' Most importantly, Nicholas is led by his adventures through a particular learning process which he articulates as follows: 'We have – my sister and I have – learnt nothing in our journeyings so strongly as we've learned what happens to the kindest, and the noblest and the gentlest people, when their souls are tainted by the touch of money.' While Kate corroborates this, Frank Cheeryble protests that his own uncles Mr Charles and Mr Ned Cheeryble have not been so tainted – 'Have they been made ignoble, or ungentle, or unkind?' – and on this point hinges the strongest political question of the play. There are two types of capitalists:

Ralph Nickleby is the wicked uncle–financial speculator; the Cheeryble brothers, Frank's far from wicked uncles, represent philanthropy in action. The question is, does Dickens – and after him, Edgar – tell us that the Cheerybles can exist, and therefore that political solutions may be found in the charitable actions of good-hearted capitalists?

Edgar was persuaded by Orwell's thesis that Dickens's social position was at root 'If men *would* behave decently the world *would* be decent.'[46] It is of the essence that the play is about Dickens's wishfulness, a wish for the Cheerybles to be a possibility. Edgar asserted:

> Like all great writers he was exploring a contradiction of which he was not necessarily fully aware, and the contradiction which he was exploring was, can you have capitalism with a feudal face? Can you have all the thrust and energy and vibrancy and teemingness which clearly attracted Dickens about the city, can you have that while preserving the loyalties and obligations of rural life, and Dickens's answer is 'Oh, I wish you could'. It's a *wishing*. No doubt he was more or less optimistic about that on good or bad days. One of the absolute reasons that we wanted to preserve the distance between the adaptation and the original work is to say, actually we think Dickens is being a bit optimistic here.

The RSC actors 'were expressing a huge, collective "wouldn't it be good if" aspiration, as they watched and told the unfolding events. This distancing device, which in Brecht is supposed to clear the mind of emotion, had in our case the effect of directing and deepening the audience's own visceral longing for Ralph's vision of the world to be disproved.'[47]

If the distanced presentation of *Nickleby* is one important way in which the adaptation interrogates Dickens's social thinking, the other is the alteration of the ending of the novel. Following on from Orwell's discussion of Dickens's saccharine endings (where the ideal is to be found in sheltered domesticity), Edgar's version challenged the audience on the notion of the philanthropic capitalist. He has a new Smike replacing the now dead original character in Dotheboys Hall; and the symmetry of the Christmas family photograph image is broken by Nicholas's leaving to hold that child out to the audience. There is a complexity to the final image; Edgar talked in interview of 'Cheeryble-isation':

> The end [of the novel] is about the Cheeryble-isation of the entire Nickleby family, literally, in that Kate marries into it and has a lot of little Cheeryble babies, the Cheerybles have brought about the Madeleine–Nicholas match and they financially enable it by Nicholas becoming a partner, so everyone becomes a Cheeryble in the end. If you look at that last passage [in the novel], it's all about the relation to the firm of the Cheeryble brothers. Nicholas became a partner in the Cheeryble brothers' firm, then he bought his old house. What did he buy it with? The money he made out of that business. And so when we turn all that into a Christmas card and when we point out there are actually still children outside in the snow, and when Nicholas leaves the Christmas card and walks out into the snow, with his wife and his sister looking at him alarmed by what's happened, and when he holds the child up to us, he is, it seems to me very clearly, and the play dramatically effectively, asking the audience the question as to whether the Cheerybles can exist, whether actually the solution is to be found in individual philanthropy, and the message of the adaptation is, no, it probably isn't.

The anti-Dickensian ending warns the 1980 audience against the Thatcherite emphasis on families and individuals, and suggests that there is (and must be) such a thing as 'society' and collective values.[48]

Edgar points out that 'the 1830s were in many ways a mirror of our own times' with regard to the technological revolution and loss of certainties.[49] In 1980 his own political thinking was shifting. He was himself 'very much in the arena of the contradiction between aspiration and the voluntarist urge to bring about the New Jerusalem, and the practical actuality of the problems of socialism in practice'. At the start of the rehearsal process of *Nickleby* he had just returned from a year in America where he had deliberately not written anything, and he had had time to consider his politics. This was during the period when the Thatcher revolution was happening in Britain. He had been reassessing the legacy of the 1960s (as we have seen in relation to *Mary Barnes*), talking to American Thatcherites about the imminent right-wing revolution, and reading about the Soviet Union (research that prepared him to write *Maydays*). His thinking resulted in two realisations. The first was this: 'The crucial thing that detached me from residual Trotskyism was that you had to take responsibility for the East. You couldn't say as the Trotskyites do that actually existing socialism was of no relevance to the aspiration for "true socialism".' The parallel realisation was that 'Social democracy was confronting a profound crisis in this country, but also in other countries, and was a huge problem in the United States also with Carter. There were continua with the problems in the Soviet Union. The mental process was we had to take responsibility for the East, because what was increasingly clear was that there wasn't going to be a [left-wing] revolution in the West.'

Edgar had accepted the economic problems under existing socialist regimes and his own awareness of the contradiction between socialist aspiration and achievement is part of the fabric of the 'wishing' of *Nickleby*. The Dickens adaptation is in this sense a crucial political cornerstone of Edgar's career, where the notion of 'if only' preoccupied adaptor as well as novelist. In Edgar's opinion, *Nickleby*'s huge success was a triumph for the moral 'that material self-interest is neither the first nor the most effective motor of human behaviour';[50] the play's success in particular in 1980, he felt, was because 'a year into Thatcher, our audiences wanted to be assured that there was more to life than money'.[51] Audiences of *Nickleby* were encouraged to take sides in a morality play for the 1980s.

The Strange Case of Dr Jekyll and Mr Hyde

The debate about moral behaviour is explicitly scrutinised in Edgar's 1991 stage adaptation, which takes a central preoccupation of the nineteenth century, the dual personality, and rereads it in the light of millennial demons. Stevenson's archetypal novella has found an enduring popularity through theatre and film adaptations; this version of *The Strange Case of Dr Jekyll and Mr Hyde* for the RSC at the Barbican Theatre defies the expectations engendered by all of them. It is about Stevenson; it is about middle-age desires and their repression; it is about the social parallels between our 'gauzy times' and Stevenson's. At its emotional centre are two

74

men, the outwardly respectable bourgeois doctor and the fiendish younger man who 'pops out' to commit rape and murder when Jekyll can no longer 'hide' him. The decision to have two actors representing, respectively, the ego and the id is an innovation that allows debate between the moralist and individualist positions and, most interestingly, allows for a love story: 'The story expresses an absolutely universal experience, the sense we all sometimes have of two parts of our personality tugging against one another, I see it as a perverted sort of love story.'[52] The story begins with self-hatred as Jekyll attempts to deny Hyde's feelings. At the end of Act One Hyde taunts his partner: 'Do you know what I canna fathom? Why you're so afeared of what you want. Why you're so afeared of what's inside of you ... And why you're so afeared of me.' We see his murderous attack on a child which reawakens memories in Jekyll of 'last time' and 'the time before'. Jekyll is forced to admit: 'Feels – wonderful' and Hyde triumphantly drives the point home: 'It's you. It's you. It's you.' Towards the end of the play Jekyll conclusively comes to the realisation that the vice that Hyde represents could have been integrated into his personality to positive moral advantage: 'if I was the break on your extremities of vice, you were the check on the excesses of my virtue.'

In performance, the excitement of the scenes between these two characters (played by Roger Allam and Simon Russell Beale) was partly due to a homoerotic quality, a *frisson* particularly exacted by the passing of the purple transformation fluid from one man's mouth to the other; but the power was primarily that of ideas in action. Edgar was interested in the way in which serial killers and child abuse offenders have often attempted to deny those criminal aspects of their personality:

> I chose to do it with two people in order to demonstrate that we cannot separate off bits of our lives. People who are lucky enough not to have uncontrollable urges say 'Oh well, people who abuse their children are completely different sorts of people from me. They are monsters and I am not a monster'. You get people themselves who are subsequently going to be found to have abused their own children saying 'If you find out who's done this to my child, I'll string them up' – it's not just an alibi, but, quite genuinely, people have found it necessary to cut off, and my allegation would be that's *why* they can do it, that, if you keep your life whole, if you confront and challenge the wicked

side of your own personality, then that's the way to resolve those contradictions. That's what the play is arguing. Jekyll is seeking to cut off something which is uncutoffable and undistinguishable. He has not been invaded by Hyde. Hyde was always there, and Hyde needs to be confronted and defeated within one man, which is what happens in the end.

Edgar gives Jekyll a sister, a self-contained New Woman whose widow status and two children underline her mental strength in contrast to his own frailty. However, Katherine's physical vertigo hints at the secret that emerges at the end of the play: 'Teddy', the Edward Hyde aspect of her brother's personality, had violently assaulted her as a child in a jealous rage over their father's indifference to him and affection for her. The life-size painting of the father accrues symbolic significance throughout the play. He was the person Jekyll loved more than anyone in the world, yet he could never gain his approval, and the notebooks of this 'fiend in human form' contain the scientific formulae whereby transformation into Hyde is possible. The father–child relationship is echoed in Jekyll's relationship to his 'old son' Hyde, and in Annie's relationship to her abusive father, encapsulating the subject of duality: for Jekyll's father was a genius as well as a beast; Jekyll himself is a self-righteous prig as well as a lion of virtue; and Annie's father is 'soft enough when sober'. This emphasis on the father reflects Robert Louis Stevenson's brutal rejection by his own father, an action caused by the son's declaration of atheism, and it is relevant that Jekyll is mocked by Hyde when he is at prayer. In this sense, on one level, the play is 'about' Stevenson as *Nickleby* is 'about' Dickens.

There is a further comparison in that, just as the novels *Nickleby* and *Jekyll* 'book-end the heroic period of what we think of as high Victorian England', so the adaptations 'frame an echoing period of our own history', the beginning and end of the Thatcher government.[53] If in 1980 *Nickleby*'s success had been found in its anti-materialist theme, then in 1991 *Jekyll* was aimed at a *fin de siècle* audience who would respond to certain social parallels. Edgar explained his intentions:

> *Nickleby* is about the uncertainties of the world as it moves into the great capitalist boom in the middle of the nineteenth century,

76

and *Jekyll* is about the period after that boom had run out of steam and a period of retrospective doubt and anxiety. Clearly, that was very comparable with the atmosphere at the beginning of the great Thatcher boom and the end of it. At the beginning, in 1981, people felt change was necessary but they were very alarmed and disturbed by what was occurring in terms of rising unemployment and subsequently the riots and so on. We're now living in a period at the end of Thatcherism, again with people feeling it was good and necessary, but it actually didn't address the various fundamental things that the market can't address – and, indeed, if you rely totally on the market, will not be addressed – individual questions of responsibility and the whole critique of greed and so on.

Comparisons are explicitly made with the child abuse issue (which in 1885 was a concern especially in the form of child prostitution) and the homeless on the streets of the West End; and in general about 'the very ether of the times', the hastening 'to the century's end' and the accompanying release of inhumanity. Act One Scene Five is largely a discussion scene between three bachelors well up in both literature and science. Into the mouths of Utterson, Lanyon and Jekyll, Edgar puts a discussion of *Faust*, the neurological disorder Tourette's Syndrome, the two sides of the brain, and contemporary social phenomena ranging from sanitary conditions to New Womanhood, which reaches its climax in Utterson's discussion of 'these our gauzy times'.

Utterson's fears lead him to long to reinforce borders between 'the classes, and the races, and the genders, and perhaps who knows within ourselves'. His peroration is a prose poem of insecurity which very effectively finds resonances with late twentieth-century British audiences grappling with the terrors of AIDS, increased racial violence in the major cities, and nightly news bulletins of bloody civil wars in countries close to home:

For I am of a mind you see, that we live inside a little dish of light, surrounded by a black infinity of darkness. And it seems the darkness is forever clawing at the light, that our circle of security is shrinking, like a crumbling shoreline lapped by an insistent sea. For there are demons lurking out there in the darkness, gentlemen, and if we take a step beyond our gates, I tell you, they will have us.

77

The demons 'out there' and 'within' constitute the play's subject; and the play has a strong affiliation to *Mary Barnes* in that it is surely stressing that 'the personal is political'; that a new code of moral behaviour must be sought, otherwise the right-wing Uttersons will claim the territory. Indeed, just as Mary Barnes learns to love herself, so Jekyll goes through that essential process and takes personal responsibility for his actions.

Jekyll ran at the Barbican Theatre over Christmas and New Year. The audience and some of the critics were expecting a Christmas 'chiller', an occasional piece for the festive season. They were not satisfied in this aspect, although, among the magic 'illusions', there was an exceptionally fine transformation from Jekyll to Hyde set in a railway carriage (along with which the words 'Describe me' were truly chilling). The main focus of the production was on techniques of domestic realism. A revolve, on which were constructed three lavish, naturalistic Victorian domestic interiors, imprisoned most of the action in the centre of the vast Barbican stage. This undoubtedly detracted from the intensity of the psychological impact so crucial to the play. There was some use of less literal techniques that were much more suitable to the text and the space. The literary origins of the piece were at certain moments made explicit by projections of pages of the Stevenson novella (which fragmented as the revolve turned, signalling the transformation of Jekyll's personality). There were attempts at expressionist lighting and sound effects, with repeated leitmotifs of eerie musical punctuation, use of voice-over and mocking laughter. An argument could be made that a second production in a more intimate theatre would benefit from a more consistent application of the freer production techniques.

Michael Billington's notice ingeniously constructed a dialectic between Dr Jekyll and Mr Hyde, who 'compare notes' after the first night performance.[54] The earnest Dr Jekyll argues in positive appreciation of giving 'the old tale topical relevance', while his opposite number argues that 'Stevenson was not writing an anti-Thatcherite social tract. He created a powerful shocker that has endured for over a century because it preys on our own private fears and fantasies. By laboriously spelling out its implications, Mr Edgar leaves nothing to our imaginations. He proves yet again that "le vice anglais" is adaptation.' Despite the balance of the presentation here, there is little doubt that Billington's own reiterated opinion is against adaptation. One of his recent polemics argues in general terms against adaptation:

> Adaptation is only vindicated when it is driven by fierce moral fervour (Lyubimov's productions of *Crime and Punishment* and *The Possessed*) or by powerful critical insight (Hampton's *Les Liaisons Dangereuses*). Otherwise, it is a lazy way of avoiding responsibility to living writers.[55]

It is undeniable that David Edgar's four adaptations for the stage are driven by fierce moral fervour and powerful critical insight. Moreover, in answer to Billington's protests cited at the head of this chapter: Edgar has reworked melodrama into subtlety, writes primarily through the medium of irony, always strives to provide a sense of the original author's vision, and his strongest commitment is to reveal contemporary relevance in the old material. His adaptations are real plays.

4

Distress Signals: *Teendreams*, *Maydays* and *That Summer*

I am sure that the extraordinary resilience and tenacity of various
forms of social idealism has something to tell us about the
importance to the species of the notion of human collective
emancipation, even if we know that our reach in this matter will
always exceed our grasp.   David Edgar, 1991[1]

In terms of the story that I have always been interested in telling,
I have always been interested in disillusion, in the political
consequences of disillusion.   David Edgar, 1992[2]

David Edgar's decision to make theatrical records of the crisis of
the left in Britain in the Thatcher years is an index of his tenacity
rather than his defection. In *Teendreams* (1979), *Maydays* (1983),
and *That Summer* (1987), the challenge is to confront the
contradictions, disappointments and failures of class-based
revolutionary socialism and to work through 'a fair amount of
dirty political washing'. Edgar was in the awkward position of
'explaining public events in a privatised age' and there were
certain risks in drawing attention to 'the yawning gap between the
world as we'd like it to be, in the heat of the night, and the one we
actually confront in the cold light of dawn'.[3]

In their refusal to label individuals as villains, these three plays
continue *Destiny*'s approach to characterisation. The error would
be to equate this strategy with even-handedness; on the contrary,
Edgar is by no means objective. In each of these plays there is an
anti-defeatist expression of renewal of faith in socialist values,
particularly as embodied in progressive movements outside the
tradition of class-based analysis, and there is a particular interest in
the resistance of women. By the late 1970s, as we have seen,

Edgar's research had led him to withdraw from the Trotskyist position: 'The Trotskyist Left has, for years, been presenting what I call alibi politics – a series of alibis for not solving the central political problem of organising a revolutionary working-class movement in the West – a series of "not me sir", "not my fault sir", "nothing to do with me sir" sort of excuses.'[4] There simply was not going to be a left-wing revolution in Western Europe and there was no denying that the Eastern European collectivist societies were bureaucratic and dictatorial. It is perhaps not surprising that Edgar's determination to keep the vision of collectivism emerges most strongly from these plays, as if the tenacious pursuit of disclosing the disillusion leads inevitably to the need for the phoenix to rise.

Against the background of an increasingly right-wing Britain, and a policy of individualism, encouragement of greed and chauvinism, Edgar finds a kernel of resistance and altruism intrinsic to human nature. His analysis in the early 1980s was as follows (as pertinent for *Teendreams* and *That Summer* as for *Maydays*):

> The mistake that the left always make is to leave the question of human nature open to be defined by the right, because Marxism is supposed to be a science and human behaviour a function of material circumstance.
>
> We presently have two definitions of human nature, that people are entirely motivated by personal greed [and/or] atavistic tribalism, spending their days making money and their nights supporting West Ham or the Task Force. If there is a message in *Maydays*, it is that the urge to protest, the urge to resist, and the outrage at injustice are just as human.[5]

These plays are ultimately concerned with a moral stance that argues for a politics of resistance despite the evidence of disillusion.

Teendreams

Teendreams was written in collaboration with Susan Todd for the company Monstrous Regiment, a performers' collective committed to socialism and feminism. The company was founded in 1975; it aimed to put women centre stage, be a consciousness-raising group, give women opportunities for work, promote new writing and explore women's hitherto invisible history. The Women's Movement in Britain, with its rallying cry of 'the personal is political', was taking off and flying, and for the founder members of Monstrous Regiment there was a euphoric sense of 'being in the right place at the right time, in step with a great movement in history'.[6] Men were not excluded: 'We looked on our project as a shared one: men and women working together to create a new kind of theatre.'[7] Ironically, however, the involvement of women with revolutionary socialism had reinforced an unexpected consciousness: 'More and more women were noticing that the famous sexual and political revolution of the 1960s just meant more better sex for the men; and that commitment to left-wing ideas meant more licking envelopes and making tea for the women.'[8] *Teendreams* problematises women's experience on the left.

David Edgar's enthusiasm for working with the company partly stemmed from an interest in usefully and relevantly addressing a particular audience. He saw Monstrous Regiment as a bridge between the Royal Court and a wider audience involved in socialist struggle. The company could, out of their own experience, address such an audience with authority and with controversial subject matter.[9] A challenge could be issued: 'There is no point in arguing to that audience that women have had a raw deal. There is a point in doing what I tried to do in *Teendreams*. *Teendreams* attempted to take feminism as given and then explore some of its contradictions and some of its problems, with a view to presenting the audience to itself.'[10]

The research and writing process merits some detailed attention. Edgar had noted that 'sexual politics is an area of theory and practice on which socialists have tended to be at best woolly and at worst downright reactionary'.[11] He set about personally reversing this tendency by inviting Susan Todd to be his immediate collaborator and seeking a collective nourishing of the text through discussion workshops with other leading feminists such as Eve Brook, Beatrix Campbell and Angela McRobbie. Susan Todd had a pioneering background as director, writer and actor for the earliest 1970s women's theatre groups. She had directed and performed in the first Monstrous Regiment play *Scum: Death,*

Destruction and Dirty Washing, and other work for the company had included writing and directing (with Ann Mitchell) the play 'Kiss and Kill'; her 'intellect and passion had been a guiding force in the first years' of the company.[12] In interview, Susan Todd stressed the group's commitment to new writing: 'We were very in love with the idea of the writer's voice. We were working partly in opposition to devising, which our experience had led us to believe was sloppy and bland. We were completely dependent on new writing because the work that we needed to do and the things we needed to say didn't exist.'[13] The initial intention was that Edgar would write a play about violence among young women, and precise ideas were discussed:

> David was specifically interested in writing a play which dealt in some way with the history of the last ten years, 1968–1978. What he wanted to do was to chart the process of the growth and development of someone who had been a revolutionary in 1968. He was particularly interested in people he considered to be political renegades, who were left-wing in their youth, then rubbished it. And his intellectual project was a defence of a continued revolutionary politics. We talked a lot about what it is that keeps people going, what it is that keeps their political faith alive, how it is born in them.

The two characters Frances and Rosie were discussed. The former (more Edgar's character) had an intellectual political faith and the latter (more Susan Todd's character) came to find a need for a voice as a result of her life experience. Further, it was intended that the two schoolgirl figures Trisha and Denise (influenced by characters in 'Kiss and Kill') were to become a focus for an examination of the new generation experiencing a post-1968 society.

Factual material was gathered from two sources. Angela McRobbie's research at the Birmingham Centre for Cultural Studies was centred on teenage magazines and their effect on the expectations of young women. Newspaper accounts of bullying among girls and resultant suicide attempts by victims were also useful. The company was then presented with a scenario for discussion, and it was at that point that prominent socialist and feminist women came in to join the group. They talked about their experience in 1968, the effect of consciousness-raising groups, their leaving marriages in the late 1960s, and the way certain ideals had been very central to their lives and had changed them. This workshop process clarified the character Frances and her need for a shift in commitment from the radical left to a new feminist politics. Finally, ten days were spent when Edgar and Susan Todd together mapped out a scene-to-scene synopsis, using Edgar's idea of a retrospective structure. Edgar then wrote the play from the sum of that work.

Teendreams deals with moral questions of how to behave. A biblical text is the key to the play: 'When I was a child, I spake as a child, I understood as a child, I thought as a child; but when I became a man, I put away childish things' (One Corinthians 13:11). Frances, the radical activist schoolteacher, recalls the 'tatty teenage fantasy' that she lived by, that 'was going to be a blueprint for The Changing of the World'. This disillusionment with revolutionary politics at first appears to be the substance of the play's persuasion when Frances questions her socialist and feminist ideals after her pupil Trisha's suicide attempt. Trisha's 'teendreams' are based on the romantic fantasy she has learnt from magazines: 'His life's been just spent waiting for a girl like you. He lost his head to you in that first moment that you met but was too shy to say.' This Never-Never Land model of the world is shattered by Frances' influence. Frances reassesses her original choice of a socialist ideology and realises that the decision was not rational, that it was a reaching for identity, an instinctive seizure of a structure to escape sadness and loneliness. The key speech uses Marxist jargon as 'teendream' argot comparable to Trisha's magazine clichés. It is prefaced by the One Corinthians text, and it is the testing point of the play, the fracturing of a life-lie:

> FRANCES. Well, now. How does it go? When I was a child ... I spoke as a child, but when ... I can't remember how it ends. Something about growing up, and you can't be childish any more. St Paul. In One Corinthians.
>
> *She makes to go, then turns back.*
>
> You see, the *real* mistake, was thinking that that need, the need to think those things, was a rational decision. To convince oneself that one had woken up, one morning, had a

glance in the mirror, and *decided, seen* that all of history's the struggle of the classes, fancy that, that capital creates the means of its own overthrow, of course, that, well I never, there appears to be this contradiction between the social methods of production and the private ownership of capital, well glory be, and all those rational cosmetics, smeared in layers across that sad and lonely, desperate little face that I had seen, that morning, in the mirror. Blueprint, change the world. In fact, a blueprint to escape the world. And me. And I've been on the run, from me, this seven years, and now at last I'm going to turn me in.

I'm sorry we were wrong.

The images here of the mirror and the cosmetics parallel the icons of Trisha's masking kit; Denise screams at Trisha, 'Moisturisers, creams, mascara, powders, spotstick, lipstick, shadow, what the fuck's a blusher? ... So a'n't you got a face? Face of your own?' The enslaving hold of a rigid and determinist idea of the world is common to Trisha and Frances. The ripping apart of that mask is part of the overall theme of change. Frances retreats to her parents' safe, comfortable middle-class home.

The play defies the expectation set up by this narrative progression. Frances is resurrected from despair by her memory of a promise to Rosie and will persevere in seeking for revolutionary alternatives. All through the play we are exposed to the struggle to learn from experience and recognise a need for change and progression however painful this might be. The play depicts women positively taking hold of their lives once a point of no return is reached and a seeming death is passed through: Rosie's marriage, Trisha's romantic fantasy, Frances's faith in revolutionary socialism, are all toppled. There are ironies and paradoxes on the journey. The parody agitprop play in Scene Six is a socialist–feminist morality: 'It's a marriage play. Tony's the Church and State and I'm the little woman wedded unto Capital' explains Anne (who is 'dressed in a parody wedding gown, festooned with pots, pans, chains and symbols of degradation'). This glimpse of a propagandist play-within-the-play is a strong self-parody, ironically highlighting the absence of such absolutism in *Teendreams'* own meaning.

The problem is that of making socialist and feminist politics compatible. Frances argues: 'I personally don't think it's possible to emancipate our sex without emancipating the working class. I don't think you can just change your lifestyle and the rest follows. I don't think you can change the insides of people's heads without changing what's outside them first'; and 'I just do find it difficult, to take that seriously a group of people arguing that the Queen's exploited by her footmen and her stable boys.' This contradiction remains with the audience to resolve as the action unfolds. Another question is raised through Rosie's situation. Her progress away from marital oppression demonstrates a characteristic journey for many women in the late 1960s and early 1970s. She does no paid work but we see her paid in kind for her wifely labour when Howard gives her jewellery trinkets. When the point is raised in Scene Seven that many women would love not to work the arena is once again open for debate: how can oppressions be measured one against the other? And when Trisha attempts suicide and Denise's delinquency extends from stealing and gambling to smashing windows, Brewer, the boorish right-wing male teacher, can goad Frances: 'you've transferred your agonies and insecurities and pain on to two schoolgirls, and what's happened is that you've destroyed them by your arrogant conviction that their choices, what they've chosen as their lives, their interests, their dreams, are worthy of contempt.' Is Brewer oppressing Frances through male superiority and defending himself against women's independence, or does he have understanding that she lacks? He points out that once Trisha's femininity props were taken away she had nothing left, and that Denise's alternative was to adopt aggressive masculinity. These sound arguments from the right are typical of Edgar's balanced approach to characterisation.

The structure of the play is complex with a non-linear time scheme. There are nineteen short scenes in the revised collected *Plays* version. The first scene set in 1975 shows Trisha's suicide attempt and the second scene follows on with Frances's reaction and disillusion. The action then flashes back for thirteen scenes, first to 1968, then to 1972, then to the 1975 events leading up to Scene One. Scene Sixteen takes us to the present action and partly repeats Scene Two. Scene Seventeen follows on chronologically with Rosie's visit to Trisha's hospital bed. Scene Eighteen is an epilogue to Frances's story with its own flashback to 1961. The final scene is a coda to the action set in the future, offering short synopses of the characters' subsequent lives through the five narrative voices of Trisha, Frances, Rosie, Denise and Ruth. Edgar had strong ideological reasons for this largely retrospective structure:

> We wanted to take the model of youthful idealism turning into middle-aged cynicism and despair, a very hoary old plot model, and to turn it round. By starting the play with the suicide and repeating the second speech of the play, we intended the audience to assume that was going to be the last scene, and that we were doing that plot model of disillusionment; but then have the characters actually coping in a way which was perhaps more realistic than the heights of idealistic revolutionism and, in a sense, beyond it, a progression. That was an attempt to *go through* an argument which has been formulated in terms of a dramatic convention, set up a theatrical expectation and then deny it. In taking the conventional theatrical form of a conventional ideological model, using it and disrupting it – not merely disrupting the audience as an end in itself – we attempted to provide a critique of that plot device's ideological basis and function.[14]

While the structural complexity does not take the weight of this justification – the narrative is unwieldy and potentially confusing – it does challenge the audience to make connections between the historical story concerned with the 1968 generation of women and the contemporary story of the schoolgirls. If it needed (as it did) more focus, it was a brave experiment, demonstrating Edgar's continuing refusal to be reductively simple.

There are three versions of the ending in published texts. Edgar has indicated 'hints of the possibility of alternative ways of developing'.[15] The first (1979) ending showed Frances and Rosie dressed up for a night out. This established their strong bond, but what of the future? In the revised (1987) version, synopses of the future are offered. Frances, for example, writes a well-received novel, 'though some feminist reviewers weren't quite sure how to read its tone', and the implication is that she has progressed from any categorisable feminist model in her understanding of life experience (but it is left as an imprecise hint, neatly avoiding the 'how' of the progress). The lyrical last lines of the play come down firmly on the side of 'dreams' as positive; yet there is a sinister undertone of music: Vivaldi's 'Winter' indicates harsh new times in which a vision of collective emancipation would be hard to realise. In the re-revised (1991) *Plays: Three* version, through tiny alterations, and in particular a mention of market forces, a more precise reference is made to the Thatcher years through which the women, with their sustained ideals and in their united front, will resist oppression. This stronger index of less optimistic times had first been written specifically for a production at the Guildhall School of Drama in May 1991.

When the play toured in its first (1979) production to Sheffield, Bradford, York, Bingley, Brighton, Birmingham and the ICA in London, Susan Todd played Rosie, 'her' character. The production attracted audiences interested in moral problem plays as well as socialist movement audiences, and especially women. They came to see a piece stressing the importance of commitment to a code of personal morality and revealing certain flaws in models of socialist and feminist analysis. In his essay 'The Morals Dilemma' (1987) Edgar offers the argument that 'the rampant individualism and the aggressive chauvinism of Thatcherite culture is a function of the reassertion of masculinity and the anti-feminist backlash'. He develops the point: 'Much of the familial and sexual violence we see in the inner cities and on the estates (and, as it ought to, but perhaps shouldn't, go without saying, behind the privet hedge and beyond the raked driveway) is a function of this pressing crisis of masculinity', and concludes that, instead of looking to the family institution alone to transmit moral codes (as traditionally), there should be and already are prototypes of models of 'effective "elective kinship" ', 'new moral communities'. These models should be and are 'based around codes of interpersonal and social behaviour appropriate to our times'; indeed 'a kinship based on a shared oppression can be as mutually sustaining as that of the family'.[16] There is no doubt that *Teendreams* bears the seriousness of this conviction.

The touring production of *Teendreams* was intrinsically that of poor theatre, with multiple roles, minimal set and props, and strong emphasis on recorded music to set the period. Its theatrical liveliness lies especially in the use of stylised language, with its conflicting jargons (Marxist, chauvinist, teenage magazine-speak); the interest of adult actors playing teenagers; and, above all, the passion of the clash of ideas. There is a particular energy in the scenes between the teenagers and it is here that Edgar achieves a core of feeling through violence and threat. Trisha's suffering when the object of her misguided desire has got into a clinch with her best friend; Denise's ripping down of Trisha's pictures (and, symbolically, her world of romance); the bullying shown in the Youth Club scene: these are the moments where the adolescent distress is put centre stage, the personalities of the young girls are allowed to live, and the theatrical takes over the ideas without losing their force. The need to find successful ways of embodying ideas is the essential problem for the research playwright. It is *Maydays* that tests that problem more than any other of Edgar's plays.

Maydays

Maydays is a play of considerable passion characterised especially by Edgar's familiar refusal to simplify. It is punctuated with long, highly-wrought and intense set pieces of speeches. It is packed with ideas and world historical points of reference. There are appropriations from Trotsky, Marx, T.S. Eliot, W.B. Yeats, Lenin and Lennon. The action encompasses the Soviet invasion of Hungary in 1956, the 'Un-Americans' of the 1950s, the situationists, the Vietnam war, CND and the Greenham Common peace camp. The text has a prefacing political chronology from 1956 to 1981, an appendix listing a selection of Maydays, and quotations prefacing each act. The action takes place from 1945 to the early 1980s. There are fifty-three characters. The settings are in four countries: England, Hungary, the United States and the Soviet Union. The controlling cerebralism is thoroughly theatricalised through irony, parody, an intricate pattern of cross-references, characters who represent three generations of socialism, and a fast-moving pace of events sweeping along to the positive conclusion. There is a strong emphasis on spectacle and an excitement that stems from the bold scale of the play, an energy more Marlovian than Shakespearian, as Edgar points out: '*Maydays* is about as grand a narrative play as it's possible to be this side of *Tamburlaine the Great*.'[17] It would be difficult to find another play in the post-war British tradition with such 'grandeur', intellectual *gravitas* and meticulous detail about revolutionary socialism. The question that vexed several commentators was, why should this subject be presented in 1983 in the London main house of a prestigious national company? Why should taxes subsidise a production of a piece centred on the ups and downs of the extreme left? Meanwhile, those on the revolutionary left protested about the intrinsic danger of displaying such blatant disillusionment and negative criticism to an RSC audience: for indeed, Edgar had unconsciously found within himself the courage demanded by Peter Hall in his *Diaries* commentary on *Destiny*: 'If only Edgar had had the courage to be as critical of the extreme left as he is of the right.'[18] A furious multi-layered debate in the national press greeted the RSC production and it is to that furore that attention should be given.

A publicity article emphasised that *Maydays* was 'the first new play by an author under 40 to reach the RSC's large stage for 5 years'.[19] Moreover, it was Edgar's first original play for a main stage. Several people in the *Maydays* company had worked on earlier RSC productions of Edgar's plays. Ron Daniels directed. Bob Peck played the Soviet dissident Lermontov; certain of the audience may have remembered his roles as Cleaver in *Destiny* and John Browdie and Sir Mulberry Hawk in *Nickleby*. Stephen Oliver composed the music. Di Seymour (set designer for *Destiny*) was responsible for costume design. There was an intrinsic 'follow that' subtext to the project as no member of the theatre-going public could have been unaware of *Nickleby*'s triumph. The problem was self-evident: 'I don't think you can write honest plays about the contemporary world that get fifteen-minute ovations.'[20]

This was a contemporary play for the new Barbican stage which bestowed an immediate 'public forum' quality, and the configuration of the times contributed to the expectation. Edgar commented:

> In the early eighties when the Barbican first opened it had a very successful two seasons. Generally it did have a buzz about it. It was in 1983 which was the year of the Foot General Election debacle; it was the year after the Falklands, and two years after the riots; the Evil Empire was still stalking the world; and Greenham Common, the starkness of that confrontation, was a present reality. The Barbican felt a grand public arena.

Given this buzz, it could be seen as frustrating in the extreme that Robert Cushman in the *Observer* felt that it was a 'misconception that the world needs a monster play about politics on a subsidised stage',[21] all the more so given that Ron Daniels had internally defended *Maydays* when the RSC had objected at one point 'because the issues were too political: David wasn't tackling the humanity of *Nickleby* but political issues'.[22] Daniels understood that 'This time it was a huge risk, that was deliberately taken by the RSC, to put this huge play on the Barbican stage and make a statement of our commitment at the time to new writing, not to David in particular, but to new writing and the world we lived in.'

Edgar, who felt himself that *Maydays* was the 'most risky' play he had written,[23] had conceived it specifically for Shakespearian actors and the Barbican stage:

> It was written to be done in the Barbican. I wrote it in order to solve a problem. The RSC hadn't had a very successful time with new work on its main stages, really since the *Destiny* period. In the late seventies it didn't have a successful time. There were a couple of projects that didn't work out and then there was a period when no new work was done at all apart from adaptations like *Nickleby* and so when it moved to the Barbican it would have been very easy (as the Barbican's even larger than the Aldwych) to say, well, new work doesn't work on the RSC main London stage, we've got a splendid small auditorium in the Pit, we should accept that the main stage is the arena of the classics ... A group of us in the RSC felt very strongly that we should put on a new, non-musical play on that stage. So it was very much written to be on that stage. I mean, the reason there's a train in the play is because I wanted to write a play that couldn't be done in the Pit.[24]

Ron Daniels (as we have seen with regard to *Destiny*) has stressed the importance for Edgar's work of the specialised training of RSC actors. With *Maydays* this was crucial:

> Our actors were used to dealing with huge soliloquies. David knew who he was writing for. From way back in the seventies we talked about the RSC's two theatres cross-feeding each other, the fact that The Other Place would bring a contemporary awareness to our main house work, whereas the main house would provide actors with an imaginative dimension, which was not possible if it was continually just dealing with small intimate material.

91

The subject was very obviously the one fly in the ointment. This was not so as far as the cast was concerned who, although they were not the committed socialists of the ilk of Monstrous Regiment, looked to David Edgar for elucidation and commentary. They received analysis in abundance. The rehearsal process involved 'teach-in' elements, with the rehearsal room turned into a relevant environment with a chronology and pictures from the 1960s posted up; videotapes such as the series *Years of Lightning* (a compilation of rock songs and newsreels) were shown; and the events were discussed. It was acknowledged that the playwright's own life experience was at the core of the play, with the result that affectionate pastiche of Edgar's personality became a performance element. The contrast with the *Teendreams* ensemble is stark: *Maydays* in text and to an extent in performance was very much the product of one person's commitment and thinking.

That thinking was about the authoritarian right. *Maydays* is about Thatcherism, written in the first flowering of the Social Democratic Party when the parliamentary Labour Party was in fragmented crisis. It explores Thatcherism by taking what seems to be a surprising route: an examination of defection from the extreme left. Edgar's perception was centred on the thesis that defectors to the right retain that very authoritarianism that caused their defection from the left: 'the paradox of defection is that the one thing people retain is the reason they left. Most people leave revolutionary parties, and communist parties in particular, because they joined out of ideals of liberation and freedom, but find that communism in operation is authoritarian. But what they take over with them is that authoritarianism.'[25] He had formed this conclusion both through his own observation of Margaret Thatcher's advisers: 'many who surround Mrs Thatcher in a formal or informal advisory capacity, started life on the other side'[26] and also through absorption of a quantity of research on defection. In particular, Edgar was impressed by Isaac Deutscher's *Heretics and Renegades* from which there is a quotation prefacing Act Two: 'Whatever the shades of individual attitudes, as a rule the intellectual ex-Communist ceases to oppose capitalism. Often he rallies to its defence, and he brings to this job the lack of scruple, the narrow-mindedness, the disregard for truth, and the intense hatred with which Stalinism has inbred him. He remains a sectarian. He is an inverted Stalinist.' Edgar commented that the central characters of *Maydays* – Weiner, Crowther, and Glass – embody 'the notion of the political defector who becomes the equally rapacious mirror image of him or herself'. The invitation to the Barbican audience was to look at the Conservative Party in a new light.

The argument was thus very specific, based on a particular insight into the distinction between the authoritarian and libertarian right. Edgar detailed his intended meaning as follows:

> What the play argued was that one of the reasons why the right was so heartless and Manichean in the early eighties was because much of its culture was created by people who'd come from the left, people who'd lost belief in the ends but kept the means. Everybody who had been on the left has confronted the fact, as Stephen Spender put it, that in order to be a Communist you are required to sacrifice the reasons that made you one. Everybody who has been on the left who has been seriously and properly engaged with the idea of possibly bringing about a socialist revolution knows that that is a real and fervent contradiction, and I was able to explore it in a way that was positive to the left by pointing out that one of the most unfortunate by-products of that phenomenon was that it created these monsters on the right. There's this whole series of people, three generations of people, who defect. What they do, they end up having exactly the same monstrosity of behaviour but with none of the idealism and the progressive impulses on the other side of the tracks.

Those who negatively criticised the play had precise although diverse reasons: defection is not a crucial subject; parliamentary politics is more relevant to British political reality than the extra-parliamentary left; the play confirms prejudice against the revolutionary left. Clearly, those who accepted its subject accepted the validity of the Barbican as public forum; and this proposition will be examined after an analysis of the play.

The American Jew Teddy Weiner, the northern English working-class Jeremy Crowther, and the English middle-class vicar's son Martin Glass are paradigmatic figures of, respectively, the 1930s, 1950s and 1960s generations of revolutionary socialist defectors. Martin Glass is closer to the playwright's own lived experience than any other character in the canon and that inner truth manifests itself proportionately in the play. We are allowed to follow Martin's political journey, his personal relationships (in particular with Jeremy Crowther and Amanda Price) and his ultimate volte-face in the depth denied to Turner in *Destiny*: 'Martin's story is true. It's true because a lot of it did happen to me and a lot of people I know. I knew Martin before I started writing a great deal better than I knew Dennis Turner. Obviously *Maydays* was personal in a way that *Destiny* wasn't personal, because there was nobody in *Destiny* I shared my life experience with in any direct way, whereas there were huge amounts in *Maydays* that were sections of life I'd lived through.' Although we can read Martin as an existentialist tragic hero who makes the wrong choice, it would be a mistake to ignore the structure of the narrative which, in its complexity, projects a meaning beyond the individual. That structure reaches out to Eastern Europe and by inclusion especially of the story of Lermontov an emphasis is placed on the continuing need for resistance. It is this perspective that offers a conclusion positive to the left.

Act One requires the audience to make connections between nine scenes spread out over twenty-five years. A skilled interweaving of precise historical reference and personal repercussion maintains a montage structure. The device is cinematic in its use of close-up and longshot, demonstrating social realism through placing the individual in an historical context:

> I didn't want the play merely to be a series of psychological case studies – I wanted to set three generations of defectors within an analysis of the 25 years of history covered by the play. So what I hoped would happen was that the audience would recognise the characters from the inside, but be able, simultaneously, like a sudden film-cut from close-up to wide-angle, to look at how these individual journeys were defined by the collective journey of an epoch.[27]

This epic strategy allows us to see the nodal points of revolutionary disillusionment. An interesting exemplary use of such a filmic 'cut' occurs in the juxtaposition of Scenes Two and Three. Scene Two is a 'wide-angle' scene set in 1956 Hungary, historically concerned with the Soviet invasion; in Scene Three we understand the effect of that invasion on Jeremy who, as a revolutionary socialist, has left the Communist Party because of it. The scene-to-scene cause and effect (with its stress on the impact of social and historical forces on the individual) is accompanied by an overall narrative structure. The characterisation of Clara, for example, is crucial to the overall structure; she is introduced in Act One Scene Two, is treated badly by Lermontov, and reappears towards the end of Act Three to impress on us that Lermontov's imprisonment in labour camps was prompted by betrayal and revenge. The play becomes a mock-Jacobean tragedy as the theme of revenge recurs in others' experience, placing the individual within a collective and exemplary story; as the theme draws to a head in Act Three Scene Five, the action takes place in a hotel's Jacobean suite under a Jacobean painting.

Parallelisms, often ironical, always involving direct echoes in language, are structural foundations. A key example occurs in Act One Scene Six and is paralleled in Act Three Scene Four. In each scene Martin is wooed by a hardliner. In the earlier scene James Grain attempts to recruit Martin for the left in an historical year for the revolutionary left, 1968. In the later scene Hugh Trelawney attempts to recruit Martin for the right in an historical year for the revolutionary right, 1979. Each recruiter criticises Martin's political journalism and dissects his vocabulary, using similar rhetoric but substituting crucial words. The word 'duty' obsesses Trelawney as much as the words 'working class' obsess Grain. In each case Martin is judged to be politically wrong. This parallelism not only points to the way in which Martin is forced to bend with the times; it also confirms a major theme in *Maydays*. That theme concerns the use of rhetoric.

An examination of language as an imperfect code capable of manipulation weaves constantly in and out of the fabric of the play. As well as offering a pattern of echoes for ironical narrative purpose, Edgar asks us to question vocabulary as a vehicle for meaning altogether. In an intimate moment of emotional upheaval Martin parodies the television show *Take Your Pick* where candidates were asked to 'Rearrange the following into a well-known phrase or saying': 'Something I've You Always Rotten Fancied.' The implications are that emotions can only have obscure expression in words and that language is a game we play to cover feeling. On a larger, public level, the entire play wrestles with the issue of 'what we mean by socialism'. Jeremy Crowther addresses the audience in the prologue, casting them as 'a large, enthusiastic – even triumphant – crowd' of Young Communists in 1945 and, as red flags fly, red banners swirl and red streamers billow, he provides the theme: 'Comrades, we have been asked a thousand times what we mean by socialism. As throughout the continent the toiling masses rise to liberate themselves from tyranny, to fashion with their own hands their own New Jerusalem, we can at last say: *this* is what we meant.' The irony is profound: Jeremy will end up on the far right, having repressed the 'childish' self who had notions of the New Jerusalem. An emphatic scrutiny of the inadequacies of language, and the gap between rhetoric and meaning, words and truth, the pressing for exact definition that is never forthcoming as phrases are appropriated and meaning slides and slithers: this is the key to the play and the reality of the 'meaning' of socialism is unlocked in this slippery context.

Throughout the play it is Amanda who takes seriously her responsibility to 'complete the building of the New Jerusalem'. These particular words, 'New Jerusalem', take on earnest or ironical or hopeful or phantasmagorical connotations depending on context. The words 'liberty', 'liberation', and 'freedom' are questioned constantly. The Trotsky phrase 'human dust' is used earnestly by James, ironically by Martin, then rejectingly by Martin, and finally it is appropriated by Jeremy for the right. The words that Hamlet played on, 'kind' and 'kindred', are several times probed in order to state the essential contradiction: does socialism 'mean' loving one's kind (working towards the emancipation of 'mankind') but not loving people; communality but not the individual, and not one's own immediate family? And is it better to pursue a course of action according to what one 'thinks' or what one 'feels'? What are the 'ultimate realities' of Soviet Communist Party jargon? Was the coarse vocabulary of that Party a means of giving a voice to the voiceless or should it be derided?

Political betrayal manifests itself through use of inversion of rhetorical language, exemplified in Martin and Phil's code, 'Red Barcelona'. This is a reference to an incident in the Spanish Civil War where the anarchists were killed by the Communists, a betrayal of all that the anarchists had worked towards in their collectivisation programme. Martin expands:

In the beginning, it was just, the communists were saying that the anarchists were wrong. Mistaken. Incorrect.
Then their mistakes and incorrectitude were 'objectively' in the interests of the fascists.
Then 'objectively' the anarchists were fascists.
Then each individual anarchist became an actual, subjective, conscious Nazi.
Ergo, my dog's a cat.

The television version of *Maydays* (structured in two films, 'Going Over' and 'Coming Back') makes explicit the theme of the slipperiness of language in *Through the Looking Glass* references used as voice-over:

'When *I* use a word,' Humpty Dumpty said, 'it means exactly what I want it to mean, neither more nor less.' ... 'The question is' said Alice, 'whether you *can* make words mean so many different things.' ... But Humpty disagrees. 'The question *is*,' said Humpty Dumpty, 'which is to be master – that is all.'

This version takes as leitmotif the One Corinthians reference used in *Teendreams* (and so profound does Edgar judge its significance to be that it would again be deployed in 'Buying a Landslide'). The question is: should one 'put away childish things'? Is revolutionary socialism childish? Or are there new forms of resistance that could supplant those tried, tested and failed?

The multifaceted title of the stage play dialectically prepares the ground for the evaluation of socialism's 'meaning'. As the *May Day Manifesto 1968* defines it: 'May Day, for many hundreds of years, has been a people's holiday: a celebration of growth on the land ... coming out of this history, May Day has been an international festival – a demonstration and commitment – of the labour movement.'[28] At the end of Act One, Amanda, the voice of wisdom and resistance, declares 'We must all remember all the May Days ... We must remember, we must absolutely not forget the superhuman things that human beings can and have achieved.' She is speaking on May Day in 1970. Towards the end of the play Clara reminds the exile Lermontov of 'those superhuman tasks' achieved in the Soviet Union; it is January 1979, the beginning of a new era of the authoritarian right in Britain. In the climactic banquet scene in Act Three Scene Six, when Lermontov celebrates resistance, he echoes Amanda and Clara. In the RSC production his speech directly indicted the Barbican audience in 'this room':

> You see, I look around this room, and I don't see faces which have ever seen the world through wire. Yours are not gaolers' faces. But perhaps they are the faces of the people who employ the gaolers.
> Faces which cannot remember, if they ever knew, the superhuman things that people can achieve, when for a moment they forget what they've been told they are.

There is no doubt that these invocations to remember, and the stress on the actuality of superhuman achievement (and hence on its potential for recurrence) embody a central vision of the play. Yet, as the American Cathy Weiner utters Act One's curtain line, she uncovers another side to the theme of the meaning of socialism: 'It's May Day. Mayday Mayday.' The pun is the antithesis to the thesis of 'remembering' and it indicates an international warning of distress.

At the very end of the play comes the synthesis. Korolenko is determined to expose conditions in the Soviet coalmines (and perhaps prompts us to see a parallel with miners' conditions in Britain); he is seen with the academic Pugachev who, we assume, has received, for smuggling abroad, the manifesto of the unofficial miners' union. Korolenko has been brutally punished in a Soviet hospital and labour camp for his 'mania' for justice. When Pugachev asks how long he will last (in his struggle) Korolenko replies with the final words in the play: 'Who knows? "May Days".' The title words have become a symbol of justice and resistance, and are inevitably still linked with Amanda. Her protest at an arms base (an unnamed but obvious Greenham Common), her 'urge to stop the planet being blown to blazes', is evidence of a resurrectionary quality in the socialist ideal, a May Day in its third sense of springtime renewal. The early 1980s Barbican audience was thus encouraged to take on board Lermontov's rebuke; they must not give way to despair because one (Stalinist) form of socialism has failed: for a new left vision is emergent from the demise of the old, linking East and West.

The last scene of *Maydays* importantly defines resistance as part of human nature. Edgar commented:

The point in the last scene of *Maydays* is that the altruistic urge, the egalitarian urge, the urge to improve society, the urge to redress grievances, and to particularly redress disparities, is as much part of being human as either of the two alternatives on offer, which are basically the two alternatives that Conservatism offers.

An exchange between Amanda and Martin encapsulates this faith at the heart of Edgar's purpose as playwright. Ironically, Martin (whom we first met as a seventeen-year-old engaged in CND) is now, over twenty years later, living in the family vicarage adjacent to the Greenham Common-like arms base and is seeking to oust women protesters who have camped on his property:

> AMANDA. And of course you may say that the urge to stop the planet being blown to blazes is a form of brute, material self-interest –
>
> MARTIN. Well, that's certainly an argument –
>
> AMANDA. Or that to want those aeroplanes to be removed is merely good old British national pride –
>
> MARTIN. Well, nobody likes Yanks –
>
> AMANDA. But I think in fact that in the end what they are doing, what we are all trying to do, in our many different ways, can only be accounted for by something in the nature of our species which resents, rejects and ultimately will resist a world that is demonstrably wrong and in this case dramatically wrong and mad and unjust and unfair.
> And I wonder, Martin, if you ever really felt like that.
> Or, if you did, if you can still remember.
>
> MARTIN. No.
>
> *Pause.*
>
> No, as it happens, I don't think I do.

Edgar clarified the argument: 'She's positing three things there: one, brute, material self-interest; the second, nationalism; the third, resistance to unfairness, and actually that's as much part of being human as the other two. The Conservative idea that somehow tribalism and individual greed are natural (which they clearly are)

99

whereas the altruistic urge is unnatural, is a sort of constructed false notion, is as false as to say the opposite.' The urge to challenge unfairness is seen as an intrinsic quality, natural to the species.

That quality is denied by Martin. Martin does not 'think' he remembers he 'felt' like that. He has cut off from his feelings because he does not want to be vulnerable, and he has run from despair into choices that remake his sense of being in the world. When we first meet Martin, his Sartrean adolescent poem 'Resist' and his CND affiliation indicate his strong potential for altruism which is cut short when disillusionment with the far left and his treatment by the party Socialist Vanguard lead him to defection. He is the saddest character in the play, and can be read in Sartrean terms as an existentialist tragic hero, a man who cannot build on his choices and impulse to resistance, and ends up living in bad faith. Edgar made a Shakespearian analogy: 'The play very clearly says that Martin made a mistake. It's *Coriolanus*: those tribunes *are* irritating but his response is to turn on the good bits of Rome as well as the bureaucratic tiresome bits.'

There is an acute and detailed examination of what Martin 'thinks' and 'feels' throughout, and of the contradictions he suffers. In particular, his Party disapproves of Martin's defence of his friend Phil (whose situationist terrorism is deemed politically wrong in the context of industrial revolutionary action) and in this context he is attacked by James Grain for what he 'thinks' and 'does'. Conversely, because Martin withdraws his support for Phil, he is attacked by Ron for what he does not 'appear to feel'. The problem for Martin is in miniature one of the grand themes of the play: should he support 'kind' or 'kindred'? The party scene (Act Two Scene Seven) is the turning-point for Martin, set in the 'wide-angle' context of Mayday 1975 and the Vietnamese victory. His defection speech satirises the left rhetoric of 'devilish social-democrats' and 'dastardly reformists', and he cannot rationalise his emotional reactions, cannot negotiate between what he thinks and feels. The driving force behind the speech is a discovery, a paradox, expressed pithily by Stephen Spender: 'The Communist, having joined the Party, has had to castrate himself of the reasons that made him one.'[29] Martin echoes the Spender realisation: 'I think it is the whole idea ... that to be a communist you must purge yourself of the instincts and beliefs that made you one.'

100

Martin's concern is that the sense of justice and compassion that led him to Communism had to be left behind and that a hard, ugly notion of 'human dust' had to be substituted, 'that there's no morality except the interests of the revolution'. He rejects the morality of the Party when he protests 'I don't believe, I can't believe, I actually refuse to be required by anybody to believe, that anyone is human dust.'

Martin's mentor is Jeremy and, at the beginning of Act Three, when Martin takes Jeremy's hand, he signals that he will follow in his mentor's path. Martin's choices now are clearly a product of his lack of negotiation between what he thinks and feels: 'What the distinction between thought and feeling disguises is that somehow the intellect is the false bit and the emotions are real ... But the relationship of thinking to feeling is, one hopes, that instinct is mediated by reason and vice-versa. Martin's great mistake is to make an absolute distinction between them, and so he becomes very vulnerable, therefore he constructs these models of the world and then when anything goes wrong with them he feels betrayed.'[30] In Act Three Scene Six Martin questions Jeremy on the authoritarian principle of government as represented by the academic Trelawney. Trelawney leads a hard-right pressure group, the Committee in Defence of Liberty; he is ironically the former Minister of State whom Phil had attempted to assassinate. Trelawney argues for a right-wing form of the state authoritarianism that Martin had condemned in Stalinism: he considers Martin very useful, a defector who has '*seen* the future and ... *know*[s] it doesn't work'. Jeremy supports Trelawney to the hilt, arguing that there is too much freedom, a 'disease' that, if we do not understand it 'will destroy us all'. Following Lermontov's banquet speech, Martin interrogates Jeremy about Trelawney's 'brave new world', one that seems to promise capital punishment, suppression, censorship and compulsory Army service. Jeremy's methods of persuasion induce Martin to seek his advice. Martin is told to go home. Home, in Jeremy's sense, is middle-class privilege, that privilege represented by Mrs Glass in the vicarage scene. This is indeed where Martin ends up, repressing his 'resisting' self. However, that rebellious self is the 'real' self, the Sartrean choice of being, that Martin betrays: 'When Jeremy says to him "Go Home", Martin thinks he's going back to what he really is, but he isn't. What he really is is that boy protesting against nuclear

101

weapons on the parade ground.'[31] Martin had chosen his own values against his family; he ends up negating 'what he really is'.

Martin's surname is allegorical. Edgar explained:

> The play started life with a single image which was a man standing in front of a mirror saying things that he could never have thought before, that he could never have articulated before: things like 'the unions have too much power' or 'actually men are better than women at doing certain things' with the sense of relief at being able finally to articulate. It arose out of an incident I'd read about, about some 1930s defectors in the US, people who were Communists in the thirties in the States, and they all seemed to have had a moment when suddenly they were able to articulate their new-forged phoenix-like right-wing beliefs, and realised that they had thought that for some time.[32]

By the end of the play, Martin has become the mirror image of himself; he is the 'glass' wherein we can see a pattern of defectors; and the glass is ultimately transparent in the sense that his 'real self' no longer exists. This is plainly signified in the television version of the play, where a mirror becomes a symbolic piece of furniture. The metaphor is reinforced when Martin practises his defection speech while looking at his reflection in a triple mirror. He turns the two side panels so that he cannot see reflections of prints of a Che Guevara poster and the Black Power protest at the 1968 Olympics; he is blanking out left icons, symbols of his revolutionary self. At the very end of the second television film 'Coming Back' (the conclusion of the entire version), Martin declares, 'for the first time since my childhood, I feel, obviously literally, but more important, existentially, at home'. His words are self-deceit for, after he locks himself into his comfortable vicarage property, he catches sight of himself in the mirror. We see stills from his life. The final image is: 'The mirror above the fireplace in the vicarage parlour. Nothing reflected in the mirror. There's no one there.' Existentially, Martin has, in fact, ceased to be.

Conversely, Lermontov, the Soviet dissident, refuses to accept authoritarianism in Britain. Ironically, his imprisonment for attempting to circulate a petition for the freedom to demonstrate, as reported in *The Times*, has effected Jeremy's shift of allegiance rightwards. Lermontov is an exception to the Deutscher model of the disillusioned defector. The Press advance on Lermontov at

Frankfurt airport babbling questions in various languages while he has 'no words to say' and the emphasis from Act Two Scene Eight onwards is on the gulf between language and meaning. Lermontov has renounced the argot of the Soviet Communist Party, but Clara reminds him in Act Three Scene Five that education in that vocabulary has at least given the people a voice. In the words of that 'arch', 'coarse', and 'breathless' vocabulary, Lermontov has 'been seduced into the camp of the most bellicose cold war imperialists'. In Britain he is fêted by the hard right and discovers that he retains the truths beneath the Party rhetoric.

Because Lermontov is unsure of the English language, he fights hard to pinpoint meaning. In Act Three Scene Five he echoes Paloczi's words, themselves an echo of his own in Act One Scene Two: 'Do I have to spell it out in semaphore?' He tries to learn a new vocabulary and with it a set of values where the concept of 'freedom' does not seem to be attached to human rights protest, and where small minority groups campaigning for freedom are labelled 'cranks and crazies'. A convention established in Act Three Scene Three assumes that when Lermontov and Paloczi speak alone they are speaking Russian. The banquet scene, the award ceremony in Act Three Scene Six, is where this convention comes into its own. The scene has been compared by David Edgar and Robert Cushman to the Taddley Patriotic League meeting scene in *Destiny*, a public scene that 'goes wrong'.[33] The right (specifically the Committee for the Defence of Liberty) is trying to claim Lermontov for their cause: he is an obvious example of someone who has suffered horribly under the Soviet regime. Teddy Weiner, the American Communist Party defector from the thirties generation, makes a speech against 'agitation', 'subversion', and 'hooligans' in the arts, law and education. He speaks of binding all citizens in 'nationhood' (very much *Destiny* territory). Lermontov gets up to make his speech, prepared for him on cards by Paloczi. He deviates from the written speech, refuses the award and walks off stage. He reinforces the key point of the play by pointing out that 'the same variety of people' applaud state control on their own side but oppose it on the other. It is a strong and coherent 'learning scene' for the audience. As Edgar commented, this scene is typical of his work in its record of public embarrassment:

The Lermontov speech arose very much out of its situation, which was a formal dinner, and standing up to make a speech at a formal dinner, and the sort of embarrassment of somebody not too secure with the language who's in a very formal situation, and all the politeness and protocols of that: that was the kind of mechanism, in the same way as the *Destiny* scene, where the way you learnt things was through the recognisable process of that sort of meeting, and those events couldn't have occurred in the same way in any other context.[34]

Ron Daniels has also compared *Maydays* with *Destiny*:

Maydays was about the disappointment with ideology and the possibilities of change in a wider sense, disappointment with the Labour Party, the onset of self-confident Thatcherism; worse than that, the collapse of the ideology of the left in England and in Hungary on a huge scale: disillusionment. These issues are hot only for the intellectual, the socialist. That's why *Destiny* was politically more exciting. *Destiny* wasn't a reflection. *Maydays* was looking back at a time and thinking 'Where did we go wrong, where did we go right, where does the flame survive', but it wasn't a play about a hot issue.

Maydays worked well at the Barbican, playing to 67 per cent capacity houses. The stage itself was, as ever, a difficulty, despite the fluid and fast-paced changes. Edgar acknowledged the vastness of the space: 'I think the Barbican is a very, very difficult stage for work that involves, as my play does, a large number of duologues. It's a Wagnerian play in that its scale of operation is very large, but an awful lot of the time there are only two or three people on at any one time; unlike in Wagner, they're not singing.'[35] In 1992 he elaborated: 'The Barbican is twenty feet too wide. The scenes that people remember are the scenes with huge things happening: the train, the airport. Tony Sher standing in the middle of the stage on his own with the CND badge was wonderful. The difficulty was the little domestic scenes which were on trucks – for example, the scene where Martin re-meets up with Jeremy – that scene went for less than it perhaps should have, these two little people in the midst of this vast space.'

Those who condemned *Maydays* were not preoccupied with its theatrical qualities, however, but its treatment of politics in that privileged space. There were two principal attacks on the play, by John McGrath and Peter Jenkins. For McGrath, *Maydays* was a dangerous betrayal of the left to the middle-class enemy: 'I do think it's a shame ... that when David Edgar writes *Maydays* for the Royal Shakespeare Company he finds himself presenting images of his former comrades to his former enemies and, indeed, his present enemies, which is distorted and wrong – it denigrates [his] work and motives, and I find that tragic and inexcusable.'[36] Edgar felt that such criticism carried 'the implication that political theatre is advertising and you don't show off the bad side of your product'; moreover that it is only if one believes that 'all is right with the revolutionary world then it is a betrayal. It was the people who didn't believe the linen was dirty who criticised washing it in public.' Edgar's own complex awareness of left positions and his own disillusionment were predicaments that he had always had personally to confront (in particular the repercussions in the West of Stalinist events in the East). To ignore the deficiencies on the left would, in this sense, be the true betrayal. As for the RSC audience, Edgar is 'not patient with the notion that you self-censor plays on the grounds of the audience you're likely to get, that there are some things you can say in the privacy of your own Bush Theatre or your own working-men's club which you're not allowed to say in the Barbican. Part of one's artistic integrity is saying the same things to different audiences, possibly in different forms. *Teendreams* was an attempt to say in a different form what *Maydays* went on to say.' Edgar's interest is in the contradictions of the socialist struggle and the need to maintain that resistance despite those contradictions; the implication is that the RSC audience has the sophistication not to find in the meaning of the play a rejection of socialism. Edgar defended himself against McGrath: 'I do think ... that it's highly dangerous to argue that left-wing playmakers shouldn't honestly confront the undoubted crisis that socialism is presently facing, in case some non-socialist might overhear and snitch on them.'[37]

McGrath also regarded the subject of defection itself as not a 'burning issue',[38] while Peter Jenkins condemned the wider subject of revolutionary politics in an impassioned *Guardian* article: 'How to play around with the politics of fantasy' (26 October 1983). Jenkins's diatribe misstated the essence of *Maydays* as follows: '[Edgar] writes a history of our times around the notion that between 1968 and 1975 a revolution in Britain was necessary, possible, desirable and betrayed.' He extrapolated from this his thesis: 'The politics of the play are thus a politics of fantasy bearing scant relation to what was actually happening in the world and in Britain during that time, and the aspirations and preoccupations of real people.' He demanded: 'If *Maydays* is a memo from left-to-left – better tactics next time, comrades – what is it doing on the stage of the RSC masquerading as a political play about our times?' and concluded with a general statement: 'A political theatre can tell us little and will have no truth or force to it, if its exponents must blind themselves to the real world.' David Edgar's written response, 'A shortsighted view of the defectors' decades' (29 October 1983) emphasises firstly that the play does not purport to be a history of British politics since 1945. Given that, he goes on to point out that revolutionary politics in the 1960s and early 1970s in America, France, Britain and elsewhere, through various movements (such as black civil rights, ecology and women's liberation) has 'irreversibly altered the perceptions and behaviour of millions and millions of real people in both their public and their private lives'. He condemns Jenkins's misreading that Martin Glass moves to a 'fascist' position and corrects: Glass moves 'from the revolutionary left via a kind of right-wing libertarianism, towards a kind of traditionalist Toryism which is becoming increasingly fashionable among academics, comment- ators, and indeed politicians close to the heart of the Conservative Party'. Peter Jenkins was himself a defector, from soft Labour left to a social democratic position in the first flowering of the SDP.

In 1992 Edgar reiterated his deep conviction of the importance of *Maydays*' subject:

> There's nothing more irritating than being told: 'I enjoyed Mr Shakespeare's play *Hamlet* but it would have been better if it had been about an old man dividing his kingdom between three daughters.' The play did not claim to be about parliamentary politics. It claimed to be no more than it was. Its claim was itself. Having said that, is it like doing a play about the Amish or the Mormons and saying you're doing a history of Christianity (which is what the Jenkins claim was)? Saying, this is such a peripheral, minor, sideline, little irrelevant lunatic tributary, that somehow the very act of telling that story on that scale implied it was more important than it was. Events since then have

demonstrated this to be the case not in entirely happy ways. It is certainly the case that the experience of seduction by Communism, seduction by the Bolshevik ideal, is a central experience of the twentieth century which has had a crucial effect on Western politics. It seems to me no question that one of social democracy's many problems is the decline of Communism in the East, because people have understood that there are many points of contact between the two, that Sweden is a bit more like Russia was than Britain is; there are certain things about egalitarian social policies, welfare socialism and so on, which are in common between soft socialism and revolutionary socialism, so it does seem to me to be a central experience for the whole of Europe.

The point was that the play was not solely about British revolutionary socialism, but about East and West, the impact of East on West, and 'distress signals' in the socialist movement and its impact on the new right: a subject of strong relevance.

It was Michael Billington who lauded the play and its place on the Barbican stage. In his *Guardian* review 'New maps of revolution' (21 October 1983) he was unequivocal: 'David Edgar's *Maydays* is exactly what the Barbican is for: a big public play on a big public theme ... For me it was a heartening evening because it showed drama doing what it alone can: analysing the nation's conscience in a large public arena.' A week later, in a long article, 'Maydays manifesto' (28 October 1983), he argued that 'all great political drama, in fact, is about the inter-action of principles and psychology' and rightly indicated how *Maydays* connects private and public behaviour. Billington also took the opportunity to make an impassioned response to Robert Cushman, demonstrating his profound commitment to theatre about politics:

Do we actually need, in Robert Cushman's phrase, monster plays about politics on subsidised stages? I would say 'Yes' for a variety of reasons. One is that politics is a naturally theatrical subject combining, as it does, ideals, causes, issues with the quirks and oddities of the human temperament. Another is that plays with a large historical canvas generate their own excitement ... Whatever you think of Edgar's play ... [it] *occupies* [its] ... space with enormous vigour. And a third reason is that the theatre is a wonderful public forum for initiating discussion and debate and for taking the moral temperature of the nation: a play like *Maydays*, although it can be seen by only a thousand or so people a night, has already triggered off an enormous amount of heated argument about the supposed failure of the Left in Britain.

Billington concluded affirmatively and memorably: 'a theatre that cuts itself off from politics cuts itself off from life.'

The importance of *Maydays* was surely that the subject had indeed been introduced into the subsidised arena, especially (as with *Destiny*) due to Ron Daniels's support. The play provided public debate about revolutionary politics and public debate about political theatre. What is Edgar's most ambitious, authoritative, referential and personal play had been the focal point of a discussion crucial to the future of the theatre in Britain. The public money accorded to its production achieved that discussion. The play connected to a lot of Edgar's journalism, especially his essays about the distinction between the authoritarian and libertarian right;[39] together, the play and the essays embodied a perception about the Conservative Party that could influence people's thinking. His argument that 'contemporary conservativism, in Britain and elsewhere, cannot be understood without understanding the role of defectors within it'[40] offered a warning, pinpointing the essential problem of the times as far as he considered it to be.

For David Edgar personally, the importance of *Maydays* cannot be overstated; it embodies the central subject of his entire canon and is the play that he ranks most highly:

> Somebody at Bristol University said that all of my career was a preparation for *Maydays* and there is a sense in which that is true. In terms of the story I have always been interested in telling, I have always been interested in disillusion, in the political consequences of disillusion. To a certain extent that is what happens in *Destiny*: in *Destiny* it's a man [Turner] who defects from the Conservative Party to the far right; there's the debate at the end of *Mary Barnes* about where the community failed. This goes back to *I'm Talking about Jerusalem* and *Their Very Own and Golden City*, and a whole vast literature of disillusion: *Darkness at Noon*; Orwell. That experience of disillusion with the great metanarrative ideal has interested me because I've always been confronted with it. I've taken up

Destiny, Royal Shakespeare Company, The Other Place,
Stratford-upon-Avon, 1976. Ian McDiarmid as Turner.

Destiny, Royal Shakespeare Company,
The Other Place, Stratford-upon-Avon, 1976.
Left to right: John Nettles as Maxwell,
Ian McDiarmid as Turner.

Mary Barnes,
Birmingham Repertory Theatre Studio, 1978.
Left to right: Patti Love as Mary,
Simon Callow as Eddie.

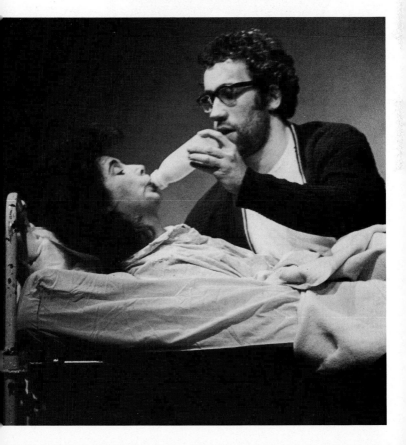

The Life and Adventures of Nicholas Nickleby,
Royal Shakespeare Company, Aldwych Theatre, London, 1980.
Roger Rees as Nicholas.

Maydays, Royal Shakespeare Company, Barbican Theatre,
London 1983. Left to right: Don Fellows as Teddy Weiner,
Bob Peck as Pavel Lermontov.

Entertaining Strangers, National Theatre at the Cottesloe Theatre, London, 1987. Left to Right:
Tim Piggot-Smith as Henry Moule, members of the company.

The Shape of the Table,
Royal National Theatre at the Cottesloe Theatre,
London, 1990.

Pentecost, Young Vic Theatre, London, 1995.
Left to right: Jan Ravens as Gabriella Pecs,
Charles Kay as Oliver Davenport.

political views in the past which have had to change. It's deeply personal in that sense. Insofar as *Maydays* confronts political disillusion as its sole central subject and confronts it in a very wide way which covers a wide variety of examples drawn from a whole three different generations, three different parts of the world, it stands as the apex of that, and you can see certain plays building up to it, and you can certainly see *The Shape of the Table* and 'Buying a Landslide' coming from it. If there were some sort of strange desert island in which only one of your plays could be allowed to survive, there's no question in my mind that that would be the play.

That Summer

The straitened circumstances of British theatre in the late 1980s imposed a necessity for small-scale productions. Edgar turned this situation to his advantage, finding a political subject that invited a dramatic (rather than epic) form.[41] Whereas *Maydays* derives its entire complex structure from its examination of the British, East European and American post-war left, *That Summer* is, in contrast, directly concerned with psychology and emotion. This two-act domestic play with effective clarity demonstrates the way the 1984–1985 miners' strike brought together working-class miners and intellectual urban socialists. It is not a documentary play about the strike (which had divided families, and which had not ensued from a ballot); it is a play about personal relationships, and the bonding that results from the dissolving of prejudices. Premièred in July 1987 at the Hampstead Theatre, it played for six weeks; a liberal metropolitan audience far removed from the South Wales pits could thus retrospectively assess the effect of the strike on a particular family. The structural framework aids this process: a prologue to the main action involves Cressida as 'an intruder from another time' and the resolution to the action is followed by an epilogue which takes place one year after the strike. Historical perspective is built into the narrative by this framing device as it is in *Teendreams*. The action itself follows the pattern of exposition, development of problems, and resolution, in the genre of social comedy. Edgar felt that realism was the 'correct form for the play' because he wanted to deal with the reality of 'what that year was really about: the building of personal relationships in action (nay, even "forged in struggle") in a way that strengthened as well as challenged the participants, whatever the immediate outcome.'[42] Psychologically realistic characters interact in a domestic setting: 'The new factor was those relationships – everybody has stories, and all the strike literature comments on it. So how do you deal with it? You put people in a house together, in a confined space, and watch the sparks fly.'[43]

Howard is an Oxford academic and his subject is history; he is a product of the 1960s left with a son called Daniel after the hero (Cohn-Bendit) of the 1968 May events. Daniel is miserably accompanying his father and his stepmother Cressida on holiday in North Wales. This strongly politicised middle-class family entertains two strangers, teenage girls from miners' families (a situation drawn directly from David Edgar's own experience in the summer of 1984). The gay schoolteacher, Terry, is another guest. Cressida's idealism about the strike contrasts with her older husband's ambivalence in the light of his 1960s experience. This is one strand of a network of conflicts including those between the 'Minerettes' (Michele and Frankie) and the hosts; Michele and Terry, Daniel and Howard, Frankie and Cressida. The girls enter a new cultural dimension where exotic cooking is the province of the husband; where witty, articulate people consult the *I Ching* and write on the 1930s British left and Spain for television (Howard) or have professions in alternative medicine (Cressida). They are cross-questioned and patronised about their own cultural environment and preferences. Running throughout the action is the farcical business of mistaken conclusions, social *faux pas*, inappropriate dress, food rituals, secrets, and focus on Cressida's adultery and suspected pregnancy. The farce conventions serve to indicate social, marital and generational gulfs.

The essential political reference point is put by a striking miner. Alun, Michele's father, says that the strike is not 'about wages and conditions ... it's about survival. Not just for us, but for our kids.' It is spelt out that the suppression of potential in all senses is actualised by threat of pit closures. Job opportunities, ability to pursue talents and enthusiasms, capacity to transcend under-privileged conditions: all these are threatened with destruction under the ruthlessness of Thatcherite attitudes to the people concerned. Although the middle-class hosts are compassionate, they are not suffering, and it is this division that is so appropriately

110

summed up at the end of Act One in Frankie's image of the skating rink and the 'posh girl'. The speech is at the same time the most savage and the most moving in the entire play:

> FRANKIE. Well, all I said was. That you know they call her 'iron maiden'. But I don't see her in that light at all. (*Pause*.) Like, I see her like those posh girls at the rink in Swansea, gliding so easy 'cross the ice, like they haven't got a care. 'Cos you see, I think, to her, we're only frozen faces. Faces, frozen in the ice, for her to glide upon. I think she skates on people's faces. (*Pause*.) And let's be frank. However much you care, you're the spectators. You are looking on. While we – we're looking up.

When Howard subsequently makes Frankie the gift of a pair of ice-skates, the issue is raised of whether he goes towards empowering her to fulfil her potential to leave a community of the oppressed. To what extent can the intellectual socialist 'spectators' be participants in the struggle? It is Howard who understands the gross sentimentality of romanticising the mining communities at the time of the General Strike as a pre-commercialised people's cultural paradise: 'I imagine, actually, that an aggressive, tribal and, might we say, machismo culture was just as prevalent in 1926 as 1984.' And ironically it is the sixteen-year-old Daniel who punctures what he imagines to be Howard's own equally sentimental images of the contemporary reality: 'Sure, for you, it's "The Rhondda", clenched fists and stirring music and lodge banners fluttering in the wind. But for them, it's dull and grimy and there aren't any decent shops or discos, and it's – just the fucking boring place they live in.' Michele acknowledges to Terry: 'It can be – restricted. Rather tight. If you don't fit.' Terry did not 'fit' because of his sexual difference, yet a strong part of his identity lies in his commitment to activism with the workers. When towards the end of the play Michele swaps badges with Terry (hers, the NUM; his, the pink triangle), she makes amends for her former prejudice and helps Terry to feel comfortable with his sexual identity. Terry is also accepted by Alun, and their affectionate parting ritual of touch offers evidence that their friendship is unaltered, and that Terry is able to belong fully to two communities that are equally important for his sense of self.

111

While Alun learns to accept that support 'from the anti-nuclear' can be positive, solidarity from what seems to be an alien source, it is Cressida who provides the strongest link with the future of socialist redirection. Cressida is 'flying free' as a result both of her involvement with the strike and her sexual involvement with a 'Trot at Cowley' who gave her 'the most dazzling of summers'. Howard, by contrast, is vasectomised and his literal infertility is matched by his political impotence. The essence of the play depends on its movement towards Howard's willingness to bring up Cressida's child by another man: the marriage is strengthened by the conception and birth of that child. Howard and Cressida end the play with two children, and those children have been conceived in momentous political times. Cressida's pregnancy is on one level symbolic of her fertile political activism which rekindles Howard's political involvement. Cressida's betrayal of fidelity has been necessary to bring about renewed commitment, and the consequences of the strike (the learning process effected by personal relationships across the class divide) will be nurtured by intellectual socialists, man and woman equally. While the male characters make several gibes at hardline feminists, it is made obvious that true emancipation is possible through marriage that coexists on several planes. Howard and Cressida were originally attracted by their shared political conviction; by the end of the play their marriage is saved and they are bonded by protection of a new child, thereby taking that conviction into the future. That summer was the most fertile of summers: 'I think we might have found the strength and perspicuity, to find that door, that secret door, and open it, and go beyond our cosy room, to something new.'

By March 1985 the miners had returned to work, with no resolution to the twelve months' strike. The government talked of victory, but the NUM president Arthur Scargill emphatically denied that it was a defeat.[44] In the epilogue to *That Summer*, Terry's opinion is that the miners 'were betrayed. They were let down.' The pit closures crisis is reverberating in the 1990s. The stand against oppression must continue in the new generation, as Cressida's metaphor of the door makes evident: 'once we've found the new door, once the old paint's cracked, the locks turned and the hinges loosened, then we'll always know it's there. And even if *we* never open it again, we'll pass it on.' This image of passing on to the new generation is crucial to all three of the plays that depict the 'distress signals' of socialism. In the final analysis, and despite the troubled contradictions that are the focus of *Teendreams*, *Maydays* and *That Summer*, there is hope for the future as well as elegy for the more straightforward convictions of the past. Howard's elegiac commentary on the summer of 1967 and those who peopled its resistance, 'That time. That summer', is transmuted into the strength of Cressida's 'Today. This time. This summer', a defiant call for resistance in the mid-1980s. Edgar's later plays were to answer the call in the face of new and more threatening obstacles to sexual and political freedom.

5

Theatre of Community:
Entertaining Strangers and *Heartlanders*

The essence of the community play is that it is democratic,
populist and, at its best, capable of exploring the tensions within
a society ... the community play, when it works, is socialism in
action.   Michael Billington, 1992[1]

Entertaining Strangers

On 18 November 1985 *Entertaining Strangers* opened in St Mary's
Church, Dorchester. Edgar's 'play for Dorchester' was the tenth of
Ann Jellicoe's large-scale projects for a specific local geographically defined community in south-west England. Jellicoe, playwright and director, had pioneered the community play in 1978,
founding the Colway Theatre Trust, and offering a model for a type
of theatre that has been taken up all over Britain and in other
countries. In their participatory and celebratory characteristics,
community plays resemble festivals and carnivals: Jellicoe was
attempting to achieve 'a vision of theatre and art which is part of
life, not simply set aside in some special building which we walk
by and ignore'.[2] The new theatrical form that Jellicoe created
involved an invitation to huge numbers of local people to take part
in theatrical experience. She justifiably states: 'Nothing like it had
ever happened before. The nearest was probably the medieval
mystery plays and Oberammergau.'[3] The Dorchester *Entertaining
Strangers* was a carnivalesque epic for a cast of over 180 local
people.

114

It was indeed the emotional charge of working with large numbers of people that attracted Edgar to Jellicoe's invitation. He was compelled by the emotional experience of seeing the Lyme Regis community play and wanted to move out of metropolitan theatre for a while. Jellicoe suggested the characters of Henry Moule and Sarah Eldridge based on the historical Dorchester townspeople of those names, and a team of local historian researchers was set up. Edgar went into the community of Dorchester, giving public talks (including one at the Conservative Club) about the project. Politically, Jellicoe's model involves an integration of the various classes and sections of what she describes as 'a very right-wing, even feudal community'.[4] She is adamant that 'political' plays will not serve this population: 'The Colway Theatre Trust comes to a town to help reconcile a community, hopefully to enrich it. Politics are divisive. We strongly feel that the humanising effect of our work is far more productive than stirring up political confrontation.'[5] Her justification for inviting professional socialist playwrights into the territory is that they best relate to 'ordinary' people. Nevertheless, as Baz Kershaw has demonstrated, this set-up cannot be 'altogether neutral'.[6]

Although it would be wrong to call the process of making *Entertaining Strangers* 'revolutionary' or even (after Augusto Boal's community theatre work in São Paulo) 'a rehearsal for the revolution',[7] it was inevitable that the participants would be changed by the event, and that some cultural and social learning would take place. The play has a sharply defined political content and Moule's political education involves a call for resistance to oppression. Given this subject and the temporary democratisation of the process, a shift in attitude (however slight) towards the 'feudalism' of the community was at the very least extremely likely. The cast included some people involved in agricultural trades, some who worked at the local brewery featured in the play, and many connected with the schools (parents, librarians and so on). The owner of the brewery financed the play (and some years later sponsored a second Dorchester community play). Although Edgar initially worried about such 'free advertising',[8] that aspect ceased to be an issue: the sponsorship was mutually beneficial to play and sponsor, and the brewery story itself was richly dramatic and provided large numbers of parts for women.

The empowering and liberating effect on the cast was firstly to do with the anti-hierarchical joining together of local people and professionals (writer, designer, composer and stage manager, as well as Ann Jellicoe herself as director, were from the profession). A further empowerment had to do with the type of play the local people were encouraged to engage with. As Edgar put it, 'What happened was that there were a lot of people who, naturally and perfectly predictably and perfectly properly, if left to their own devices, would have done a production of *Witness for the Prosecution*; these people were opened up to other matter. These south-western towns are very conservative places and I think what we absolutely did was enable people on what was for them a fairly radical wing of that to engage with the *avant-garde*.'[9] Thirdly, Edgar was rightly convinced that 'The fact that the play was about the town and the fact that the play was built by and with them was very important', posing 'just a slight challenge to the spirit of the age'. The egalitarian process of playmaking enabled local participants to engage with what Michael Billington has defined as 'socialism in action'.[10]

The audience was mostly drawn from the local catchment area and watched a story unfold about people of that locality. Although they were not encouraged to be 'spect-actors' in an approximation of Augusto Boal's method,[11] they did mingle with the actors in the promenade situation of the performance (which took place in the public space of the church). People they might well know personally took on the roles of their nineteenth-century forebears. The emotional significance of this for everyone concerned cannot be over-emphasised: people were embodying and celebrating their own community. Since the theatre of Athens in the fifth century BC, there has recurred the theme of 'our town' and those involved in *Entertaining Strangers* received a message that (simply put) is 'Your life has meaning because it's part of a structure'. In this kind of theatre the 'local history' aspect takes on a grand elevation, a ritual quality, and in its first context *Entertaining Strangers* was a myth play in this sense. Furthermore, the story of the play has a potent mythic quality. In interview, Ann Jellicoe pinpointed this aspect: 'It is the myth of the man who is hated by the people and yet rescues the people. It's so powerful, that image. It's a very, very basic powerful story.'[12] Henry Moule is a Methodist fundamentalist clergyman who is hated as much for his disregard for people's

116

enjoyment (as reflected in his prohibitive attitude to alcohol, sex and festivities) as for his disregard for their needs (as reflected in his dismissal of the church orchestra). Moule takes punishment from the people but his heroism is proved in the 1854 cholera epidemic.

Edgar recognised early on that Jellicoe's community projects are not types of pageant but types of carnival:

> *Entertaining Strangers* ... has (and must have) some of the elements of pageant, of huge, almost self-contained units of action or sequences of event, passing the fixed point of the audience's perception. What is wrong with pageant is that it is *merely* processional, lacking the dynamic of purpose, a medium of heritage rather than history. Carnival, on the other hand, is full of life and aim, even if those aims can be contradictory, and its vivacity crackling with danger. And increasingly I think that what Ann Jellicoe has created over the years are not plays or pageants, but kinds of carnival, and it is that reality which provides the sense of an event not just of commitment and energy but of moral force and artistic scale.[13]

He became drawn to a theory of drama that was especially congruent with the spirit of his play. *Entertaining Strangers* actively embraces renewal and revival, demonstrating a fracturing of hardened positions as people unbend towards each other in a time of great need. The play ultimately achieves a strength of conviction about Utopian possibility. Mikhail Bakhtin has described carnival as an anti-hierarchical topsy-turvydom, a short-lived egalitarian Utopia:

> It is like life itself, but shaped according to a certain pattern of play ... it does not acknowledge any distinction between actors and spectators ... Carnival is not a spectacle seen by the people; they live in it, and everyone participates because its very idea embraces all the people. While carnival lasts, there is no other life outside it. During carnival time life is subject only to its laws, that is, the laws of its own freedom. It has a universal spirit, it is a special condition of the entire world, of the world's revival and renewal, in which all take part.[14]

In Dorchester, the conditions of carnival (in particular, audience participation in a public space, sudden shifts of focus and multi-focus) were the basis for the conventions of a new carnivalesque theatre form. The Dorchester *Entertaining Strangers* is an example of the folk culture that carnival is essentially part of: a people's egalitarian celebratory event.

In 1987 the play was given a further life in a new version for the National Theatre. It was directed by Peter Hall and starred Judi Dench and Tim Pigott-Smith. Although the Dorchester version is published, it is this version that is preserved in Edgar's collected *Plays*. If the first version was a myth play for the people, gaining from the emotional scale of the event, with a celebration of 'our town' at its heart, the second version is a more poetic, richer, theatrically developed piece that relies less on narrative and is more experimental in form. It is this text, with its exciting potential for performance, that is worth analysing in some detail. The event at the Cottesloe Theatre was considerably different from that at St Mary's Church, Dorchester. The transition of the play to the National has aroused an amount of contentious commentary, along the lines of the professional theatre's 'plundering the energies and resources of the people'.[15] This is not justifiable for several reasons. The National *Entertaining Strangers* is a different text, a new play for a different context. The new context altered the play's purpose and sharpened the political aspect of the material in contemporary terms. A play of socialist conviction entered the dominant cultural context with the potential to raise the awareness of an audience drawn not from a local community but assembling from much wider afield and encompassing international tourists to London. If they would come in any case to see professional star actors, this was a lure that could be turned to useful purpose by the political content. The unique experience of 'the people' was over and the new situation received a new play.

The Literary Manager of the National had attended Edgar's public reading of *Entertaining Strangers* in Dorchester; he had encouraged Peter Hall to read it. Edgar commented:

> I accepted the invitation from the National because I wanted the play to have another life and I was already by then aware that there were certain dramatic theories I found attractive which one could usefully apply to this piece of work. The National behaved absolutely exemplarily with Dorchester. The people were actually rather complimented that the National had taken up their play. The notion that this was a raid in which primitive frescoes were ripped off the wall and turned up at the Tate

behind glass is a very bad analogy. The play had already happened. It wasn't taken away and plundered. It was finished. We went down to Dorchester and saw people who'd been involved with the play. People who wanted to come up and see rehearsals were allowed to. There was a great group treat when they came up to see the play.

The revised piece centres on a *Maydays* theme: it concerns the love of 'kind' and the love of 'kindred':

> One of the sharpest accusations Conservatives fire at the Left concerns the supposed contradiction between love for all humanity and caring for people you actually know (as Burke puts it, the apparent mutual exclusiveness of love of 'kind' and 'kindred'). In the course of *Entertaining Strangers*, the cleric Henry Moule discovers an almost superhuman care for strangers, but he cannot apply this lesson to relations with his own son. While the brewer Sarah Eldridge, desperately loving of her own, cannot extend that love beyond her doors. It seems to me clear that both forms of love are limited and insufficient. The first has blighted the socialist experiment, the second challenges the moral pretensions of the enterprise culture.[16]

These insights came after the Dorchester production, and the relationship of Sarah Eldridge and Henry Moule is developed to emphasise their complementary capacities for love. Both characters learn to change and this gives promise for the possibility of contemporary social renewal.

In the National Theatre context, removed from the Dorchester emphasis on re-enacting the past of specific actual individuals, a sharp analogy with the spirit of the 1980s slotted into place. The play elucidates a division on the right between entrepreneurial endeavour and religious fundamentalism. The business zeal of Sarah is quintessentially Thatcherite and her emphasis on the family links closely with a social climate where the Prime Minister could declare that, 'There is no such thing as society.'[17] In Act One Scene Ten, Sarah states that she will not 'waste time wallowing in silly sentiment, 'bout folks I don't know and I can't do nothing for'. She is Sarah our contemporary, embodying the ethos of the 1980s which emphasised Victorian and family values. She sells beer, making profits for her individual and family well-being, denying responsibility for its effects on those who buy it. During the course of the play we see a drunk soldier buying sex with a girl of twelve, and a moral question is raised about social responsibility for child prostitution and the resultant abandonment of unwanted babies. Capitalism is linked in this sense with moral corruption. The solution is not to stop selling beer (as Moule believes) but to develop better social conditions so that the poor do not have to sell their bodies. Sarah's denial of any responsibility in the current poor social conditions as Moule describes them emphasises the tunnel vision of the business mentality: her love for 'kind' is non-existent.

Moreover, another uncomfortable resonance existed for the National audience. By 1987 the AIDS epidemic had been given public airing, a certain amount of panic had set in, and there immediately ensued morally judgemental analyses and fundamentalist conceits that the viral illness was a punishment visited on those who had sinned. When the cholera epidemic is seen by Moule in judgemental terms, the analogy clicks home: 'it is my belief, that this dreadful sickness is a visitation of God's just and wrathful judgement on His sinful and forgetful children' (Act Two Scene Four). And when Sarah maintains a self-evidently misguided opinion – 'It won't spread. For 'tis a – a disease of – the afflicted. The already wretched, sickly, and debased. It will not touch us, Emily' (Act Two Scene Three) – she could be as well speaking with the assured certainty of heterosexual bigots in the late 1980s.

In form the new version was deeply influenced by the Bakhtinian theory of carnival. The Cottesloe Theatre had been the site for a much acclaimed promenade production of Tony Harrison's adaptation of the medieval mystery plays.[18] Edgar was well aware of the analogy between the mystery plays and Jellicoe's community plays and, with regard to the overwhelming experience of the closing song in Howard Barker's community play 'The Poor Man's Friend', he had made a specific analogy to the National production: 'I think the only recent experience I find remotely akin to it was that of seeing the National Theatre *Mysteries* cycle.'[19] The problem he faced was how to create a similar experience given the fact that the Dorchester story did not have the same emotional power outside that town. The huge cast was replaced by a cast of twenty-three and there had to be found 'some kind of metaphorical surrogate for the sheer power of Dorchester's numbers (and the emotional strength of the fact that the play was performed in a church established by one of the central characters, within a stone's throw of a brewery founded by the other)'.[20] That surrogate is the Mummers' Play, fragments of which punctuate the new version. The Mummers' Play is a treatment of the nature cycle akin to a fertility ritual; its theme of resurrection celebrates the cycle of life and death.

Edgar's intention was clearly to embody a shared feeling in the audience by means of a choric device enriching the basic storyline. That shared feeling was inchoate, inexpressible in normalistic language, involving a deep-lying mystery about life itself. Edgar explains:

> In outline, *Entertaining Strangers* is about the attempt to impose two eminently Victorian values on an English county town in the process of transformation from an essentially rural to an urban society. Both sets of beliefs are found wanting, in face of the older and more basic realities which emerge to challenge them during the course of the play. These realities – and the ancient mysteries that both acknowledge and confront them – are represented in the new version by fragments from a mummers' play, which is sometimes actually happening, but more often takes the form of a snatch or echo in the mind.[21]

It is valuable to cite W. B. Yeats's term 'emotion of multitude' in this context. Yeats asked for a form uniquely capable of expressing archetypal realities that could not be verbalised. His admirable essay sheds light on Edgar's endeavour. Yeats argued that:

> The Greek drama has got the emotion of multitude from its chorus, which called up famous sorrows, even all the gods and all heroes, to witness, as it were, some well-ordered fable, some action separated but for this from all but itself ... The Shakespearian drama gets the emotion of multitude out of the sub-plot which copies the main plot, much as a shadow upon the wall copies one's body in the firelight ... Ibsen and Maeterlinck have, on the other hand, created a new form, for they get multitude from the wild duck in the attic, or from the crown at the bottom of the fountain, vague symbols that set the mind wandering from idea to idea, emotion to emotion. Indeed all the great masters have understood that there cannot be great art

121

without the little limited life of the fable, which is always better the simpler it is, and the rich, far-wandering, many-imaged life of the half-seen world beyond it.[22]

In the new *Entertaining Strangers*, the Mummers' Play snatches serve to evoke 'emotion of multitude', setting 'the mind wandering from idea to idea, emotion to emotion', finding a shared feeling about the cycle of life and death.

Edgar had discovered a key reference in Bakhtin's book on Rabelais. Bakhtin cited 'the traditional function of the ancient feast of fools, which is to evoke the ritual of the dying and reborn king'.[23] Edgar would attempt to capture the quality of carnival in his play through such ritual in the Mummers' Play elements. It was the exploration of contradiction in carnival that most excited him, its capacity 'to express the opposite in the same plane'.[24] He argues in his essay 'Festivals of the Oppressed' that the essence of our time lies in horrifying contradiction between desirable and actual human behaviour, citing the 1984–1985 miners' strike where vicious acts coexisted with acts of bravery. In theatrical practice, carnivalesque form would allow for a simultaneous representation of contradiction (rather than the dialectical argument where thesis, antithesis and synthesis are shown separately), a more sensuous representation of the fusion and movement of life. He quotes Bakhtin:

All that exists dies and is born simultaneously, combines the past and the future, the obsolete and the youthful, the old truth and the new truth. However small the part of the existing world we have chosen we shall find in it the same fusion. And this fusion is deeply dynamic: all that exists, both in the whole and in each of its parts, is in the act of becoming.[25]

Edgar's enthusiasm for this dynamic aspect of carnival and his willingness to experiment theatrically to fulfil its implications leads to the strong archetypal impact of the second version of *Entertaining Strangers*. The spiritual 'what could be' aspect of the play, its Utopianism, is expressed through a new form that seeks to combine Brechtian cerebralism with Bakhtinian carnival.

The new theatricality of the written text is particularly impressive. Structurally there are nineteen scenes, many of which involve sudden shifts of focus, beats within the scenes that are also numbered. Act One Scene One, for example, shifts from verse Mummers' Play presentation (the St George and the Dragon story) to what at first seems to be a play-within-the-play at the Green Dragon Inn, Dorchester, towards 1829. This second beat of the scene is in prose dialogue: it sets up the conflict between Sarah and Moule who attain a parallelism with St George and the Dragon, and it makes comic use of two glove puppets. The third beat shifts to nineteenth century narrators in *Nickleby* choric mode (in prose) and then, finally, to a higher level of the set where the St George Mummer has a stanza of verse (the second choric mode in the play). Throughout there is a linguistically and visually emphasised contrast between Dorchester (prose chorus) and Fordington (a more primitive, verse chorus of Mummers) that accentuates the contrast between respectable town and poor slum. The Bakhtinian fusion of contradictions is thus captured in social terms until, by the end of Act One, disease and therefore death are seen to rest side by side with life, in simultaneous coexistence, a more mysterious level of ambivalence:

> MOULE. I say – there is a stranger in our midst. His name is Cholera.
>
> SOME. Cholera.
>
> ALL. Cholera.
>
> *Blackout.*

By the end of the play the disease is explicable in social and sanitary terms. It is Moule who makes a great leap of realisation. He has heroically helped the sick and dying despite the animosity towards his killjoy prohibitions and the attacks against him in Fordington. Through his altruism he has stopped the disease spreading. In a typical Edgaresque interruption of a public award ceremony he makes his great speech of resistance. The blame for cholera lies at the door of the managers of Prince Albert's estate. The labourers 'live crushed into a space which cannot overreach five acres, and which has become a great sink into which the excremental filth of all the neighbouring parishes is poured'. He insists, movingly and stirringly:

> I will not rest until this wrong is righted. For it is a species of
> oppression, and it will and should provoke resistance. And I say
> all this as one to whom, until these dreadful happenings
> occurred, such views as I now entertain were strangers.

Moule has made a political conversion. Cholera is the result not of
people's behaviour but of landowners' negligence. He has learnt
not to judge morally the sufferers of disease; he has learnt to
examine the social and political causes of poverty which lead to
disease.

The title is as multi-layered as that of *Maydays*. The repeated
motif of 'entertaining strangers' is quoted from a biblical text (and
it is interesting to locate Edgar's increasing use of such motifs
from *Teendreams* onwards, adding a referential richness to his
work). Hebrews 13:1 reads:

> Let brotherly love continue. Be not forgetful to entertain
> strangers; for thereby some have entertained angels unawares.

There are ironies: cholera is a 'stranger'; if it is an angel in disguise
it is because it teaches a lesson about moral judgementalism. And
when Moule recognises in Act Two Scene Five that he has seen
'angels unawares' he is simultaneously unsympathetic towards his
son's relationship with the servant girl Fanny. Moule's action
concerning the pregnant girl will be one cause of his son's suicide.
He cannot find love for 'kindred'. Yet, by the point of his political
conversion (discussed above) he has implicitly connected with his
son's view of the world. In Act Two Scene Seven, his son Horace,
as Poor Law Inspector, simultaneously envisions 'the towers of
Jerusalem' and talks bitterly about the human actuality of the poor
killing their babies. This is a lucid expression of two central
themes: the fusion of opposites, and the gap between experience
and vision. The father's political education comes too late for
reconciliation with his son.

Sarah's daughters are the 'angels' whose philanthropic action
Moule has witnessed in the powerful vision scene of Act Two
Scene Four (Beat Seven). It is Sarah herself (in the central section
of the final scene) who points the morals concerning the theme of
the opposition between love of kind and love of kindred:

124

And it do take me some time to appreciate. That until we loose
the bonds of strangers, then the cup we raise behind our gates is
gall.

But also, that the strangers we must entertain include our own.
And the bonds we loose are not just theirs, but ours.

Subsequent to Moule's and Sarah's reconciliation in the
churchyard, Moule shows that he has absorbed this lesson when
he judges the pregnant young woman: 'Her fault is grave ... But,
maybe. There are even graver.'

It is Sarah too who points to the resurrection motif at the core of
the play. The motif is of the Mummers' narrative and the seasonal
ritual of death into life, winter into spring:

For we must remember, must we not, that like trees men have
roots and trunks, which thrust up to the sky, but also branches
which stretch out to other men, and touch them.

Pause.

For only thus may we divine – from what, strange soil, may
green things grow.

The dead Mummer has been resurrected and has seen 'the Holy
City'. The motif of the New Jerusalem recurs throughout as it does
in *Maydays*, but in this Utopian play, following on from the
positive conversions and reconciliations that we have seen, the
ideal society seems not unrealisable. The entire company gathers
for the final song: they too are 'resurrected', whether their
characters have died or have been victims. The image in the final
wassailing song of poor plough boys outside the big, rich house at
Christmas begs for the social distinctions to be levelled in a new
society:

And you pretty maid with your silver-headed pin
Pray open the door and let us come in

It is Edgar's theme of the triumph of human capacity for altruism
and resistance that implies the move forward in social terms.

The new experimental theatricality of *Entertaining Strangers* has
the following characteristics: huge spectacular set pieces (such as

the Races, and the Crimean procession); comic scenes of familial interaction; nightmarish expressionism (Moule's Revelations scene of Act Two Scene Four Beat Seven); song (children's menacing Plague songs, hymns, sentimental party pieces such as 'Grey Hawk' in Act One Scene Seven); public gatherings that go awry; verse and prose choric narrative; a repeated resonant biblical motif; tableaux; and sudden shifts of focus. Yet throughout there is a strong traditional element of conflict, of a story with beginning, middle and end. A tiny scene such as Act Two Scene Four Beat One, where people boil clothes in a copper and children sing a song, can without dialogue and through juxtaposition chillingly sum up the impact of the cholera threat, exemplifying the succinct visual and rhythmic quality of the play. In Act Two there is an increasing use of verse or song at the ends of scenes as Mummers or children crystallise emotion through rhythmic expression and visual representation which exactly sum up mood. An example of the strong gestural signs in the play is seen when (in Act One Scene Three Beat Two) an offer of a penknife symbolises the proffering of God's grace. There are chilling emotional build-ups such as in Act Two Scene Four Beat Two when Martha Lock's son dies. She demands biblical consolation from Moule; and a snatch of a Mummer's verse rounds off the scene, summing up the poverty of Martha's family's existence:

Here come I old Poor and Mean
Hardly worthy to be seen,
Half be starved and t'other half blind
With a well-ricked back and a broken mind.

It is above all a visionary, symbolist quality that is memorable. The story is archetypal, the vision Utopian:

MOULE. Saw. Three angels. Saw. Three strangers. And I John ... saw the Holy City. New Jerusalem. And behold I make all things new.

Perhaps it was in production terms a risk that Edgar allowed his Mummers to be 'real' as well as 'echoes' or 'snatches' in the mind. Their masked presence embodies the symbolist power of the play and demands a symbolist representation which the National

126

production did not pursue effectively. There was a (rather restricted) promenade situation and the new poetic text was not fully actualised in performance. The play's power rests with a visionary, mythic theme and an exact and precise and delicate theatrical experimentation that must find an equivalent in production. There is in *Entertaining Strangers* a yearning and poetic subtext that conjures up the ambivalence of life and holds out the hope of social and spiritual resurrection.

Heartlanders

David Edgar has noted that there have been very successful urban community plays 'often involving groups drawn from the widest possible class and ethnic spectra', demonstrating 'a perhaps unexpected potential for carnivalesque theatre in the urban environment'.[26] The celebratory play he wrote in collaboration with Stephen Bill and Anne Devlin for the City of Birmingham's centenary year, *Heartlanders* (1989), is just such a play; a brief summary will serve to indicate the positive energy of this type of theatre. It had a huge cast of 300 citizens of Birmingham and was performed on the Birmingham Repertory Theatre's main stage. It brings together English, Welsh, Asian, Irish and Afro-Caribbean people in its characters, and its scenes range in setting from pizzeria to ante-natal class, from hair salon to Diwali ceremony in a Hindu temple. The play amply illustrates the contradictions of city life and is full of humour. The three collaborative playwrights each wrote a strand, and Margaret's story, the woman looking for her daughter, is unmistakably Edgar's strand, hallmarked by its use of language. The play ends in two ritual ceremonies, Diwali and Christmas, a hymn is sung, and (as in *Teendreams*) the story of the characters' immediate future lives is narrated. A baby has been born, and the very ending celebrates the mystery of new life, in an atmosphere of reconciliation, harmony and quest fulfilled. There is much talk of 'community' in the play, revealing the multiple uses to which this slippery term may be put. The tramp Ernest is 'returned' to the 'community'; Margaret talks of Joel's 'community'; and the play itself celebrates Birmingham, a city where many races jostle against each other.

The project of *Heartlanders* was clearly very distinct from that of Dorchester. Chris Parr, who directed it, has commented on Edgar's informed understanding of the process of creating a play with local people.[27] Edgar's sensitivity to this aspect had been gained from his Dorchester experience. Although there was no 'community' to create in the way that there was in Dorchester because people were drawn from all over Birmingham, there is still the sense at the core of the community play of group celebration (here, a celebration of diverse cultures). In his essay 'From Metroland to the Medicis: The Cultural Politics of the City State', Edgar asks: 'How do alignments based on locality, origin, religion, sexuality work with each other? What are the cultural consequences of a continent increasingly defined by migration and the breaking-down of traditional patterns of affinity?'[28] In *Heartlanders* he shows ways in which 'in the cities ... cultures meet, clash and, who knows, may eventually cohere'.[29] Edgar's community plays are 'socialism in action'.

6

Theatre of Nation:
The Shape of the Table,
'Parallel Bars' and
'Buying a Landslide'

This was the year communism in Eastern Europe died.
1949–1989 R.I.P. And the epitaph might be:

> Nothing in his life
> Became him like the leaving it

The thing that was comprehensively installed in the newly
defined territories of Poland, Czechoslovakia, Hungary,
Romania and Bulgaria, and in the newly created German
Democratic Republic after 1949, the thing called, according to
viewpoint, 'socialism', 'totalitarianism', 'Stalinism',
'politbureaucratic dictatorship', 'real existing socialism', 'state
capitalism', 'dictatorship over needs', or, most neutrally, 'the
Soviet-type system' – that thing will never walk again. And
arguably, if we can no longer talk of communism we should no
longer talk of Eastern Europe, at least with a capital 'E' for
Eastern. Instead, we shall have central Europe again, east central
Europe, south-eastern Europe, eastern Europe with a small 'e'
and, above all, individual peoples, nations and states.

Timothy Garton Ash, 1990[1]

Should we talk about this as a revolution? Someone asks. For
after all, in our linguistic context the word 'revolution' has a
clear sub-text of violence. A 'peaceful revolution' sounds like a
contradiction in terms. A rather academic point, you might think.
But actually a great deal of what is happening is precisely about
words: about finding new, plain, true words rather than the old
mendacious phrases with which people have lived for so long.

The drafting committees try to ensure that from the outset the Forum's statements are in fresh language. Alas they do not always succeed. The communiqués, with their repetition of acronyms ... soon begin to sound like old officialese.

Timothy Garton Ash, 1990[2]

The Shape of the Table

Whereas *Entertaining Strangers* and *Heartlanders* are concerned with communities within Britain, *The Shape of the Table* poses questions about the disintegration of the 'community' of Eastern Europe and the integration of a new Europe, raising urgent issues about nationalism and internationalism. The play foresees the bloodshed of civil war and racism that the emergence of a released nationalist fervour would so horrifyingly call into being in the former Iron Curtain countries:

> SPASSOV. The voices whispering in simple people's ears. The people who felt safe before. The demons that we're letting loose. And indeed the Europe we're rejoining.

Far from unequivocally welcoming the 1989 liberation from totalitarian regimes in Eastern Europe, Edgar had written a prescient tragedy. He probes the notion of freedom itself, asking whether people need freedom 'to' or 'from': is freedom from fear, insecurity, unemployment and homelessness more a need than freedom to buy Western products or to exercise entrepreneurial zeal? An interest in language as political code and euphemism permeates the play, linking it firmly with *Maydays* (where the discussion of the word 'freedom' is part of a similar dissection of political vocabulary). Indeed, *The Shape of the Table* refocuses the Eastern European strand of *Maydays* in the light of the 1989 revolutionary events.

The play was scheduled to open in the Cottesloe Theatre on 8 November 1990, the day before the first anniversary of the opening of the Berlin Wall and the day after the anniversary of the 1917 Russian Revolution. In the course of its run it developed an added exquisite appropriateness: on 22 November Margaret Thatcher was forced to resign after eleven continuous years as Prime Minister. The immediate subject of transference of power (in this contemporary case within the governing party) could hardly have been more timely for a British audience who could read the play with reference to a current political crisis. And when the play was produced in Bucharest in December 1991 the audience also responded to it with immediacy, giving it a new reading very close to their own circumstances in post-revolutionary Romania. One measure of the play's potency lies in its scrutiny of recurrent archetypal political issues.

Edgar raises perennial questions about power. Why do people want power? Is the fact of having power more important than what is done with it? How is political power transferred and what are the minutiae of that process of negotiation? How do the successors to power avoid turning into copies of their corrupt predecessors? Have the leaders as individuals betrayed the people through their abuse of power or is the governing party system at fault? How does political rhetoric obscure revelations about abuse of power? Edgar's participation in hundreds of political meetings accounted for his fascination with the meeting-room discussion rather than the revolutionary protests on the streets. His being invited by the *Guardian* to review the first crop of books in English on the 1989 revolutions (an invitation that indicated respect for Edgar's knowledge about Eastern European Communism) eminently qualified him to write on the subject.[3]

From the start he saw his play in wider terms as belonging to a tradition of political drama:

> There are two great political stories. One is about how you give up power – the story of *Richard II* and *King Lear*. The other is about how, when you've got power, you avoid turning into the people you've taken it from – *Henry IV*, I suppose. Both of these were present [in the 1989 events] and people were concentrating on the second one – which comes into the second half of the play – but apparently ignoring the first. That's where I started from. The second thing I was interested in was the wonderfully strong images we saw on television of the great events in the streets; bells in Prague, the flags with the holes cut in the middle in Romania, the sparklers on the Berlin Wall, and so on. I wanted really to look behind all that at what was going on in the meeting rooms. One is very struck by the contrast between those grand, simple, majestic images and the detailed reality of the negotiations.[4]

The primary visual images of *The Shape of the Table* are those of the negotiating table itself and the dirty windows beyond which, 'out there', the people are rioting. The characters are informed politicians debating the future of their country in a moment of historical crisis and this choice allows the demonstration of political process and political change to be more authoritative: the emotions attached to political ambiguities are expressed by characters who are aware of the situation they are involved in. Had Edgar written about the street demonstrations that articulacy of power would have been denied him. Whereas in his 1992 film script 'Parallel Bars' he writes about the Romanian people involved in that specific revolution, it is of the essence of *The Shape of the Table* that we are looking at a fictional country and archetypal political issues.

The play is set in one meeting room, formerly a Banqueting Hall, in a baroque palace. The action spans two months in 1989, November and December, in a fictional country of Eastern Europe. This is neither Poland nor Czechoslovakia, neither Hungary nor Romania, neither Bulgaria nor the German Democratic Republic but a fictional amalgam of all of them. Edgar wanted to explore the similar characteristics of the 1989 revolutions. The determined avoidance of a particular place and the factual basis create a semi-documentary technique that would, in theory, allow the playwright to hold back judgement of specific actual individuals:

> I suppose the play hovers over the Czech/Hungarian/Polish border, and has rather more limbs in Czechoslovakia than the other two. But what I hope people will accept is the idea of a world parallel to the real world, where you have fictional people who are clearly based on real people, but have different names and different histories. You enter into a deal with the audience, which says this person is like that historical person, but they're not the same. So you're not setting up to be an advocate, nor indeed a prosecuting counsel for that historical person.[5]

This technique could create difficulties; people could apply a valid test of the documentary and say 'This isn't what really happened in Czechoslovakia (or Hungary, or Poland)' and a good production needs to consider carefully how to retain the 'fictional country' aspect. This is particularly important as Pavel Prus, the dissident writer who becomes President, has obvious elements of Vaclav Havel; Victor Spassov, the 'bourgeois restorationist' is to an extent modelled on Dubcek; and the opposition group Public Platform has resonances with Civic Forum. Nevertheless, this is not Czechoslovakia, giving Edgar licence to trace what could have happened.

The structure of two acts in six scenes is that of the realistic well-made play, focusing on meetings and debate in a room to show in microcosm the state of the country. Each character serves as a connecting medium for the social, political and moral issues under debate, individual personalities are not condemned, and there is an incisive ability to record the positive and negative poles of the historical events and political shifts under examination. A parallelism of quasi-heroic action links Lutz (the ousted hardliner First Secretary) and Prus: at the beginning a document that would have secured his release from prison is burnt by Prus and at the end a similar releasing document is torn up by Lutz. In each case, the individual chooses responsibility and commitment, refusing to lie, accepting blame. It is the personality of Lutz that is intriguing, because (in the familiar pattern of *Destiny* and *Maydays*) he is by no means a villain. The character grows from a position of lying bureaucratic ugliness to that of moral voice.

In the first scene this working-class First Secretary shows his capacity to contemplate violence against the demonstrators and his unjustified faith in the inclination of the Soviet Union to come to his aid. In the second scene he lies about the reaction at the 26th February Auto Plant meeting and is demoted to Chair of the General Federation of Trade Unions; however, by Act Two Scene One his moral conviction about 'reneging on our promise to the working class to end the crime of capital accumulation and the exploitation of one man by another' begins to sound less like automatic Communist jargon and more like sincere protest in the face of frightening future possibilities. Lutz's rediscovered moral integrity is heard clearly in the final scene when he debates with his successor. In Lutz's moving speech about socialist vision it is established that he fought against the Nazis, occupying the very room in the palace that we witness. The idealism of 1945 has now been betrayed and perverted. The proclamation of his side in 1945 was of 'futures of an unimaginable scale and splendour, in which the immense and boundless untapped energies and talents of the masses would be liberated, every peasant would be Aristotle, every worker Michelangelo'. The mirror imagery that runs through the play is brought to a climax in this speech. The great gilt-framed mirrors of this room (now no longer in place) reflected the anti-fascists in their working blouses and red armbands: 'we swore that if we ever looked into a mirror and we couldn't recognise ourselves that day, then we'd tear up our party cards and descend into oblivion.' The image of the visible physical change that lack of political integrity would bring had been used in *Maydays* with specific reference to Martin Glass's defection. Here, the image demonstrates Lutz's determination to be honest about himself. The self-accusation is a sign that the individuals have betrayed the system: 'You see, it wasn't that the working class weren't up to it. It was that we weren't up to it. We weren't betrayed by saboteurs. We didn't need to be. It was pilot error. Nothing wrong with the machine. And I've often thought, thank God they took those mirrors down.'

Lutz's conception of the Communist movement is crucial to the play's thematic design. Edgar wanted to rehabilitate morally the last generation of Communists: 'The way Lutz looks at the Communist movement and what it meant is not the way most people look at those regimes. Most people say, well, at least the people were secure. But the Communist movement did also provide an image of people very dramatically seizing productive control of vital circumstances. In the obituaries, people have rather ignored that kind of enabling, participatory side of the socialist dream. I think it was important.'[6] It would be hard for the majority of people who lived under those regimes to accept Edgar's viewpoint and this is where the 'fictional country' aspect is so important. Edgar is writing an elegy for the Marxist vision rather than a celebration of a totalitarian regime.

The fairy tale as parallel to Marx's grand view of history is a central metaphor in the play. Prus makes the analogy and his presidential term will exist in a world lacking belief in a fairy tale with a happy ending. There is a strong elegiac sense in the play that there is a precise human need for such a story, that such a shaping faith gives necessary conviction in the potential of human nature. The alternative is a level of belief that certain people have the right to be privileged at the expense of the majority, and where the ugliness of anti-Semitism and persecution of other minorities steadily gains ground. The ousted Prime Minister Kaplan is himself Jewish and has survived the Auschwitz extermination camp. Lutz has been a political prisoner in Buchenwald. At the end of the play, as the bells toll for the new President, the genie has been let out of the bottle: 'The spirit with his promises of boundless power who once unleashed turns out to be a demon.' The fairy tale stoppered the bottle; Edgar explains the analogy:

> There is a rhythm to fairy tales, and Marxism has an equivalence to that. Feudalism gives way to capitalism; then capitalism creates in its own belly the means of its own destruction, the industrial proletariat; and then the industrial proletariat takes over. The dialectic of thesis–antithesis–synthesis is there in most fairy stories. Also there is the morality-tale element; plus the element of wanting to live happily ever after – there are many ways in which the Marxist story and the fairy story are equivalent. But now that the grand story is off the agenda – a story that we have all ingested, even without realising it – it will be interesting to see how we live.[7]

The tragedy lies in the failure of human organisation to reach Utopian vision. It is implied that, although we have the end of the story of a socialist experiment begun in 1917, this is not the end of the story of socialism. The hint that people need their dream of emancipation implies that other such experiments may need to take place. Edgar's play 'is ultimately about ... whether socialism is now finally off the historical agenda. Does the idea have a future at all; and if it doesn't, what are the consequences? And what is it that has failed: a system, or individuals, or a whole idea of human nature?'[8]

The pragmatism of Prus's final stance thus raises more questions than it answers. Prus calls the real slogan of the November 1989 revolution 'Back to normal', and the dialogue ensues:

> PRUS. The message of our revolution. Please, no more adventures. No more heroism. Certainly no more unimagin-ably splendid futures. Just: let's get back to the normal ordinary way of doing things. The way that works. The way they do them in the west.
>
> LUTZ. So that's what you're going to tell them? No more fairy tales? No more grand stories? Back to normal?

135

PRUS. It is – what they want.

LUTZ. For now.

As Prus tries to become accustomed to his new suit of clothes, so he begins to be in Macbeth's position of having the robes of office ill-fitting. He has murdered a whole way of looking at the world. The secretarial assistant Monica Freie does not conceive her baby after all, symbolically pointing to the sterility of the new regime.

Edgar elaborated in interview on the dangers of the failure of Communism in Eastern Europe:

> The two ideas of egalitarianism and emancipation have come under huge threat. Two things will become increasingly challenged as a consequence. One is that it will become more possible to hold and express views about theories of genetic differences between people. As a consequence universal suffrage will come under attack. The people living under those regimes viewed themselves as being governed by peasants. The technocratic classes who brought about their overthrow take the view that 'We were run for forty years by people who should have stayed on the factory floor where they belonged.' Now that egalitarian political theories have collapsed, it seems to me quite possible that the western intelligentsia may become attracted by anti-democratic, elitist ideas.[9]

Part of the warning in the play is that the stability would (in the short run, at any rate) give way to race and class antagonisms. This has been a justified warning, particularly so with regard to the chaos, hatred and bloodshed in the former Yugoslavia, and with neo-Nazism surfacing all over Europe (and especially in Germany). Given Edgar's warning about universal suffrage, the alternatives to the 'fairy story' world view could indeed be demonic.

The collapse of a particular political order is theatricalised in the metaphor of the table that changes its shape. In Act One, the huge rectangular table covered with a cloth, its settings impeccably formal, around which the members of the government rigidly move or at which they sit in prescribed places, represents the inflexible disguise of political unity of the Communist countries in the Eastern bloc. The table dominates the caucus room which has itself

136

been the historical site of constitution decisions over the years, was once Nazi headquarters, and was formerly a ballroom with mirrors. Now the politicians can only see their reflections in the dirty glass of the tall windows that separate them from the people. They are shielded from the demonstrations we hear outside, reading words, writing words, and making decisions removed from the needs of the populace. When Prus the window-cleaner and critic of fairy tales arrives, history starts to shift. In a letter from prison, read out by Vladislav in the first scene, Prus had stated: 'More and more, I feel that I am actually inside a fairy story, a land where everything is possible because nothing's what it seems.' When, at the end of Act One, negotiations have revealed that socialism and democracy 'are not in all ways necessarily identical', full talks between opposition and government can proceed: the peaceful revolution has happened without any smashed windows.

The question arises of the constitution of the talks, who sits where, and it is Kaplan who pinpoints the shift that has occurred. The moment is the most spectacular in a play with minimal visual emphasis:

> KAPLAN. Oh, you know, I really don't think that will prove a problem. For, Mr Prus, I think we're entering, or we have entered, now, your magic land where everything is possible, and things aren't always what they seem.
>
> *He pulls the tablecloth off the great table. It is revealed to be a number of smaller tables, of modern manufacture, set together to form the big rectangle. He pulls the end of one of the smaller tables away from the others, to demonstrate the geometric possibilities.*
>
> I'd say there's room for everyone.

With the entrance of Spassov, the first act comes to a close. The impression of unity has been deceptive. In the RNT production the green cloth hid many small, ugly, uneven, differently patterned, formica-topped café tables, metaphor of the reality beneath the mask. The countries can split apart and can each move away from the previous domination of the Soviet Union. Each has a different nationalist possibility. The initial slight political change is demonstrated by Kaplan.

Edgar continues to develop the visual allegory of the political situation throughout Act Two. The tables in Act Two Scene One are covered in crisp white cloths, and are formed into three sides of a big square. This meeting area separates the gathered political groups into parties. The opposition has been allowed to take part in a formal meeting, sides are able to negotiate across the room, and the one-Party system has been replaced. In the RNT production a small centre table supported a floral arrangement, its only function a decorative one. In Act Two Scene Two one of the tables of the square arrangement has been removed, leaving an L-shape. The move from Communism has progressed further, breaking with the past (Spassov will not be up for President). In the play's final scene one table pushed to the side is left. In the RNT production this was the small table from Act Two Scene One. Lutz's overcoat and scarf are on the table. In the last moments, he sits by the table, having locked himself in that historical room. The bells ring for the inauguration of the new President. Here, the small table symbolically signifies the individual, in stark contrast to the original grand rectangular table's symbolic representation of the system. Various readings can be taken from this. Politics are at the starting-point again of the individual (who was there throughout the socialist experiment but was submerged in the whole Party machine). The inflexible restrictive structure has gone but the vulnerable individual is left: will there be a new politics glorifying the individual or will the individual need to build up a new structure, a new socialism to protect him/herself? Does the visual metaphor involve recognition of Lutz's failure to serve the system? Although this reading is slightly balanced by Freie's comment: 'It isn't right that individuals should take the blame', Lutz has indeed chosen to take the blame, and the ending is potently moving.

The visual metaphor of the changing shape of the table is valuable as a teaching device for the audience. Symbolism and allegory within naturalism are present throughout the tradition of naturalism, from the plays of Ibsen, Chekhov and Strindberg onwards. Edgar's device is on one level comparable with the use of the cherry orchard in Chekhov's last play, where the orchard's changing status and the first attempt at destruction of the trees signify the end of one era and the emergence of new hope for the future. In Chekhov's play we find an ambivalence: there is both sadness and hope in the symbol of destruction, just as the changing shape of the table in Edgar's play signifies a mixture of despair at failure and potential for the future. The elegiac quality is unmistakable in each play. However, it is also interesting to speculate that Edgar's early use of the demonstrative visual device in his agitprop plays for the General Will has stood him in good stead here, an influence more Brechtian than Chekhovian, more allegorical than symbolist, in the final analysis. The title of the play points to the metaphor, ensuring that the audience go to the heart of the play's meaning.

The narrative works at a fast pace, propelled by characters who represent various political strands in Europe. Edgar represents in Kaplan the 'reasonably liberal-minded but basically machine Communist'; in Milev, 'a younger generation hardliner who didn't have the experience of the partisan struggle during the war, and the only one of the four central Communist figures still active at the end of the play'; in Vladislav, 'a young technocratic apparatchik' in the pay of Moscow.[10] Kaplan enjoys the irony that the Soviet Union set in motion this revolution and yet had twenty years earlier violently suppressed the liberal revolution that Spassov had attempted. His comment to Spassov is typically Edgaresque: 'As Marx perceptively reminds us, the events of history occurring twice. First time as tragedy, the second time as farce.' The perception is one Edgar often adduces and yet the ironical events are not surprising to the audience whose attention to the news reports from Eastern Europe in 1989 is assumed. Edgar's compensation is 'to capture the sense of what it was like when you didn't know the ending':

It's very difficult for the audience to take that programme out of their minds. The way I chose to do that dramatically was to have everyone constantly thrown by the speed of events. Each scene ends with some sort of resolution and a sense of what happens next; then the next scene comes and the goalposts have moved and the stakes are upped. The character you think has just won is suddenly out on his ear. And each shift is a surprise to somebody. Each is a moment when you think you've got to a point of rest and you haven't.[11]

The speed of events is demonstrated through a struggle for power. Divisions between members within the ruling party and divisions between members of Public Platform ensure an interest in individuals in conflict. On the opposition, the role of Victor Spassov is particularly important. The young secretary for Public Platform, Victoria Brodskaya, has been named after him and her passionate outburst in Act Two Scene One demonstrates the former First Secretary's importance to the new generation. In terms of social system, he represents in his ideas 'the third way'. Edgar commented: 'the next point you get to after you realise that Communism itself is under threat and the Party will not stay in power however it reforms itself, is to confront the question of the third way, a kind of social democracy based on the precepts of the Prague Spring, and in many ways the Hungarian Uprising of '56. Spassov represents that aspiration, and the question is raised as to whether that too is a view that history has now overtaken.'[12]

In a play that centres on debate it is the use of language as code and euphemism that most reveals the hypocrisy of this Eastern European regime. Edgar stated: 'There is the extraordinary way in which those regimes used language to obfuscate and obscure, and in a way the play ... is about the liberation of language. When people start talking there is a great contest over what things are called. That contest over meaning is a very critical one in the play, and also, I think, a dramatic one, in as much as you're often aware of the contrast between the way people say things and what they're saying.'[13] Timothy Garton Ash reported on the need of the 1989 revolutionaries to find new words to replace 'the old mendacious phrases'.[14] In the dramatisation of this aspect of the 1989 revolutions, the play excels. The debate is made interesting and amusing by a meticulous and ruthless exposure of the use of code.

At first, when the politically-correct jargon is not used, corrections are made. In Act One Scene Two, when Vladislav refers to Spassov's 'programme of reform', Lutz jogs him into the correct code:

LUTZ. Programme of 'reform'?

VLADISLAV. I'm sorry. Bourgeois restoration.

LUTZ. Right.

The Spassov 'New Morning' programme must be seen as negative because that is the Party line, and the term chosen connotes

140

betrayal of Communist principle. The Soviet Union is 'our great friend and neighbour' or 'our eastern ally'. The tiny details of vocabulary are pored over in the scrutiny of documents, and the anxiety of such attention to detail filters into bickering over individuals' non-official expressions of opinion. Edgar's device is to highlight such an expression and then to repeat it whereupon it becomes a double joke. One example of this tactic concerns the word 'welsh'. In Act One Scene Three Milev is picked up by Kaplan for use of this crude expression:

> MILEV. Well, as long as you don't welsh on it –

> KAPLAN. Comrade Milev, the word 'welsh' is really not appropriate to a conversation between colleagues in a government, or comrades in a party.

In Act Two Scene One Milev gets his own back:

> VLADISLAV. In other words, what's happening is that you are reneging on agreements of three days ago.

> MILEV. Or welshing, even.

In the meticulous detail of debate, Kaplan can point out that the word 'restoration' 'has its own meaning. As well as being code.' The opposition continue to break the code. Are offers in a document 'only words' or do the words have meaning behind them? Crucially, Prus juxtaposes two forms of words about the post-Spassov years, shattering the euphemism involved: 'we do insist that any investigation of the last 20 years covers the last 20 years, and not just what the government insists on calling "the period of the consolidation", following "receipt of international fraternal help". Which we, we think more accurately, call "the period of the suppression after the invasion".'

In interview, Edgar has elaborated on his twin interests in language in *The Shape of the Table*. Firstly, in a wider sense: 'The theatre is wonderful at dealing with situations where what is said and what is being seen and what is being meant are three different things. It's almost a definition of the drama, and therefore a language that is based around not saying what you mean is very

141

intriguing for a playwright.' Secondly, the interest is in the specific events and their effect on language:

> What basically happened in 1989 was the codes broke down. The codes ceased to function in the way they had functioned. The code that most dramatically ceased to function was the socialist code, the code that we all had a common purpose, and you attach what you want to that common purpose. I think certain codes surrounding phrases like 'geopolitical realities' and 'our neighbours to the east' broke down because Gorbachev broke them down in the GDR by saying 'You're on your own'. The assumption that things would not be allowed to go too far (either because the Soviets would invade or would insist on some sort of military takeover as an option, as in 1981 in Poland) ceased to be an option, so the whole set of codes related to that idea ceased to work. To a certain extent all the countries had employed those codes about limits and accepting realities and so on. I also got very amused by and interested in codes about human things going wrong, 'temporary shortcomings' and 'minor complications' and all of that, used in a slightly odd way like 'temporary shortcoming of the telephone'. Those were again codes that stopped working: 'No, this isn't a "temporary shortcoming"! This is "the phone's not working"!'

The ramifications of 1989 were to shape a new Europe: 'essentially we're talking about all of us, all Europe, and about the kind of Europe we are going to find ourselves part of.'[15] When the Romanian première of *The Shape of the Table* took place at the Bulandra Theatre in Bucharest in December 1991, changes of emphasis in the light of the specific Romanian post-revolutionary experience were made by the director. The play was seen as being about the way the Communists manipulated and controlled. The anti-Semitic reference (associated with Kaplan) was cut to enhance lack of sympathy with the Communists. Edgar noted that 'In the second act it became increasingly clear that a play about power's relinquishment had been effectively transformed into a play about men attempting to cling on to it for dear life.'[16] The final scene most clearly showed the new reading:

> In London, this scene was an elegy to broken ideals; in Bucharest it was a reminder of their continued strength; a strength confirmed when – as the new President leaves – the

142

deposed dictator turns to the retained Secretarial Assistant and asks, in gleeful incredulity, "So they kept you on?" For us, this was a light-hearted acknowledgement of the new President's sense of irony; in Romania it confirmed that the old structures are not yet fully dismantled, and may yet have another day.[17]

Movingly, although this was a major production at a prestigious theatre, tangerines were not available as stage props (or indeed at all) and oranges were not to be found in numbers. In Act One Scene Three a single orange replaced the mound of tangerines used in the London production. The wife of the former Minister of Culture had translated the play; the former Minister confirmed to Edgar: 'You have an Eastern European soul.'[18] The representation of the argument and the detail of bureaucratic style were found to be accurate in an Eastern European country.

The Shape of the Table was the third play in 1990 about the events of late 1989 by English socialist playwrights. Caryl Churchill's *Mad Forest* (at the Central School of Speech and Drama, then the Royal Court, with a run in Bucharest) was premièred first (in June) to great critical acclaim. It is a 'Play from Romania', a play of empathy, thoroughly Aristotelian in its treatment of and appeal to emotional experience. As a result it does not incite debate about the political questions it raises. *Moscow Gold*, by Tariq Ali and Howard Brenton, on the RSC's main house stage at the Barbican from the end of September, is a history of the Soviet socialist experiment from 1917 (a brief prologue spectacular), leaping to 1982, and then covering events until 1989. These events are dramatised in a carnivalesque theatrical style but the political material is not editorialised in sufficient depth to provoke new debate. Edgar's play, by contrast, engages in debate concerning the issues of contemporary politics with the sensitivity and intelligence that encourage the audience to continue that debate outside the theatre. In November 1990, when the Conservative government ousted Thatcher, and when the whole of Europe – East and West – was passing through a time of turmoil and trying to find a new identity, *The Shape of the Table* approached the essential issues with a sense of balance.

'Parallel Bars'

Whereas *The Shape of the Table* is a dramatic account of the ideological values involved in the 1989 revolutions, focusing on politicians and intellectuals engaged in debate in order to show the political and moral meaning in the turbulence, the other side of the revolutionary action is dramatised in 'Parallel Bars'. In the 1991 film script, action is shown on the streets of Romanian cities, on the road from Timişoara to Bucharest, in the National Art Museum and in individuals' homes. People are caught up in that action without pointedly intellectualising it. The cerebralism of *The Shape of the Table* is complemented in 'Parallel Bars' by the conjuring up of a mood of danger and violence. The focus on men in *The Shape of the Table* is complemented by a focus on women in 'Parallel Bars'. The emphasis is on the people as hero of the revolution. Zoë Florescu is an Olympic champion gymnast. She is an important figure in a regime where sport was used as metaphor for national achievement, but her true heroism emerges in the revolution. She performs a handstand on the parallel scaffolding sections of a building works, thereby proving her identity to the police in Bucharest and saving her new friends from prison. The parallel bars are supposed to be 'only for the men', confirming one point of the film: the women are disengaged from the role of childbearing (either through choice or physical sterility) and prove themselves in other ways.

Edgar offers a richly layered action, allowing political points to emerge from the detail of personal relationships, biblical parallelism and reference to the visual arts. The Brueghel painting *The Massacre of the Innocents* is a recurrent structural motif, pointing to the conditions of the revolution. Throughout, we see ordinary people responding to the revolution with acts of bravery: the curator saves paintings from the National Museum; one character is shot dead when he uses his body as shield for his friend. The heroes are both those who die so that others may be saved and also those who use their skills for others' benefit. A toast is made: 'To doing what we do. To doctors healing. Artists making art. And to restorers and curators – well, restoring. Preserving what is cultivated, civilised and great, for the health not merely of our own but future generations.' The biblical sentence 'O you of little faith' resounds repeatedly. Cumulatively, the heroic action of

'Parallel Bars' offers evidence that the audience should retain faith in human altruistic potential.

'Buying a Landslide'

In 'Buying a Landslide' (1992), Edgar temporarily leaves aside the political issues of the Eastern bloc countries to articulate the corruption at the heart of American capitalism. The contemporary action takes place over a weekend at the 'ocean-view hilltop home' of Walter Partin, Conservative Republican senatorial candidate. Partin's consultants stage-manage a simulation of the imminent television electoral debate between Partin and his Democrat opponent, Philip Kautsky. Edgar's model is the classic American stage play: 'that classic, almost thirties whodunnit situation of a group of people isolated for a weekend for a common purpose who then fall rapidly into dispute with accusations of betrayal and revenge.'[19] The television medium clearly suited the subject of the play, which was shot in New York with American actors. It is the Michael Tyne character who interested Edgar. Tyne is (in the *Maydays* mould) a defector: he has moved to the right from a 1960s student revolutionary position. This libertarian economist has been hired to simulate Kautsky, and indeed is also acting his former self; he is representing views he once held: 'The fact that he was engaged to give his best shots to things and opinions he now despised in order for those opinions to be defeated was obviously a very exciting irony.'

Tyne has defected not because of disillusionment with the ends of the left but with the authoritarian means. In particular, he has been affected by the treatment of a woman comrade whose pregnancy coincided 'with a drive in the collective against petty-bourgeois individualism ... so the collective had a meeting about her condition and decided that in the interests of the revolution her pregnancy should be terminated'. Kautsky, the father of the baby, had argued for the necessity for this abortion. It is thus well psychologically motivated that Tyne should both want revenge on Kautsky and that he should in the course of the play be shaken by another case of an abused pregnant woman. Tyne discovers and exposes the scandal that Robert Rutherford, campaign chairman, has secured illegal financial backing by flying arms to Nicaragua in exchange for cocaine. A Mexican peasant farmer has died in Partin's home, victim both of a cocaine package bursting inside her pregnant body and also of a doctor who – out of fear that the scandal will be discovered – gives her an injection instead of getting her to hospital.

Tyne's sensitivity to this individual's plight is seen as a flaw by fellow defector Teddy Weinfeld. Weinfeld, a Marxist in the 1930s and defector to the right, is clearly modelled on the *Maydays* character Teddy Weiner. Early on in the play, the motif of One Corinthians is re-rehearsed in a new context, as is the *Maydays* emphasis on the split between thinking and feeling:

> WEINFELD. 'When I was a child, I spake as a child, I understood
> as a child: but when I became a man, I put away childish things'
> ... St Paul to the Corinthians ... For the point is, that it's easy to
> change what you think. The tricky thing, is to abandon what you
> feel. Because it isn't the authoritarianism, the intellectual
> contempt, the cruelty. It's the other things that have got to go.
> The rigour. The élan. And the – romance. To defect is to betray
> the person who you once were. And worse, the person you still
> are. Because, in fact: it's growing up.

At the end of the play Weinfeld taunts Tyne: 'So. A man who's put off childish things? Hell, come on. It was just an accident ... The woman. Sure, awful. Sure, a tragedy. But worth destroying a political career? Or even two? Welcome to grown-up city, Mr Tyne.'

Tyne has exposed the scandal during the simulation. His choice is now whether to inform Kautsky. In the final scene we see Tyne watching the actual television debate; witness on television Partin stealing Tyne's own political rhetoric; then see Tyne leaving a telephone message for Kautsky. It seems that Tyne has not after all been able to betray his former self in the face of a corrupt Republican campaign. The ending is ambivalent, the story deliberately not completed, leaving the audience to feel unresolved and to debate the issues in their own minds.

Partin is schooled very like Turner in *Destiny*, changing his tune as his campaign managers find obstacles in the argument. His words are so much window-dressing, and he is forced to employ the correct codes for public acceptance just as the Communists in

The Shape of the Table are forced. The title is double-edged. It alludes on the one hand to the reference that Mary-Jane reminds us of: 'Didn't Joe Kennedy tell Jack, I'll buy you the Presidency, but I'm damned if I'm buying you a landslide?' The second reference is to Partin's house: we discover that it is about to slide down into the sea with the next storm, metaphorically encapsulating the corruption of his campaign and of America itself. Homophobia, religious fundamentalism, restrictive immigration, and anti-abortion are some of the issues that emerge during the weekend. The assembled advisers are hopelessly divided, their Republicanism an umbrella for phobia and prejudice. The question is raised of what the people want, and Partin supplies an answer for the 1990s:

> PARTIN. The trouble is, folks just don't *want* to think the place they live is built on shifting sand. They remember, in the 60s, all those cracks and fissures in the crust, and the nasty things that crawled up through. They've had enough of risk and challenge. They want home. Even if, hell, 'home' slid into the ocean long ago. They don't want platforms. They want prophecies. They don't want promises, but dreams. So you offer them a vision of a shining city on a hill, so high the waves can't reach it. And, why not?

Edgar discussed Partin's comment on the spirit of the times in the context of the American presidential electoral campaign of Autumn 1992:

> The most interesting thing about this campaign was Ross Perot who was basically saying 'I have no programme. I have no policy. Trust me'. And, in fact, if you look at America in many ways that may be what people now need. And one of the things that's coming out of Eastern Europe is a whole series of figures (some of whom run out of steam, as prophets do) like Havel, like Walesa, like Yeltsin, without a particular programme, or with programmes that mutate and change, but who are actually saying, 'The world's a very difficult and dangerous place. Follow me.' In a way it's an outgrowth of the revival of interest in the spiritual and while rewriting the play that's been one of the things I've been increasingly aware of and have been increasingly emphasising.[20]

147

'Buying a Landslide' expresses the particular political spirit of the 1990s as it affects America. Nevertheless Edgar's keen interest in Eastern Europe re-emerges in these comparisons he makes with the Czech Republic, Poland and Russia: *Pentecost* returns to the discussion conducted in *Maydays*, *The Shape of the Table* and 'Parallel Bars'.

7

Pentecost

And when the day of Pentecost was fully come, they were all
with one accord in one place. And suddenly there came a sound
from heaven as of a rushing mighty wind, and it filled all the
house where they were sitting. And there appeared unto them
cloven tongues like as of fire, and it sat upon each of them. And
they were all filled with the Holy Ghost, and began to speak with
other tongues, as the Spirit gave them utterance. And there were
dwelling at Jerusalem Jews, devout men, out of every nation
under heaven. Now when this was noised abroad, the multitude
came together, and were confounded, because that every man
heard them speak in his own language.   Acts 2: 1–6

How communities of difference relate to each other in an
increasingly globalised but also fractured world is the big human
question we will confront in the new century. Because it is an
essentially cultural question (as opposed to the questions posed
by traditional Marxism or entrepreneurial liberalism), it will
inevitably put the arts in the foreground, particularly the
narrative arts, as people seek ever more desperately to construct,
deconstruct and reassemble stories that make sense of the world.
                                              David Edgar, 1994[1]

Pentecost was first performed at The Other Place, the smallest of
the Royal Shakespeare Company's three theatre spaces in
Stratford-upon-Avon, on 12 October 1994. Five years after the
collapse of the Berlin Wall, Edgar took as his subject the new
Europe. Into a play of powerful narrative, engrossingly argued
ideas and surprising structural shifts, there comes a final shocking
visual image of German-speaking commandos bursting through the
wall of a church. This *coup de théâtre* is a paradigm for the
devastation and dissolution that the post-1989 years have
witnessed. The abandoned church is set near the border of an

unnamed south-east European country which has throughout its troubled history struggled with invasion, occupation and oppression. On the church's wall is a twelfth-century fresco which is claimed to be the biggest art discovery since Pompeii, prompting a revised understanding of 600 years of European civilisation. The fresco is of hybrid Eastern and Western provenance; its incorporation of perspective and three-dimensional figures 100 years before Giotto's use of these techniques in Northern Italy affirms that culture is built out of a collision of influences. The destruction of the fresco has been ordered under the benign eye of the Minister for Preservation of National Monuments, one of the many ironies that give this play a particular density and richness.

If the image of a wall that comes tumbling down is on one level a crux in recent European political iconography, it is also an image from the Judaeo-Christian narrative by which for twenty centuries people have tried to make sense of their lives. *Pentecost* gives unique expression to the millennial sensibility. It is based on the biblical stories of the Tower of Babel (Genesis 11: 1–9) and Pentecost (Acts 2: 1–13), moving in its structural patterning from Act One: Babel to Act Two: Pentecost. The account of Babel is a pessimistic story of hubris. There is one language on earth and people try to build a tower with its top in the heavens. To prevent this act of human pride, God makes people speak many languages so that there is no mutual understanding. Northrop Frye has contended that, 'Whenever we construct a system of thought to unite earth with heaven, the story of the Tower of Babel recurs: we discover that after all we can't quite make it, and that what we have in the meantime is a plurality of languages.'[2] In Edgar's understanding, 'Communism was a sort of Esperanto, trying to create a perfect language without any of the difficulties or problems existing in language.'[3] The communist code has failed and after the 1989 'revolutions' a plurality of voices clamour for identity. In Act One the concentration on the fight for possession of the fresco involves most crucially a variety of opinions about cultural identity. The characters' voices argue across each other as Edgar reveals several perspectives in collision. In Act Two the account of Pentecost becomes relevant. This is an optimistic story of divine grace in its redemptive power. The Holy Spirit comes to reveal the Christian message; when the apostles deliver the sermon in 'tongues', the message is understood by all people whatever their own language happens to be. In Scene Six of *Pentecost* a story is told in a language that no one present understands and yet the outline of the story is comprehended. This is the Pentecostal moment of the play, a visionary glimpse of 'how communities of difference can relate to each other without losing a sense of what makes them what they are'.[4] The vision is complex and Michael Attenborough, the director of the first production, has given it succinct expression: 'You're asking people to celebrate difference, celebrate the particularity of individual cultures, but at the same time accept the idea that it could be that within those individual cultures will be cross-fertilised ideas and influences.'[5]

The structure of the play is consciously broken-backed. *Pentecost* is itself a cultural hybrid. In Act One there is a closely-argued dialectical cerebralism which opens expectations that this is to be a play of ideas centring on a small number of characters. The plot is at first contained within a detective story genre. In this whodunnit we want to find out who painted the fresco. Gabriella Pecs, an art curator working at the National Museum of the fictional country of the play, presents her case to Oliver Davenport, the English art historian who serves in this genre as the detective who investigates the origin of the fresco she has discovered. The American–Jewish Leo Katz is the second distinguished art historian who arrives on the scene. Leo takes the role of the Police Superintendent who says 'You've got it all wrong': he argues for the fresco not to be restored. Gabriella has started to wipe away the painting on top of the fresco. We see a socialist realist painting of heroic revolutionary workers enthusiastically waving a red flag. As Gabriella removes bricks from the wall of the church, she seems to cut a hole in the flag. Edgar is offering us an image that speaks simultaneously of the collapse of the Berlin Wall and of the holes cut in flags in that same moment of the 'great turnaround' of 1989. The metaphor of artistic restoration is analogous to the political 'restoration' (rather than 'revolution') of 1989. Throughout the play we see layers of art history peeled back as more of the medieval fresco is revealed beneath the Communist painting. The image is of older cultural identities remaining intact throughout the forty years of Communist rule, of religious conviction beneath materialist surface. Part of the argument that ensues is to do with the value of the Communist years. Should the fight against Fascism be forgotten, all that history obliterated? Were the Communist years in many ways as ugly a reign of terror as that of Nazi Germany? A trial (a typically Edgaresque meeting scene) is organised to serve sentence on the restoration issue. The magistrate Anna Jedlikova, a former dissident, decrees that the fresco must not be removed from the church, and by metaphorical implication that Communist history must be remembered. What is at stake here is the use to which the fresco is to be put, and Lenin's question about whose interests will be served by an action is appropriately, if ironically, raised.

This structural progression is abruptly interrupted when, three minutes in playing time before the end of Act One, a group of twelve armed multinational refugees bursts into the church. The abstract debate about the value and use of art objects, and about high art and low art, is sent spiralling onto a different plane. The fresco's origin has not yet been indisputably pinpointed; the energy level shoots up; the play transmutes into a thriller of another kind, a hostage drama. The refugees have brought with them one hostage, the Page Three girl, Toni Newsome; they also take as hostages Oliver, Leo, Gabriella and the fresco. The four human hostages change clothes with, and are forced to see through the eyes of four refugees: a Pakistani, an Afghan, a Kurd and a Turk. In Scene Five, which begins the second act, Yasmin, the stateless Palestinian leader of the 'huddled masses' gathered in the church, tells the deeply distressing personal histories of the asylum-seeking people. She tells stories of violence, dispossession, displacement, exploitation, imprisonment, betrayal, humiliation, inhumanity, on a vast scale and in various countries. She exposes the oppression of East by West. Leo turns attention again to the fresco and the use that can be made of it. The fresco represents the start of the Renaissance, the birth of the homocentric world view: 'Not God but Man is the measure of all things.' He points out 'the most delicious irony' (a phrase he has picked up from Yasmin): the people who rule the fictional country long 'to join the Western Club', and the shameful truth is that more value is placed on the fresco than on either refugees or hostages. The double standard has repeated itself throughout twentieth-century history:

And it's not the first time. As Dubrovnik burns, western
intellectuals write polite letters to the papers, protesting the

destruction of the architecture. Mitterand destroys a squatter camp to build a library. The camp guards at Auschwitz spend their evenings listening to Mozart on the gramophone.

Leo concludes that, perhaps 'there *is* some line, if not from Beethoven to Buchenwald, then at least to the World Bank, the IMF and NATO'. He urges Yasmin to 'underline the irony. And set your huddled masses free'; his advice to her is to threaten to burn the fresco. In his new situation, in circumstances where he can communicate with refugees, Leo has surrendered his Act One conviction that the fresco should not be removed from the church: he has seen its significance and found its use. Gabriella revises her right-wing attitude about human 'dregs' and 'world misfits'. Oliver finds wanting his 'art as artefact' theory; crucially, he admits that works of art might after all contain universal moral truths, that there are universal human values that transcend national contexts:

> Perhaps there are universal human values which we should protect. From those who threaten them.

It is this epiphany that resonates in the following scene.

In Scene Six there is another disjunctional leap. Edgar involves the audience in a ritual as the mystery of Pentecost is revealed. The debate gives way to music and dance. Transformation takes place. The gathered refugees communicate in the references and catchphrases of contemporary Western culture – 'Beam me up, Scotty'; an Elvis Presley song, for example – as well as through the languages and archetypal stories of their own cultures. Through this method of communication, stories are told that add up to one story, the optimistic Christian story of the Passion, where death is followed by resurrection, where the horrific story of the denial, torture, stripping and killing of Jesus echoes the refugees' own histories. Translation of Tunu's story (told in Sinhalese) is unnecessary because of the universal nature of its elements. Indeed, Edgar argues that there are only two types of *ur*-story:

> There are various examples of the pessimistic story – don't open the box, don't go out of the garden, don't talk to strangers – and

then there are various examples of the optimistic story: there are stories about achievement and about miracles and the Christian story is that story. The Garden of Eden is the other story it matches and complements.

When Tunu speaks of the great King Dasharatha and his wicked Queen, their son Rama and his beautiful Princess Sita, she tells an optimistic story of eventual overcoming of evil, proof of faith and a happy reign in paradise. Oliver recognises the narrative that takes us from paradise lost (the Garden of Eden) to paradise regained (the Christian story of redemption):

> Or as we might remember it: a God forbids his child the forest fruit. The child of disobedience is banished and his children are condemned to wander through the earth. But finally the God in pity sends his only son for their redemption. Who teaches them through parables and tales. Who rides unrecognised into the holy city. Prophesies his capture and his death. But promises his followers that nonetheless, in three days' time he'll prove himself the thing he claims to be.

The fresco depicts the nadir in this story, the Lamentation of Mary over the body of Jesus. When the fresco is proved to be a hybrid of East and West, this connects with the recognition that Tunu's Eastern story is resonant of the Christian story: all works of art are hybrid; all cultures are 'impure' because they cross-refer. *Pentecost* itself has this characteristic and is in essence an example of the optimistic story; Edgar points out:

> Tunu's story involves someone going on a journey, being captured and having to perform a task, which is what happened to the painting, but also what happened to Leo, Oliver and Gabriella too. They were captured and asked to perform various tasks to secure their release.

The play itself goes on to consider the possibility of redemption through faith, faith that universal human values can prevail in coexistence with the acknowledgement of separate cultural identities. The thriller becomes a mystery play in Scene Six. When Oliver offers the solution to the fresco in Scene Seven, he solves the whodunnit aspect of the play; simultaneously, he brings

154

the thriller to a climax: now that the hostages know for sure that the fresco is valuable, they will take up Leo's suggestion and threaten to burn it to secure their freedom. The two elements of the hybrid form streamline into one at the point where the East–West nature of the fresco is revealed.

The great problem of our time is not, of course, capable of such immediate solution; in Scene Seven the precious work of art and several human lives are destroyed. Edgar states the problem as follows:

> For me, what 1989 and the collapse of the Berlin Wall meant
> was that the great experiment to conquer human aggression by
> pretending that the difference between people didn't exist, had
> failed. Marxism was, in my view, a heroic attempt to recognise
> the mutual dependence of human beings on this planet. That
> having failed, the alternative that seemed to be presented very
> quickly after 1989 was people asserting their difference to a
> point of exclusivity, for people defining their culture in a very
> narrow, often nationalistic, often racial way and saying, here is
> my culture, I will now build a border, build a fortress, build
> barbed wire around it.[6]

Scene Eight is a coda to the events. The visual image of the fresco has been replaced by an image of a gaping hole in the wall. It is a window on a new world of possibilities, a space to be filled. Much of the play's fascination rests on the demonstration of the ambiguities of language, and echoes and cross-references recur in different contexts to generate new meanings. In the final moment, three words – huddled, yearning, free – evoke the poem carved on the Statue of Liberty, 'Give me your huddled masses, yearning to breathe free.' That final word has the double-edgedness that it has in *Maydays* and *The Shape of the Table*. The question is: freedom 'from' or freedom 'to'? The new 'freedom' in Eastern European countries has been centred on the market, freedom to adopt the values of the Western economic system. As Edgar makes clear, however, the urgency is for a different liberty, a post-Communist mores that could achieve a freedom from oppression for the 'huddled masses'. The audience is invited to accept that moral responsibility when they are reminded by the linguistic echo of the moment in Scene Six when the 'huddled masses' of refugees stumbled towards a shared cultural under-standing that preserves individual cultural identities.

155

The central theme that 'There is no such thing as cultural purity'[7] is highlighted by the multiplicity of languages spoken in the play. The characters from several nations speak their own languages and each also speaks (to the extent he or she knows it) Russian, or English, or Arabic. During the course of the play we hear Swedish, German, Russian, Arabic, Polish, Italian, Turkish and Sinhalese as well as the language of the fictional country in which the play is set (in fact, Bulgarian is used for this). The fictional language of Old Nagolitic is crucial to the plot; we hear the languages of computer-speak and the Communist code; there is witty playing with differences between American and British English. The predominant way in which the characters communicate (imperfectly) is through the shared argot of English as a Second Language. One purpose of using so many languages is to make each member of the audience feel the linguistic confusion. A related purpose is to argue that we must start with the separate authentic languages we already have, rather than invent a new synthetic code as Communism did. The force of the different authentic languages (including English as a Second Language) is to illustrate the argument that cultural purity does not exist. Cultures are always being enriched by the influence of other cultures. As Edgar remarked:

> People communicate across linguistic barriers imperfectly, with all sorts of mistranslations and misunderstandings, but they are really communicating, and have created all the patois and creoles and pidgins which make up what is now the most spoken language in the world, English as a Second Language. With all its imperfections and difficulties and failures, English as a Second Language seems to me the best metaphor for cultural communication, rather than Esperanto.

The delight Edgar has always taken in language idiosyncrasy is here allowed full rein. Two plot hinges skilfully involve tiny points of language. In Scene Seven Oliver discovers the origin of the fresco through a linguistic misunderstanding. In Scene Eight we learn that the church was still bugged, although a bug had been destroyed:

LEO. They bust the bug.

CZABA. Ah, wonders of your English language.

LEO. *What?*

CZABA. They bust *a* bug. *The* bug was in *the* syringe.

The point is that Slavic languages do not have articles. The complexities of language detail are wittily stressed throughout.

The fictional country is caught in the contradiction of bordering East and West. The mood of transience and liminality is set by the location of the church (on the edge of the motorway), by the location of the village it is in (near the border, on the edge of the country), and by the location of the country (on 'Europe's battlement', on the edge of Europe). Everything here is in process, fluid, just as the church has had a multiple purpose (as stable, storehouse, Museum of Atheism, Nazi 'Transit Camp', as well as a church serving Roman Catholic and Orthodox faiths in its time). We are in a fictional northern Balkan country that has a border with Germany (geographically impossible in actuality) and, as with *The Shape of the Table*, the country has aspects of several actual countries. It is politically closest to Slovakia, because its border is the Catholic–Orthodox one, the point at which a new substitute for the Berlin Wall has emerged: 'a new European order is emerging where the barriers are no longer between East and West but between relatively advanced countries ... and those which are underdeveloped.'[8] Slovakia is a model, as Edgar comments:

> It could go West and become a 'good' country like Hungary, Poland, the Czech Republic, Croatia or Slovenia; or it could go into the 'bad' side: Ukraine, Bulgaria, Romania, Serbia (the bits to the East of the new Wall).

There is a sense in which the setting is in limbo, a word of distinct meanings cited by the Concise Oxford Dictionary: ' region on border of hell'; 'prison, confinement'; 'condition of neglect or oblivion'. In the Act One fight for possession of the fresco, it is the torture chamber (Nazi 'Transit Camp') aspect of the church's identity that becomes most important.

The question posed is whether history should be erased; the partial restoration of the fresco has already scraped away names of prisoners scratched on the church wall during the Nazi period. Leo points this out, but it is Anna Jedlikova who is given the strongest story about loss of identity:

JEDLIKOVA. Worst story that I ever hear, in second world war,
    Serb children are transport to camp at Jansenovac, and they
    are so hungry that they eat cardboard tags around their neck.
    Which is their family, their age, their name. They eat their
    history. They die, and nobody remember them ... And now,
    already, here, our past is being erased. And exiles with new
    names come back, and restore old names of streets and
    squares and towns. But in fact you cannot wipe it all away,
    like a cosmetic. Because for forty years it is not normal here.
    And so we must remember. We must not eat our names.
    Otherwise, like Trotsky, we might end up with our jailer's.

The fervent cry 'we must remember' echoes Lermontov's cry of
resistance in the dinner-party scene in *Maydays* (and the voices of
Amanda and Clara in that play). The defeated president Lutz gives
the same warning in *The Shape of the Table*. Are we to forget the
power of anti-fascist resistance? Ironically, it is stressed that the
former prisoner Jedlikova is indeed the new jailer (as magistrate);
the new society has changed her identity to its opposite and we
must ask to what extent those who have power will become
corrupted by it.

In the final scene Jedlikova is again given a key speech about
identity. She binds together the clothes imagery used throughout
the play, when she tries to indicate the millennial alternatives for
Eastern Europeans:

Look. I know how it appear. What happen in this country since
great turnaround.

Slight pause.

But you must understand what we are losing during all this
century. How Communism strip away all culture from our past,
and clothe us all instead in uniform. And when we throw it off
we think, hey, we have been through all so much, we are new
kind of people, we will build new life.

Slight pause.

But we find that we are not so special. Even those of us who
suffer very much. And so yes, we turn from proletcult to Rambo,
or pornography. And you know, is may be best we march to next
millennium in silly national costume. When alternative is dress
of Arnold Schwarzenegger, or wearing nothing very much at all.

The West offers the East a culture of violence and pornography; the development of nationalisms seems a better alternative. The importance of *Pentecost* surely lies in its persuasive argument that we must progress beyond these alternatives, understanding the implications of Leo's crucial pro-refugee statement: 'we are the sum of all the people who've invaded us. We are, involuntarily, each other's guests.' When Leo says this, he ironically wears the trousers and black jersey of a German-speaking commando; it looks as if he has become an enemy but in fact his experience with refugees from many nations has changed his dogmatic way of thinking. Wrong signals of clothing have caused the death of Oliver (shot because he was wrongly identified as a refugee in his borrowed clothing). Edgar articulated the idea behind the clothes imagery:

> Communism attempted to strip us down to nakedness and start again. The solution was putting people in uniform as opposed to working with the grain of what people came with, which is the accretion of clothes, things that we have developed over time.

The clothes imagery works in tandem with the language imagery to suggest the dangers of the attempt to link cultures without taking into account their different identities.

Without a new understanding of how communities of difference can relate to each other, the future threatens to be bleak, aggressive and chaotic. Edgar has expressed his personal fear:

> I'm desperately concerned that we are about to walk into the next millennium with no firm set of ways of looking at the world that aren't terrifying, that the only grand narratives still on the block are Christian fundamentalism and nationalism and that very extreme form of free marketeering that shades so interestingly into authoritarianism wherever you push it ... The left and indeed the liberal centre, is confused and has no model which particularly works. I think that's very scary in ... a situation where new countries with great hopes are emerging and coming up against sinister realities.[9]

The urgency of *Pentecost* stems from the need to find a solution to the millennial crisis.

The formal strategies of this play mark a considerable advance for Edgar. The use of imagery is sustained throughout: the metaphor of the painting, the clothes images, the languages in which the play is written, the focus on the church wall, and the biblical resonance of title and narrative – all these operate to poeticise the meaning. The popular genres of whodunnit and thriller are parodied. Edgar has also adapted the double time-scale prevalent in contemporary fiction and drama. Moreover, he based the structure on a late Shakespearian comedy, and originally conceived Scene Six as opera. This element of pastiche, the self-consciously referential mode, the ironies and pleasures of the play, Edgar defines as specifically post-modern:

> It is a post-modern play in these ways: it wears its genres on its sleeve; it is deliberately, consciously broken-backed; it is hybrid both in form and content; you're supposed to enjoy the solution to the problem and the echo references.

Several reviewers of the first production pointed out a similarity to Tom Stoppard's *Arcadia*, which is in the contemporary genre of the literary investigation of the past. Edgar takes the double time-scale and alters it. Whereas *Arcadia* flashes forward to interlock past with present, *Pentecost* uses the present with important reference to the periods of the painting and of the fresco. The use of the fresco allows discussion of the Renaissance and analogies with the contemporary moment, but there is no scene set in (for example) Giotto's chapel at Padua. The image does the work of flashbacks. It is 'read' by art-historian characters much as the Victorian poetry and letters in A.S. Byatt's novel *Possession* are read by characters who are academics who draw conclusions about the past.

The disjunction of the play just before the interval is a strategy that Edgar discerned in *The Winter's Tale*. He emphasises the 'magic kingdom' aspect:

> The basic structure of all Shakespeare is that you have people who are close to a crisis. They are driven into the countryside; in comedy they dress up as other people and come back in and get married; in tragedy they strip naked, stay outside and die. The variants are those plays where they refuse to go out and the outside comes in to get them: *Macbeth* and *Richard III*. In *Pentecost*, as in *The Winter's Tale*, you have a triangular first act between three people. You have a major disjunction – in *Pentecost* it is both spatial and temporal, but not literally, in that it's an invasion. The outside world in this case invades and turns into a magic kingdom.

The refugees bring with them the magic kingdom, which reaches its apogee in the storytelling scene, which is equivalent to the famous bucolic scene in *The Winter's Tale*. The disjunction in *Pentecost* happens just before the interval and, as in *The Winter's Tale*, they end up going back inside. In this case they've left Oliver dead behind them – he has been stripped and dressed like someone else, and he can't change back.

The Shakespearian comic richness of *Pentecost* is compounded by a reference to the Shakespearian-sounding names of some of the new Eastern European countries; and by specific references: Illyria (*Twelfth Night*) is cited; the name Oliver comes from the character in *As You Like It*; even the word 'gobbyo' (in invented Old Nagolitic) that solves the fresco's origin obliquely refers to a character in *The Merchant of Venice*. The self-consciousness says: this is a comedy; this is in an English tradition; this is a play appropriately performed by the RSC. In the first production, the majority of actors were also in productions of Shakespeare in the main house. Edgar commented: 'Two of our actors were in nothing else, but one was Charles Kay, who's got a lot of Shakespeare experience. The fact that the others were doing Shakespeare did give them a sense of structure and shape, and a capacity to play small parts memorably.'

Edgar had originally conceived Scene Six in terms of Jacobean masque or of opera, something very much outside the rest of the action, a space of magic (akin to the magic forest in Shakespearian comedy). In this initial conception, the stories and snatches of music, the dances and biblical references, would have operated in a medley of forms, overlapping, echoing and recurring, as the stories twisted and turned from one speaker to the next: truly a 'speaking in tongues'. As it evolved from conception, through rehearsal, to performance, the scene changed. *Pentecost* had been commissioned for the Royal National Theatre's Olivier stage, for Trevor Nunn to direct. Edgar had fantasised about a collaboration between the RNT and the English National Opera, with the refugees played by opera singers. As it turned out, the Olivier was withdrawn and the Cottesloe, the smallest RNT theatre, was offered at a date in 1995. This was rejected by Edgar for two main reasons: there was now to be a substantially and unacceptably smaller cast, and

161

Trevor Nunn would not be available at that time. The play was then offered to the RSC, and accepted. Once the rehearsal process was under way, Edgar worked on the scene with the associate director and the actors cast as the refugees, while the first half of the play was rehearsed by Michael Attenborough. Through exploration of the refugees' characters in improvisation, and investigation of various storytelling techniques (with Edgar always open to the actors' suggestions), a scene of linear, sequential storytelling, rooted in naturalism, emerged. The conception of a different theatrical language (a true theatricality) for the climax of Pentecostal meaning was abandoned.

Michael Attenborough was firmly convinced that it was important to stress the recognisable humanity of the refugees:

> There is a smelly reality to the arrival of these people. They have blood, sweat and tears on them. They are real people. You are asking the audience to identify with them as real people. You go to the lengths of telling the audience in some detail about their backgrounds. They have objectives. I strongly believe that Scene Six had to be played naturalistically, and if you'd suddenly, that far into a naturalistic evening, gone stylised, it would have looked like the playwright was taking a pair of pliers and bending the characters and the events to make his point. I believed that the point would still be there if you retained the truth and the reality of it and didn't go into theatrical metaphor.

Another valid way of directing the scene would be to go boldly for the operatic quality of the initial conception, to ignore the perceived need to help the audience, to see the scene as dependent on rhythm and movement. Edgar was fully adamant (with Attenborough) that, once the scene was written in a linear form, it should be played naturalistically. There is an opportunity still firmly present in the text for a more experimental method to emerge (if Edgar felt it appropriate, for a later production, to rewrite the scene). The spiritual strength of the play is already accentuated by the church setting, biblical motif and title, and the metaphysical moment might be enhanced further.

Attenborough felt that the title was 'a good guiding light for us in terms of the experience that the play should provide for the audience. It has a religious and spiritual buzz to it, which I think is exciting for that play because it deals with something that can't be articulated.' What resists articulation is Edgar's vision of a situation where communities of difference can relate to each other while maintaining their own identities, people speaking in various tongues but going out with the same message. This deeply moral and spiritual play would have been limited by a more prosaic title. There were several alternatives that were discarded. Edgar discussed these:

> It was 'The Illyich Lamentation'. It was 'Threnos', which is the Byzantine word for lamentation. It was 'The Space on the Wall', which is about people taking down pictures of Lenin and not having anything to put up. 'The Space on the Wall' obviously had resonances of the painting, but it was too close to *The Shape of the Table*. What's nice about 'Pentecost' is that it is a single-word title, which relates it to *Maydays* and *Destiny*.

Another early choice was 'Restoration', referring to the starting point for the play, the realisation that the Eastern European 'revolutions' were often regarded in those countries not as revolutions but as 'restorations' of a pre-Communist past. This choice was rejected because it is the title of a play by Edward Bond.

Attenborough is an Executive Producer of the RSC, with a particular responsibility for new work. With his direction of *Pentecost* and *After Easter* by Anne Devlin (premièred at The Other Place on 18 May 1994), he returned the RSC (as Edgar put it) 'to its rightful place as a new-writing theatre of distinction'. *Pentecost* was developed collectively by a company with whom Edgar has had a long and successful relationship. The play's extraordinary linguistic challenges called for a company sensitive to language and with the resources to hire translators and a language specialist. Attenborough confirmed that 'the whole question of language and the use of language is central to the work that the RSC do, whether it's the sonnet work John Barton does or the way Adrian Noble approaches Shakespeare'. The venue for the play in Stratford, The Other Place, is a small, intimate, uncomfortable space on the outer reaches of the town. The alternative was the more comfortable Swan. Attenborough explained the choice:

For me, the advantage of The Other Place over the Swan is that the Swan has what I would describe as an unavoidable feel-good factor. It embraces you. It's cosy, it's warm, it's a smiley space. You actually see people smile when they walk into it. And this is not a smiley play. It's a rough, difficult, abrasive, dangerous play. I voted for The Other Place because I felt that we wanted to put the audience in that room with those people, that when somebody knocked on the door they were knocking on the door of the room you were in; if a loudhailer is shouting outside, it's shouting into the room you're in.

Attenborough was able to direct entrances from three sides, using the fixed gangways. The feeling of immediacy accentuated the urgency of the subject. The disadvantage, Attenborough felt, was that 'It was a bit like directing *Ben Hur* on a postage stamp.' The large cast meant that there was masking at times, but Attenborough was persuaded that the audience tolerated it, as they would not in a big space. A sense of danger, speed and panic was well conveyed in that rough space; the impassioned debate of the first half could be followed with concentration; and, because the venue had so successfully been used for the original production of *Destiny* almost twenty years earlier, there was a special sense of Edgar's relationship with the RSC.

Edgar complimented Robert Jones's design as 'brilliantly finished, inspired in concept: it's the best design I've ever had'. Once Jones had found solutions to the two central technical problems (the bursting through of the wall, and the various stages the painting goes through), he first contemplated a stylised design (one idea was to use bits of maps). In the end, they chose a realistic church interior, as Attenborough explained:

The more we worked on it, we saw that the play did not want to take some stylised set. You needed to believe you were in a church on a south-eastern border of Europe. The church is an emblem for what happens to the painting: it has had a multi-layered life. It was important to have a gnarled, gritty, three-dimensional feel to it, as knotty and real as possible.

The music created by Ilona Sekacz was evocative of solemn church ceremony and worship. Working with the authenticity of the set, it focused attention on the title and the metaphor of redemption.

164

The critical reception of the production was extremely positive. In particular, Michael Coveney's *Observer* notice (30 October 1994) emphasised that 'David Edgar's powerful, urgent and brilliant new play for the RSC in Stratford-upon-Avon is the first serious response in the British theatre to the tragedy of Sarajevo ... There has been no more ambitious or rewarding play in the British theatre all year.' Irving Wardle in the *Independent on Sunday* (30 October 1994) argued that 'It is the richest text to arrive on the English stage since Stoppard's *Arcadia*; and a drama on the politics of language that ranks with Friel's *Translations*.' In the end-of-year 'best new work' judgements, *Pentecost* was very highly praised.[10]

This is Edgar's most complex, detailed and rich play since *Maydays*; its tough cerebralism is complemented by wit, humour and compassion. The play develops Edgar's main preoccupations over the last fifteen years. The 1994 Birmingham Theatre Conference entitled 'All Passion Spent?' raised the question: is all the fire of 1970s political theatre now cold?[11] *Pentecost* proves that committed public theatre still exists, and that it can be thrilling. The play up-ends received forms, moving from dialectical first half to visionary second half; in an early essay, Edgar had praised plays such as Trevor Griffiths's *Comedians* that have similar structural shifts.[12] It also goes some way towards bridging the gulf between the performance art and cerebral traditions of Edgar's generation of playwrights; this is a recurring subject of Edgar's essays.[13] Edgar has praised the visual images that certain public plays (such as Bond's *Lear*) have burned onto the memory.[14] The image of the commandos bursting through the church wall is his most potent image to date.

It is a quarter of a century since Edgar began his playwriting career. His energy for the role of secretary for the times is as abundant as ever. The seriousness of his purpose is to put on the English stage the most urgent problems of contemporary history. The crisis of post-Communist Eastern Europe has been scrutinised in Tony Kushner's *Slavs!* (which had its British première at the Hampstead Theatre on 13 December 1994). Kushner phrases a key question in the last line: 'What is to be done?' If we take as an answer Samuel Beckett's bleak proposition in *Waiting for Godot*: 'Nothing to be done', we deny responsibility for the chaotic situation of contemporary Europe; we are saying that positive change cannot occur. On the contrary, as E.H. Carr has stressed, 'History in its essence is change, movement, or – if you do not cavil at the old-fashioned word – progress ... History is the long struggle of man, by the exercise of his reason, to understand his environment and to act upon it.'[15] Edgar confronts his audiences with what is most at stake in our contemporary historical situation. He insists on the importance of understanding the past and present in order to influence the future.

David Edgar continues to document in plays for theatre, television and radio the political mores of Britain, Eastern Europe and America. His early plays took a propagandist stand on specific social, moral and political issues. As his career has developed, he has tackled head-on his central theme of disillusion with the left in plays that achieve a balance of discussion. His interest in adaptation of both fiction and autobiography has centred on the contemporary moral and political meanings of the plays he has sculpted from others' writing. A focus on research and wit, contradiction and irony hallmarks the canon. He has experimented with documentary, parody, agitprop, epic, carnivalesque and realistic forms. Chris Parr launched Edgar's career with *Two Kinds of Angel* in 1970. He was there at the start and twenty-two years later he produced 'Buying a Landslide' for BBC Television. He has directed several of Edgar's plays in the intervening period. In 1992 when I asked him to sum up Edgar's career he was unequivocal:

> I agree with Oscar Lewenstein. Oscar always used to say about David that he was a political playwright who knew what he was talking about. Over the years he's become less of a participant in politics and more of an observer. It's been good for his writing.[16]

As secretary for the times, David Edgar writes with the political literacy, social vision, and critical intelligence that make him unique among his contemporaries.

Notes

Introduction

1. Elizabeth Swain, *David Edgar: Playwright and Politician*, American University Studies Series 4, English Language and Literature vol. 36, New York: Peter Lang, 1986, p. 335. Swain analyses the plays up to and including *Maydays*.
2. Murray Armstrong, 'The Cairo Commons', *Weekend Guardian*, 27–28 May 1989.
3. E.H. Carr, *What is History?* [first published by Macmillan in 1961], second edition, ed. R.W. Davies [first published in Pelican Books in 1987], Penguin, 1990, p. 30.
4. There are two relevant references in Balzac. See first: 'Théorie de la démarche' (1833) in Honoré de Balzac, *Oeuvres complètes*, vol. 39, ed. Marcel Bouteron and Henri Longnon, Paris: Louis Conard, 1938, pp. 625–6: 'Il y a dans tous les temps un homme de génie qui se fait le secrétaire de son époque: Homère, Aristote, Tacite, Shakspeare, l'Arétine, Machiavel, Rabelais, Bacon, Molière, Voltaire, ont tenu la plume sous la dictée de leurs siècles.' Translated (by Susan Painter) this is (literally) as follows: 'There is in all times a man of genius who makes himself secretary of his epoch: Homer, Aristotle, Tacitus, Shakespeare, the Aretine, Machiavelli, Rabelais, Bacon, Molière, Voltaire, have held the pen under the dictation of their centuries.' See also the famous 'Avant-propos' (1842) to *La Comédie humaine* in Honoré de Balzac, *Oeuvres complètes*, vol. 1 (in the above edition), 1953, p. xxix: 'La Société française allait être l'historien, je ne devais être que le secrétaire.' Translated (by Susan Painter) this is (literally) as follows: 'French society was going to be the historian, I needed to be only the secretary.' See the annotated Pléiade edition for a note on the 'secretary' phrase and Balzac's interpretation of it: 'Avant-propos de *La Comédie humaine*', ed. Madeleine Fargeaud, in Honoré de Balzac, *La Comédie humaine*, vol. 1, ed. Pierre-Georges Castex, Bibliothèque de la Pléiade, Paris: Gallimard, 1976, p. 1124.

5. 'Events following', *Guardian*, 27 February 1976.
6. Interview with Susan Painter, 19 July 1994.
7. See Leonard Tancock's introduction to Emile Zola, *Thérèse Raquin*, Penguin, 1962, p. 15: 'In a study of Proudhon and Courbet published in *Mes Haines* in 1866, Zola had [defined] art in these terms: *Une oeuvre d'art est un coin de la création vu a travers un tempérament.* Paraphrasing this in English, we might say that any work of art is a picture of the world, or a corner of it, distorted, coloured, arranged by the personality of the artist.'
8. David Edgar, 'On Drama-Documentary', *The Second Time as Farce: Reflections on the Drama of Mean Times*, Lawrence and Wishart, 1988, p. 58. The cream of Edgar's political and theatrical journalism up to 1988 is collected in this volume (subsequently referred to as *Second Time*).
9. Interview with Derek Paget, 15 January 1986, quoted in Paget's doctoral thesis, '*Oh What A Lovely War* and the broken tradition of Documentary Theatre', Manchester University, 1988, p. 374.
10. 'Thoughts for the Third Term', *Second Time*, op. cit., note 8, p. 12.
11. See, for example, Bob Jessop, Kevin Bonnett, Simon Bromley and Tom Ling, *Thatcherism: A Tale of Two Nations*, Cambridge: Polity Press (in association with Oxford: Basil Blackwell), 1988, p. 189.
12. 'Festivals of the Oppressed', *Second Time*, op. cit., note 8, p. 234.
13. 'Thoughts for the Third Term', *Second Time*, op. cit., note 8, p. 21.
14. 'State of Play: new work in the contemporary British theatre', *RSA Journal*, vol. CXLI no. 5440, June 1993, pp. 450–60. Edited version: 'New State of Play', *Guardian*, 1 March 1993.
15. Note that the National Theatre became the Royal National Theatre in 1988.
16. See John McGrath, *The Bone Won't Break: On Theatre and Hope in Hard Times*, Methuen, 1990; Roland Rees, *Fringe First: Pioneers of the Fringe Theatre on Record*, Oberon, 1992; and Rob Ritchie, ed., *The Joint Stock Book: The Making of a Theatre Collective*, Methuen, 1987.
17. 'State of Play', op. cit., note 14, p. 454.
18. Ibid., p. 456.
19. Ibid., p. 457.
20. Catherine Itzin, *Stages in the Revolution: Political Theatre in Britain Since 1968*, Eyre Methuen, 1980, p. 306. See pp. 306–15 for an account of the founding of the Theatre Writers' Union.
21. 'A play wot I wrote', *Guardian*, 13 July 1994.

Chapter One

1. David Edgar, 'Towards a Theatre of Dynamic Ambiguities', *Theatre Quarterly*, vol. 9 no. 33, Spring 1979, p. 6 (subsequently referred to as 'Dynamic Ambiguities'). This long interview of twenty pages with Clive Barker and Simon Trussler is by far the most detailed source of information on Edgar's career and biography, especially valuable for its analysis of the early unpublished work. A much shortened version of the interview is to be found in Simon Trussler (ed.), *New Theatre Voices of the Seventies*, Eyre Methuen, 1981, pp. 157–71.
2. 'Dynamic Ambiguities', op. cit., note 1, p. 4.
3. See Alan Sked and Chris Cook, *Post-war Britain: A Political History*, third edition, Penguin, 1990, p. 259. This book is a valuable source of reference, as is Arthur Marwick, *British Society Since 1945*, second edition, Penguin, 1990.
4. Ann McFerran, 'Relative Values', *Sunday Times Magazine*, 25 June 1989.
5. Benedict Nightingale, 'Destined to take notes on the times', *The Times*, 3 November 1990.
6. John Fox was at the College of Art until 1971 when he was appointed Senior Lecturer in the Fine Art department at Leeds Polytechnic.
7. There are several essays in which Edgar has discussed trends in the socialist theatre of his generation of playwrights. Good starting points, where Edgar covers developments in form, are 'Ten Years of Political Theatre, 1968–1978', in David Edgar, *The Second Time as Farce: Reflections on the Drama of Mean Times*, Lawrence and Wishart, 1988, pp. 24–47 (subsequently referred to as *Second Time*); and 'Public Theatre in a Private Age', ibid., pp. 160–75. Baz Kershaw, *The Politics of Performance: Radical Theatre as Cultural Intervention*, Routledge, 1992, pp. 78–86, analyses Edgar's viewpoint of the trends of performance art and agitprop. John Bull, *New British Political Dramatists*, Macmillan Modern Dramatists Series, Macmillan, 1984, pp. 1–27, has an account of these trends, and a chapter on Edgar's work, pp. 151–94, as well as a section on *Maydays*, pp. 221–5 and a useful chronology of political and historical events from 1968–83. There are several good introductions to the general area of alternative theatre: Peter Ansorge, *Disrupting the Spectacle: Five Years of Experimental and Fringe Theatre in Britain*, Pitman, 1975; Sandy Craig (ed.), *Dreams and Deconstructions: Alternative Theatre in Britain*, Ambergate, Derbyshire: Amber Lane Press, 1980; Catherine Itzin, *Stages in the Revolution: Political Theatre in Britain Since 1968*, Eyre Methuen, 1980, based on extensive interviews with theatre practitioners and with a chapter on Edgar and the General Will

company, pp. 139–51; and Clive Barker, 'From Fringe to Alternative Theatre', *Zeitschrift für Anglistik und Amerikanistik*, vol. 26 no. 1, 1978, pp. 48–62. *New Edinburgh Review*, no. 30, August 1975, is devoted to political theatre and has several articles of interest, e.g. Richard Seyd, 'The Theatre of Red Ladder', pp. 36–42, which is a detailed discussion of the problems of agitprop.

8. Interview with Susan Painter, 2 June 1992. All subsequent quotations from Chris Parr in this chapter are from this source.

9. 'Dynamic Ambiguities', op. cit., note 1, p. 5.

10. Ibid.

11. Ibid., p. 6.

12. Primary sources are Erwin Piscator, *The Political Theatre* [first published 1929], ed. and trans. Hugh Rorrison, Eyre Methuen, 1980 and Bertolt Brecht, *Brecht on Theatre*, ed. and trans. John Willett, Methuen, 1964. For an analysis of Piscator's theatrical practice, see Graham Holderness, 'Shaustück and Lehrstück: Erwin Piscator and the Politics of Theatre', in Graham Holderness (ed.), *The Politics of Theatre and Drama*, Macmillan, 1992, pp. 99–119.

13. Clive Barker, 'Alternative Theatre/Political Theatre' in Graham Holderness, op. cit., note 12, p. 26. Barker's essay, pp. 18–43, is a referentially wide-ranging piece examining the relationship between the two terms in the title. The notes refer to an extensive bibliography.

14. See Robert Hewison, *Too Much: Art and Society in the Sixties 1960–75*, Methuen, 1986, pp. 182–225.

15. Itzin, op. cit., note 7, p. 146.

16. Quoted in Richard Boon, *Brenton the Playwright*, Methuen, 1991, p. 54. For an account of the situationists' influence on Brenton, see pp. 54–6. For further information on the situationists, see Hewison, op. cit., note 14, pp. 150–1.

17. 'Ten Years of Political Theatre, 1968–1978', *Second Time*, op. cit., note 7, p. 26.

18. 'Dynamic Ambiguities', op. cit., note 1, p. 6.

19. The Living Newspaper technique originated in post-revolutionary Russian theatre; it was particularly emphasised in 1930s theatre in America. Edgar had researched aspects of the tradition: see 'Dynamic Ambiguities', op. cit., note 1, p. 7.

20. Ibid.

21. Boon, op. cit., note 16, p. 59. For further analysis, see Michael Billington's review in *One Night Stands: A Critic's View of British Theatre from 1971 to 1991*, Nick Hern Books, 1993, pp. 19–20.

22. 'Public Theatre in a Private Age', *Second Time*, op. cit., note 7, p. 161.

23. Interview with Susan Painter, 16 January 1992.

24. 'Ten Years of Political Theatre, 1968–1978', *Second Time*, op. cit., note 7, p. 46.

25. 'Dynamic Ambiguities', op. cit., note 1, p. 8.
26. David Edgar, 'Return to Base', *New Edinburgh Review*, no. 30, August 1975, p. 3.
27. 'Dynamic Ambiguities', op. cit., note 1, p. 8.
28. 'Finding Room on the Agenda for Love: A History of Gay Sweatshop' in Philip Osment (ed.), *Gay Sweatshop: Four Plays and a Company*, Methuen, 1989, p. xxi.
29. Ibid., p. xiii.
30. 'Dynamic Ambiguities', op. cit., note 1, p. 13.
31. 'Ten Years of Political Theatre, 1968–1978', *Second Time*, op. cit., note 7, p. 34. The early 1980s saw a revival of agitprop: see 'Festivals of the Oppressed', *Second Time*, op. cit., note 7, pp. 230–1. See also the discussion in 'Public Theatre in a Private Age', *Second Time*, op. cit., note 7, pp. 167–8.
32. *New Edinburgh Review*, op. cit., note 26, p. 2.
33. 'Festivals of the Oppressed', *Second Time*, op. cit., note 7, p. 230.
34. 'Dynamic Ambiguities', op. cit., note 1, p. 22.
35. David Edgar, quoted in Itzin, op. cit., note 7, p. 141.
36. 'Festivals of the Oppressed', *Second Time*, op. cit., note 7, pp. 234–5.
37. The Soviet director Meyerhold was arrested, brought to secret trial and, it is believed, shot dead in a Moscow prison in 1940 for deviating from the Socialist Realism norm. See Edward Braun, *The Theatre of Meyerhold: Revolution on the Modern Stage*, Eyre Methuen, 1979, and Robert Leach, *Vsevelod Meyerhold*, Directors in Perspective Series, Cambridge UP, 1989, for details of Meyerhold's theatre practice. See Erwin Piscator and Graham Holderness, op. cit., note 12, for discussion of form in Piscator's Germany. See Raphael Samuel, Ewan MacColl and Stuart Cosgrove, *Theatres of the Left 1880–1935: Workers' Theatre Movements in Britain and America*, Routledge and Kegan Paul, 1985, for discussions of form; in particular, 'The debate on naturalism', pp. 167–81.
38. 'Public Theatre in a Private Age', *Second Time*, op. cit., note 7, p. 169.
39. Cited in 'Ten Years of Political Theatre, 1968–1978', *Second Time*, op. cit., note 7, p. 34.
40. David Edgar, quoted in Itzin, op. cit., note 7, p. 146.

Chapter Two

1. David Edgar, 'Towards a Theatre of Dynamic Ambiguities', *Theatre Quarterly*, vol. 9 no. 33, Spring 1979, p.15 (subsequently referred to as 'Dynamic Ambiguities').

2. David Edgar, *The Second Time as Farce: Reflections on the Drama of Mean Times*, Lawrence and Wishart, 1988, p. 41 (subsequently referred to as *Second Time*).
3. Interview with Susan Painter, 29 May 1991.
4. 'Dynamic Ambiguities', op. cit., note 1, p. 14.
5. 'Festivals of the Oppressed', *Second Time*, op. cit., note 2, p. 233.
6. 'Ten Years of Political Theatre, 1968–1978', *Second Time*, op. cit., note 2, p. 36.
7. Interview with Susan Painter, 16 January 1992.
8. For McGrath's commentary on the debate see his *A Good Night Out*, Methuen, 1981 (and, in particular, pp. 33–4, pp. 47–8, pp. 62–4, p. 122). There is further discussion in Tony Mitchell's interview with McGrath: 'Popular Theatre and the Changing Perspective of the Eighties', *New Theatre Quarterly* vol. 1, no. 4, 1985, pp. 390–9. For a discussion of McGrath's position see Colin Chambers and Mike Prior, *Playwrights' Progress: Patterns of Postwar British Drama*, Oxford: Amber Lane Press, 1987, pp. 60–75. Here, Chambers and Prior contrast McGrath with Tom Stoppard in a useful analysis of 'Problems of Political Theatre'.
9. 'Dynamic Ambiguities', op. cit., note 1, p. 15.
10. Ibid, p. 18.
11. Interview with Susan Painter, 23 July 1991. All subsequent quotations from Ron Daniels in this chapter are from this source.
12. Colin Chambers, *Other Spaces: New Theatre and the RSC*, Methuen Theatrefile, Eyre Methuen and *TQ* publications, 1980, p. 45. For details of Daniels's career see pp. 44–6.
13. David Edgar, quoted in Terry Grimley, 'Enter Stage Right', *Birmingham Post*, 28 September 1976.
14. Ibid.
15. 'Dynamic Ambiguities', op. cit., note 1, p. 16.
16. See, for example, the Introduction to *Plays: Two*, Methuen, 1990, p. viii.
17. In the 1976 text the agent is an Asian character, Razak. The change was made to accommodate this point about Turner's experience. Monty replaces Razak in the revised 1978 text.
18. Interview with Susan Painter, 16 January 1992.
19. Ibid.
20. 'Dynamic Ambiguities', op. cit., note 1, p. 12.
21. *Second Time*, op. cit., note 2, pp. 69–70.
22. 'Dynamic Ambiguities', op. cit., note 1, p. 21.
23. Interview with Robert Cushman, *Talking Theatre*, BBC Radio Four, broadcast on 27 January 1988.
24. Interview with Susan Painter, 16 January 1992.
25. Ibid.

172

26. Steve Grant, 'Through the Fire', *Time Out*, 22 October 1976.
27. Interview with Susan Painter, 22 July 1991. All subsequent quotations from Ian McDiarmid in this chapter are from this source.
28. Interview with Susan Painter, 16 January 1992.
29. Op. cit., note 23.
30. Interview with Susan Painter, 16 January 1992.
31. Grimley, op. cit., note 13.
32. 'Dynamic Ambiguities', op. cit., note 1, p. 17.
33. Cited in Malcolm Page and Simon Trussler, *File on Edgar*, Methuen, 1991, p. 49.
34. Ian McDiarmid stressed these observations, op. cit., note 27.
35. Interview with Susan Painter, 21 February 1992. See 'Thoughts for the Third Term', *Second Time*, op. cit., note 2, pp. 11–12.
36. Elizabeth Swain, *David Edgar: Playwright and Politician*, American University Studies Series 4, English Language and Literature vol. 36, New York: Peter Lang, 1986, p. 146.
37. 'Dynamic Ambiguities', op. cit., note 1, p. 10.
38. Chambers, op. cit., note 12, p. 77.

Chapter Three

1. 'Call that a masterpiece? Critics list their pet hates', *Guardian*, 24 December 1991.
2. 'Adapting *Nickleby*', in David Edgar, *The Second Time as Farce: Reflections on the Drama of Mean Times*, Lawrence and Wishart, 1988, p 159 (subsequently referred to as *Second Time*).
3. Eric Bentley, *The Theatre of Commitment*, Methuen, 1968, pp. 153–4.
4. David Edgar, summing-up address at the 'Beyond Words' Birmingham University conference, 12 April 1992. Not published.
5. 'Adapting *Nickleby*', *Second Time*, op. cit., note 2, p. 145.
6. See Edward Braun, *The Theatre of Meyerhold: Revolution on the Modern Stage*, Eyre Methuen, 1979; Robert Leach, *Vsevelod Meyerhold*, Directors in Perpective Series, CUP, 1989; Bertolt Brecht, *Brecht on Theatre*, ed. and trans. John Willett, Methuen, 1964; and Erwin Piscator, *The Political Theatre* [first published 1929], ed. and trans. Hugh Rorrison, Eyre Methuen, 1980.
7. Bentley, op. cit., note 3, pp. 198–9.
8. Ibid., p. 168.
9. Billington is quoted from 'Split decision', *Guardian*, 29 November 1991. For Billington's commitment to social and political theatre see, e.g., 'Thriving on the oxygen of protest', *Guardian*, 7 May 1992.

10. The phrase is David Edgar's, in interview with Susan Painter, 21 February 1992. Unless indicated otherwise, all subsequent quotations from Edgar in this chapter are from this source.

11. David Edgar, 'Towards a Theatre of Dynamic Ambiguities', *Theatre Quarterly*, vol. 9 no. 33, Spring 1979, p. 18–20 (subsequently referred to as 'Dynamic Ambiguities').

12. Ibid., p. 23.

13. Ibid., p. 20.

14. 'Adapting *Nickleby*', *Second Time*, op. cit., note 2, p. 146.

15. Albie Sachs, *The Jail Diary of Albie Sachs*, Paladin, 1990, pp. 92–100.

16. David Edgar, cited in Malcolm Page and Simon Trussler, *File on Edgar*, Methuen, 1991, p. 53.

17. Ibid.

18. David Edgar, Introduction to *Plays: One*, Methuen, 1987, p. viii.

19. 'Dynamic Ambiguities', op. cit., note 11, p. 20.

20. David Edgar, quoted in David Ian Rabey, *British and Irish Political Drama in the Twentieth Century: Implicating the Audience*, Macmillan, 1986, p. 183.

21. Albie Sachs, *The Soft Vengeance of a Freedom Fighter*, Paladin, 1991, pp. 184–8.

22. See Carol Steinberg, 'Albie Sachs: Our Shakespearian Fool', *TDR*, no. 1 (T129), Spring 1991, pp. 194–9. Steinberg comments 'His martyrdom is starkly visible' (p. 194). In this issue of *TDR* see also Albie Sachs's 1989 talk for an African National Congress seminar, 'Preparing Ourselves for Freedom', pp. 187–93.

23. 'Dynamic Ambiguities', op. cit., note 11, p. 9.

24. 'My Hero: David Edgar on R.D. Laing', *Independent*, 3 June 1989.

25. R.D. Laing and A. Esterson, *Sanity, Madness, and the Family: Families of Schizophrenics* [first published 1964], Pelican Books, Penguin, 1970, p. 12.

26. R.D. Laing, quoted in Elizabeth Swain, *David Edgar: Playwright and Politician*, American University Studies Series 4, English Language and Literature vol. 36, New York: Peter Lang, 1986, p. 258.

27. Op. cit., note 24.

28. Interview with Susan Painter, 23 January 1992. Unless indicated otherwise, all subsequent quotations from Simon Callow are from this source.

29. Op. cit., note 24.

30. Simon Callow, *Being an Actor*, Methuen, 1984, p. 81.

31. Quoted from the interview, op. cit., note 28. See also Callow, op. cit., note 30, pp. 79–82.

32. *Second Time*, op. cit., note 2, p. 224.

33. George Orwell, 'Charles Dickens', *Collected Essays*, Mercury Books, Heinemann, 1961, p. 73.

34. Leon Rubin, *The Nicholas Nickleby Story: The Making of the Historic Royal Shakespeare Company Production*, Heinemann, 1981, p. 25.
35. Orwell, op. cit., note 33, p. 87.
36. 'A triumph of perversity', *Guardian*, 23 June 1980.
37. See Rubin, op. cit., note 34; and 'Adapting *Nickleby*', *Second Time*, op. cit., note 2, pp. 143–59, for an account of the rehearsal process.
38. See Bernard Beckerman, *Theatrical Presentation: Performer, Audience and Act*, Routledge, 1990 for appreciative discussion of *Nickleby*'s presentational techniques.
39. Lyric Theatre, Hammersmith, discussion of *Nickleby*, 26 March 1991. Not published.
40. Ros Asquith, 'A Dickens of a Play', *Time Out*, 20 June 1980.
41. 'Seeking Ourselves in the Other Place', *RSC Magazine*, no. 2, Autumn 1990, pp. 20–21.
42. Sally Beauman, 'David Edgar: Back to the Barricades', *Sunday Times*, 16 October 1983.
43. Bernard Levin, 'The Truth about Dickens in Nine Joyous Hours', *The Times*, 8 July 1980.
44. *Second Time*, op. cit., note 2, p. 19.
45. See, e.g., Colin Chambers and Mike Prior, *Playwrights' Progress: Patterns of Postwar British Drama*, Oxford: Amber Lane Press, 1987, p. 94.
46. 'Adapting *Nickleby*', *Second Time*, op. cit., note 2, p. 156.
47. Ibid., pp. 157–8.
48. Margaret Thatcher: 'There is no such thing as society. There are individual men and women, and there are families', quoted in Douglas Keay, 'Aids, Education and the Year 2,000!', *Woman's Own*, 31 October 1987, p. 10.
49. 'Adapting *Nickleby*', *Second Time*, op. cit., note 2, p. 148.
50. Introduction to *Plays: Two*, Methuen, 1990, p. xii.
51. 'Our Winter's Tale', *RSC Magazine*, no. 4, Autumn 1991, p. 23.
52. David Edgar, quoted in Michael Church, 'Altering egos for a perverted love story', *Guardian*, 15 November 1991.
53. Op.cit., note 51.
54. 'Split decision', op. cit., note 9.
55. 'First signs of the second-rate', *Guardian*, 30 July 1992.

Chapter Four

1. Introduction to *Plays: Three*, Methuen, 1991, pp. x–xi.
2. Interview with Susan Painter, 15 September 1992. Unless indicated otherwise, all subsequent quotations from David Edgar in this chapter are from this source.

3. 'Public Theatre in a Private Age', in David Edgar, *The Second Time as Farce: Reflections on the Drama of Mean Times*, Lawrence and Wishart, 1988, p. 166 and p. 172 (subsequently referred to as *Second Time*).

4. David Edgar, ' Towards a Theatre of Dynamic Ambiguities', *Theatre Quarterly*, vol. 9 no. 33, Spring 1979, p. 22 (subsequently referred to as 'Dynamic Ambiguities').

5. Francesca Simon, 'The Urge to Protest', *New Society*, 20 October 1983.

6. Gillian Hanna, *Monstrous Regiment: Four Plays and a Collective Celebration*, Nick Hern Books, 1991, p. xxix.

7. Ibid.

8. Ibid., pp. xiv–xv.

9. 'Ten Years of Political Theatre, 1968–1978', *Second Time*, op. cit., note 3, pp. 45–7.

10. Elizabeth Swain, *David Edgar: Playwright and Politician*, American University Studies Series 4, English Language and Literature vol. 36, New York: Peter Lang, 1986, p. 176.

11. Op.cit., note 9, p. 46.

12. Hanna, op. cit., note 6, p. xlix.

13. Interview with Susan Painter, 12 May 1991. Subsequent quotations from Susan Todd are from this source. Note that in 1992 Susan Todd changed her name to Lily Susan Todd; references to her in this book retain her original name to avoid confusion over publication sources.

14. David Ian Rabey, *British and Irish Political Drama in the Twentieth Century: Implicating the Audience*, Macmillan, 1986, p. 179.

15. 'Dynamic Ambiguities', op. cit., note 4, p. 20.

16. *Second Time*, op. cit., note 3, pp. 220–2.

17. Introduction to *Plays: Three*, op. cit., note 1, p. xi.

18. John Goodwin (ed), *Peter Hall's Diaries: The Story of a Dramatic Battle*, Hamish Hamilton, 1983, p. 301.

19. Sally Beauman, 'David Edgar: Back to the Barricades', *Sunday Times*, 16 October 1983.

20. Ibid.

21. Robert Cushman, 'A Matter of Tyranny', *Observer*, 23 October 1983.

22. Interview with Susan Painter, 23 July 1991. All subsequent quotations from Ron Daniels in this chapter are from this source.

23. Swain, op. cit., note 10, p. 284.

24. Interview with Robert Cushman, *Talking Theatre*, BBC Radio Four, broadcast 27 January 1988.

25. David Edgar, quoted in Simon, op. cit., note 5.

26. David Edgar, quoted in John Cunningham, 'Signals of Distress', *Guardian*, 17 October 1983.

27. 'Public Theatre in a Private Age', *Second Time*, op. cit., note 3, p. 172.

28. Raymond Williams (ed.), *May Day Manifesto 1968*, Penguin, 1968, p. 13.
29. Quoted by Edgar in the prefacing page to Act Two of the *Maydays* text: *Plays: Three*, op. cit., note 1, p. 240.
30. David Edgar, quoted in Simon, op. cit., note 5.
31. Ibid.
32. Op.cit., note 24.
33. Ibid.
34. Ibid.
35. Ibid.
36. John McGrath quoted in Tony Mitchell, 'Popular Theatre and the Changing Perspective of the Eighties', *New Theatre Quarterly*, vol. 1, no. 4, 1985, p. 395.
37. 'Festivals of the Oppressed', *Second Time*, op. cit., note 3, p. 233.
38. Op.cit., note 36.
39. See especially 'The Free or the Good', *Second Time*, op. cit., note 3, pp. 94–121.
40. 'A shortsighted view of the defectors' decades', *Guardian*, 29 October 1983.
41. For an account of the circumstances of British theatre in the late 1980s, see David Edgar, 'State of Play: new work in the contemporary British theatre', *RSA Journal*, vol. CXLI, no. 5440, June 1993, pp. 450–60. See Richard Boon, *Brenton the Playwright*, Methuen, 1991, pp. 248–52, for an account of the effects of the crisis of cuts in arts subsidy on the plays of Edgar and his contemporary political dramatists. See also the Introduction to this book.
42. Malcolm Page and Simon Trussler, *File on Edgar*, Methuen, 1991, p. 79.
43. Ibid.
44. See Geoffrey Goodman, *The Miners' Strike*, Pluto Press, 1985, pp. 200–205.

Chapter Five

1. 'The playwrights who care in the community', *Guardian*, 28 May 1992.
2. Preface (by Ann Jellicoe) to David Edgar, *Entertaining Strangers: A Play for Dorchester*, Methuen New Theatrescripts, Methuen, 1986, p. 5.
3. Ann Jellicoe, *Community Plays: How to put them on*, Methuen, 1987, p. 8.
4. Ibid., p. 122.

5. Ibid.
6. Baz Kershaw, *The Politics of Performance: Radical Theatre as Cultural Intervention*, Routledge, 1992, p. 205.
7. See 'Festivals of the Oppressed', in David Edgar, *The Second Time as Farce: Reflections on the Drama of Mean Times*, Lawrence and Wishart, 1988, p. 245 (subsequently referred to as *Second Time*).
8. Jellicoe, op. cit., note 3, p. 38.
9. Interview with Susan Painter, 25 May 1993. Unless indicated otherwise, quotations from David Edgar in this chapter are from this source.
10. Op.cit, note 1.
11. See Augusto Boal, *Theatre of the Oppressed*, trans. Charles A. and Maria-Odilia Leal McBride, Pluto Press, 1979 and Augusto Boal, *Games for Actors and Non-Actors*, trans. Adrian Jackson, Routledge, 1992, for definitions of 'spect-actor'. The best way to appreciate the term is to try out Boal's theatre games.
12. Interview with Susan Painter, 7 June 1993.
13. David Edgar, quoted in Ann Jellicoe, op. cit., note 3, p. 120.
14. Mikhail Bakhtin, *Rabelais and his World*, trans. Hélène Iswolsky [first published in English in 1968], Bloomington: Indiana UP, 1984, p. 7.
15. Graham Holderness in Graham Holderness (ed.) *The Politics of Theatre and Drama*, Macmillan, 1992, p. 11. See also in this volume Peter Reynolds, 'Community Theatre: Carnival or Camp?', pp. 84–98, with a discussion of *Entertaining Strangers* and the National Theatre on pp. 89–90.
16. Introduction, *Plays: Two*, Methuen, 1990, p. xii.
17. Margaret Thatcher, quoted in Douglas Keay, 'Aids, Education and the Year 2,000!', *Woman's Own*, 31 October 1987, p. 10.
18. Tony Harrison, *The Mysteries*, Faber, 1985. The first performance of the entire trilogy was in the Cottesloe Theatre on 19 January 1985.
19. Jellicoe, op. cit., note 3, p. 34.
20. Introduction to *Entertaining Strangers, Plays: Two*, op. cit., note 16, p. 388.
21. Ibid.
22. W.B. Yeats, 'Emotion of Multitude', *Essays and Introductions*, Macmillan, 1961, pp. 215–16.
23. 'Festivals of the Oppressed', *Second Time*, op. cit., note 7, p. 242.
24. Ibid.
25. Ibid.
26. Ibid., p. 244.
27. Interview with Susan Painter, 2 June 1992.
28. Mark Fisher and Ursula Owen (eds), *Whose Cities?*, Penguin, 1991, p. 20.
29. Ibid., p. 30.

Chapter Six

1. Timothy Garton Ash, *We the People: The Revolutions of '89: Witnessed in Warsaw, Budapest, Berlin and Prague*, Granta Books, 1990, p. 131.
2. Ibid., p. 113.
3. 'Ideology in the red', *Guardian*, 3 May 1990.
4. Martyn Clement, 'Table Talk', *Plays and Players*, November 1990, p. 7.
5. Ibid., p. 6.
6. Ibid., p. 8.
7. Lynne Truss, 'He's talking about a revolution', *Independent on Sunday*, 4 November 1990.
8. Ibid.
9. Interview with Susan Painter, 25 May 1993. Unless indicated otherwise, quotations from David Edgar in this chapter are from this source.
10. Clement, op. cit., note 4, p. 7.
11. Ibid.
12. Ibid., p. 8.
13. Ibid., p. 7.
14. Op.cit., note 2.
15. David Edgar, quoted in Steve Grant, 'Red Alert', *Time Out*, 7–14 November 1990.
16. David Edgar, 'The table turned', *Independent*, 14 December 1991.
17. Ibid.
18. David Edgar cited this comment in interview with Susan Painter, 25 May 1993.
19. David Edgar, interviewed on *Kaleidoscope*, BBC Radio Four, 2 September 1992.
20. Ibid.

Chapter Seven

1. David Edgar, 'Ripe for a dramatic revival', *Sunday Times*, 9 October 1994.
2. Northrop Frye, *Anatomy of Criticism*, Princeton, New Jersey: Princeton University Press [first published 1957], Princeton Paperback, 1971, p. 354.
3. Interview with Susan Painter, 24 November 1994. Unless indicated otherwise, all subsequent quotations from David Edgar are from this source.

4. David Edgar, interviewed on *The Late Show*, BBC2, 9 November 1994.

5. Interview with Susan Painter, 7 November 1994. All subsequent quotations from Michael Attenborough are from this source.

6. David Edgar, interviewed on *The Late Show*, op. cit., note 4.

7. David Edgar in Aleks Sierz, 'Stages of Struggle', *Red Pepper* 42, November 1994.

8. Terry Grimley, 'Metaphor for a new order', *Birmingham Post Weekend*, 8 October 1994.

9. David Edgar, interviewed on *The Late Show*, op. cit., note 4.

10. See for example Michael Billington, 'Critical theatre', *Guardian*, 28 December 1994; Michael Coveney, 'Arts review of 1994: Theatre', *Observer*, 18 December 1994; Jane Edwardes, 'The best and worst of '94: Theatre', *Time Out*, 14–21 December 1994.

11. For an interview with Edgar about the 1994 Birmingham Theatre Conference (written before the event) see Terry Grimley, 'Forget the Bard – send in the clowns', *Birmingham Post*, 21 April 1994. For an analysis of the conference see Michael Billington, 'The most significant sex change', *Guardian*, 27 April 1994.

12. See David Edgar, 'Ten Years of Political Theatre, 1968–1978', *The Second Time as Farce: Reflections on the Drama of Mean Times*, Lawrence and Wishart, 1988, p. 43 (Subsequently referred to as *Second Time*).

13. See (for example) David Edgar, 'Public Theatre in a Private Age', *Second Time*, op. cit., note 12, pp.174–5: and David Edgar, 'Ripe for a dramatic revival', *Sunday Times*, op. cit., note 1.

14. See David Edgar, 'Ten Years of Political Theatre, 1968–1978', op. cit., note 12, p. 41.

15. E.H. Carr, *What is History?* [first published by Macmillan in 1961], second edition, ed. R.W. Davies [first published by Pelican Books in 1987], Penguin, 1990, pp. 132–4.

16. Interview with Susan Painter, 2 June 1992. Oscar Lewenstein was General Manager of the Royal Court Theatre in the early 1950s, a founder member of the English Stage Company in the mid 1950s, and Artistic Director of the English Stage Company at the Royal Court from 1972 to 1975. He had worked originally with Glasgow Unity Theatre, a group committed to left politics.

Bibliography

Place of publication, unless otherwise stated, is London.

Primary Sources

i. Published plays

1. *Dick Deterred*, New York, Monthly Review Press, 1974.
2. *Two Kinds of Angel*, included in V.E. Mitchell, ed., *The London Fringe Theatre*, Burnham House, 1975.
3. *Destiny*, Methuen New Theatrescripts, 1976. Methuen Modern Plays, 1978. Included in *Plays: One*, Methuen, 1987.
4. *Wreckers*, Methuen New Theatrescripts, 1977. With an Introduction by the author and music by the 7:84 band.
5. *Ball Boys*, Pluto Press, 1978. Included in *The Best Short Plays, 1982*, Radnor, Pennsylvania, Chilton Book Company, 1982. Included in *Edgar: Shorts*, Nick Hern Books, 1989.
6. *The Jail Diary of Albie Sachs*, Rex Collings, 1978. With an Introduction. Included in *Plays: One*, Methuen, 1987.
7. *Teendreams* (with Susan Todd), Methuen New Theatrescripts, 1979. With a Note. With *Our Own People*, Methuen Modern Plays, 1988. Included in *Plays: Three*, Methuen, 1991.
8. *Mary Barnes*, Methuen Modern Plays, 1979. With an Author's Note. Included in *Plays: One*, Methuen, 1987.
9. *The Life and Adventures of Nicholas Nickleby*, Part One and Part Two, New York, Dramatists' Play Service, 1982. In two volumes with the Author's Introduction to each. Included in *Plays: Two*, Methuen, 1990.
10. *Maydays*, Methuen New Theatrescripts, 1983. Methuen Modern Plays, 1984. Included in *Plays: Three*, Methuen, 1991.
11. *Entertaining Strangers: A Play for Dorchester*, Methuen New Theatrescripts, 1985. With a Preface by Ann Jellicoe and an Author's Note.

12. *Entertaining Strangers*, new version, Methuen Modern Plays, 1988. With an Introduction. Included in *Plays: Two*, Methuen, 1990. With an Introduction and a Textual Note.
13. *O Fair Jerusalem*, included in *Plays: One*, Methuen, 1987.
14. *Saigon Rose*, included in *Plays: One*, Methuen, 1987.
15. *That Summer*, Methuen Modern Plays, 1987. Included in *Plays: Three*, Methuen, 1991.
16. *Our Own People* (with *Teendreams*), Methuen Modern Plays, 1988. Included in *Plays: Three*, Methuen, 1991.
17. *Vote for Them* (with Neil Grant), BBC Publications, 1989. With an Introduction by Neil Grant.
18. *Blood Sports*, included in *Edgar: Shorts*, Nick Hern Books, 1989.
19. *Baby Love*, included in *Edgar: Shorts*, Nick Hern Books, 1989.
20. *The National Theatre*, included in *Edgar: Shorts*, Nick Hern Books, 1989.
21. *The Midas Connection*, included in *Edgar: Shorts*, Nick Hern Books, 1989.
22. *Heartlanders* (with Stephen Bill and Anne Devlin), Nick Hern Books, 1989.
23. *Ecclesiastes*, included in *Plays: Two*, Methuen, 1990.
24. *The Shape of the Table*, Nick Hern Books, 1990.
25. *The Strange Case of Dr Jekyll and Mr Hyde*, Nick Hern Books, 1992.
26. *Pentecost*, Nick Hern Books, 1995.

Collected Plays

Plays: One (The Jail Diary of Albie Sachs, Mary Barnes, Saigon Rose, O Fair Jerusalem, Destiny), Methuen, 1987. With A Chronology of Plays and Screenplays and an Introduction by the author.
Edgar: Shorts (Blood Sports with *Ball Boys, Baby Love, The National Theatre, The Midas Connection)*, Nick Hern Books, 1989. With an Introduction by the author.
Plays: Two (Ecclesiastes, The Life and Adventures of Nicholas Nickleby Part One, *The Life and Adventures of Nicholas Nickleby* Part Two, the new version of *Entertaining Strangers)*, Methuen, 1990. With A Chronology of Plays and Screenplays, an Introduction by the author, an Introduction to *Entertaining Strangers* and a Textual Note on *Entertaining Strangers*.
Plays: Three (Our Own People, Teendreams, Maydays, That Summer), Methuen, 1991. With A Chronology of Plays and Screenplays and an Introduction by the author.

ii. Unpublished plays

Performed

1. 'A Truer Shade of Blue', 1970.
2. 'Still Life: Man in Bed', 1971.
3. 'Acid', 1971.
4. 'Bloody Rosa', 1971.
5. 'The National Interest', 1971.
6. 'Conversation in Paradise', 1971.
7. 'Tedderella', 1971.
8. 'The Rupert Show', 1972.
9. 'The End', 1972.
10. 'Excuses, Excuses', 1972.
11. 'Rent, or Caught in the Act', 1972.
12. 'State of Emergency', 1972.
13. 'England's Ireland', collaboration with Tony Bicât, Howard Brenton, Brian Clark, Francis Fuchs, David Hare and Snoo Wilson, 1972.
14. 'Road to Hanoi', a scene in 'Point 101', 1972.
15. 'Not with a Bang but a Whimper', 1972.
16. 'Death Story', 1972.
17. 'A Fart for Europe', collaboration with Howard Brenton, 1973.
18. 'Chamberlains', a section of 'Up Spaghetti Junction', 1973.
19. 'Gangsters', 1973.
20. 'The Eagle Has Landed', television play, 1973.
21. 'The Case of the Workers' Plane', 1973.
22. 'Liberated Zone', 1973.
23. 'Operation Iskra', 1973.
24. 'The Dunkirk Spirit', 1974.
25. 'The All-Singing, All-Talking Golden Oldie Rock Revival Ho Chi Minh Peace Love and Revolution Show', 1974.
26. 'Man Only Dines', 1974.
27. 'I Know What I Meant', television documentary drama, 1974.
28. 'The Owners', radio play, 1974.
29. 'Bad Buy', radio play, 1974.
30. 'Censors', television play, collaboration with Robert Muller and Hugh Whitemore, 1975.
31. 'Concorde Cabaret', shorter version of 'The Case of the Workers' Plane', 1975.
32. 'Events Following the Closure of a Motorcycle Factory', 1976.
33. 'Hero or Villain?', radio play, 1976.
34. 'The Perils of Bardfrod', collaboration with Richard Crane, 1976.
35. 'Do Something – Somebody', radio play, 1977.

36. 'Destiny', television version of stage play, 1978.
37. 'Destiny', radio version of stage play, 1979.
38. 'Saigon Rose', radio version of stage play, 1979.
39. 'The Jail Diary of Albie Sachs', radio adaptation by Madeline Sotheby of stage play, 1979.
40. 'The Jail Diary of Albie Sachs', television version of stage play, 1981.
41. 'Nicholas Nickleby', television version of stage play, 1982.
42. 'Lady Jane', film script, 1986.
43. 'Maydays', radio adaptation by Christer Brosjö of stage play, 1987.
44. 'A Movie Starring Me', radio play, 1991.
45. 'Buying a Landslide', television play, 1992.
46. 'The Shape of the Table', radio adaptation by Hilary Norrish of stage play, 1992.
47. 'That Summer', radio version of stage play, 1993.
48. 'Mary Barnes', radio version of stage play, 1995.

Unperformed scripts referred to in this book

1. 'Going Over', and 'Coming Back', television version of *Maydays*, structured in two parts, 1988.
2. 'Parallel Bars', 1991.

iii. Other Work

Short stories

'1997', *Marxism Today*, January 1984, reprinted in *The Second Time as Farce: Reflections on the Drama of Mean Times*, Lawrence and Wishart (1988).

'Novel Approaches: a Tale for New Times', *Marxism Today*, August 1989, reprinted in Martin Jacques and Stuart Hall, eds., *New Times*, Lawrence and Wishart (1989).

Collection of essays

The Second Time as Farce: Reflections on the Drama of Mean Times, Lawrence and Wishart (1988).

Political and theatre articles published in books

(Pieces reprinted in *The Second Time as Farce* are marked with an asterisk.)

'Socialist Theatre and the Bourgeois Author', in Wilfred van der Will, ed., *Workers and Writers*, Birmingham, Dept. of German, University of Birmingham (1975).

'David Edgar Comments', in James Vinson, ed., *Contemporary Dramatists*, St James's Press (1977).

*'On Drama Documentary', in Frank Pike, ed., *Ah Mischief! The Writer and Television*, Faber and Faber (1982).

*'Adapting *Nickleby*', in Robert Giddings, ed., *The Changing World of Charles Dickens*, Vision (1983).

'Bitter Harvest', in James Curran, ed., *The Future of the Left*, Cambridge, Polity Press (1984).

*'The Free or the Good', in Ruth Levitas, ed., *The Ideology of the New Right*, Cambridge, Polity Press (1985).

'From Metroland to the Medicis: The Cultural Politics of the City State', in Mark Fisher and Ursula Owen, eds., *Whose Cities?*, Penguin (1991).

Political and general articles

(Pieces reprinted in *The Second Time as Farce* are marked with an asterisk.)

'Writers' Column', *Film and Television Technician* (January 1977).

'The National Front is a Nazi Front', *Socialist Challenge* (21 July 1977).

*'Racism, Fascism and the Politics of the National Front', *Race and Class* (Autumn 1977).

'The National Front: A danger to us all', *Anti-Nazi League programme* (1978).

'Britain's National Front', *Present Tense*, New York (Spring 1978).

'Why the Front is beyond the pale', *Sunday Times* (1 October 1978).

'Reagan's Hidden Agenda: Racism and the New American Right', *Race and Class* (Winter 1981).

'Bitter Harvest', *New Socialist* (September 1983). Reprinted in James Curran, op. cit.

'Fag Ends', *New Statesman* (19 October 1984).

*'Why Live Aid Came Alive', *Marxism Today* (September 1985). Also as 'How Live Aid revived the Sixties message', *Guardian* (2 September 1985).

'The Revenger's Tragedy', *New Statesman* (21 February 1986).

*'Never Too Old', *New Socialist* (May 1986).

'It wasn't so naff in the 60s after all', *Guardian* (7 July 1986).

'Close Up: Norman Tebbit', *Marxism Today* (October 1986).

'The New Nostalgia', *Marxism Today* (March 1987).

*'The Morals Dilemma', *Marxism Today* (October 1987).

'When the Hardline is Right', *Marxism Today* (February 1988). Also as 'Hear the people sing', *Guardian* (18 January 1988).

'Trial and Error', *Time Out* (24 February–2 March 1988).

'On the Race Track', *Marxism Today* (November 1988).
'Culture Vulture', *Marxism Today* (May 1989).
'Pole position', *New Statesman* (2 June 1989).
'My Hero', *Independent Magazine* (3 June 1989).
'Farewell Clubland', *Marxism Today* (January 1990).
'A book that changed me', *Independent on Sunday* (1 April 1990).
'Are you being served?', *Marxism Today* (May 1991). Also as 'The C-
   word that puts all of us on a lower level', *Independent* (23 April 1991).
'The Final Deadline', *Marxism Today* (December 1991).
'Restoration dramas', *New Statesman and Society* (16 June 1995).
'English in Revolt', *Daily Telegraph* (15 July 1995).

Theatre and television articles

(Pieces reprinted in *The Second Time as Farce* are marked with an
asterisk; articles on specific plays are indicated in brackets).

'Something Rotten in the State of Drama', *The Month in Yorkshire*
   (February 1972).
'Against the General Will', *Plays and Players* (May 1973).
'Resident Writers', *Plays and Players* (July 1975).
'Return to Base', *New Edinburgh Review* (August 1975).
*'Political Theatre 1968–1978', *Theatre Quarterly* (Winter 1979) and
   Socialist Review (April 1978 and May 1978).
'American Culture: A cop out', *Marxism Today* (October 1980).
'Recrystallisation of the Novel', *The Times* (26 November 1980). (On
   Nickleby.)
'Putting Politics on Stage', *New Socialist* (November 1981).
'The lurking threat to radical theatre', *Guardian* (20 March 1982).
*'The Diverse Progeny of Jimmy Porter', *New Society* (6 January
   1983).
*'Adapting *Nickleby*', *The Dickensian* (Spring 1983). Reprinted in Robert
   Giddings, op. cit.
'Political Theatre', *Marxism Today* (October 1983). (On *Maydays*.)
*'Public Theatre in a Private Age', *British Theatre Institute* (Autumn 1984).
   Reprinted: *Forum Modernes Theater*, no. 1, Tubingen (1986). Edited
   version: *Times Literary Supplement* (10 September 1982); reprinted in
   Stanley Weintraub, ed., *British Dramatists since World War Two:
   Dictionary of Literary Biography*, vol. 13, Part 2, Detroit, Gale (1982).
'Why Pay's the Thing', *Guardian* (28 June 1985).
'Tooth and Claw', *City Limits* (July 1985). (On *Destiny*.)
'All aboard the A Train and join the Carnival', *Guardian* (16 November
   1985). (On *Entertaining Strangers*.)

'The New Play is the thing', *Guardian* (19 July 1986).

'Days of Excitement', *Bradford Telegraph and Argus* (27 October 1986).

'To Have and Have Not', *City Limits* (2 July 1987). (On *That Summer*.)

*'Festivals of the Oppressed', *New Formations*, no. 3 (Winter 1987); *Race and Class*, vol. 29, no. 4 (Spring 1988).

'Jingles, Jangles', *Marxism Today* (January 1988).

'Alive and Kicking', *20/20* (May 1989).

'Faction Plan', *Listener* (1 June 1989). (On *Vote for Them*.)

'Seeking Ourselves in the Other Place', *RSC Magazine*, no. 2 (Autumn 1990).

'Stage Left', *Marxism Today* (December 1990).

'Looking forward', *Independent* (8 May 1991).

'Our Winter's Tale', *RSC Magazine*, no. 4 (Autumn 1991). (On *Dr Jekyll and Mr Hyde*.)

'The table turned', *Independent* (14 December 1991). (On *The Shape of the Table*.)

'On the world stage', *Independent* (19 August 1992). (On 'Buying a Landslide'.)

'Public Theatre in a Private Age', revised version, in *Aspects of Theatre and Drama in Britain and New Zealand*, Praktikumsbüro für Lehramtsstudiengange und Lehrerfortbildung, University of Siegen (1992).

'State of Play', *RSA Journal*, vol. CXLI, no. 5440, June 1993. Edited version: 'New State of Play', *Guardian* (1 March 1993).

'Seeing isn't believing', *Sunday Times: The Culture* (22 August 1993).

'A play wot I wrote', *Guardian* (13 July 1994).

'Ripe for a dramatic revival', *Sunday Times: The Culture* (9 October 1994)

'Who'd be a playwright?', *Independent on Sunday* (27 November 1994).

Film and theatre reviews

'History without sentimentality', *Socialist Voice* (March 1977). (On Walter Bernstein: *The Front*.)

'Politics of Humours', *Times Literary Supplement* (12 September 1980). (On Nigel Williams: *Line 'em*.)

'Party Conversations', *Times Literary Supplement* (17 October 1980). (On Stephen Sewell: *Traitors*.)

Interviews

Richard Eyre, *Marxism Today* (August 1987).
Sebastian Coe, *Marxism Today* (July 1990).

Letters

'A German lesson for the nation', *Guardian* (3 June 1977). (On *Destiny*, in reply to Peter Jenkins, 1 June 1977.)
'A shortsighted view of the defectors' decades', *Guardian* (29 October 1983). (On *Maydays*, in reply to Peter Jenkins, 26 October 1983.)
'Why Clause 28 should kindly leave the stage', *Guardian* (28 January 1988).

Book reviews

(This is a list selected from the large number of book reviews Edgar has written. Pieces reprinted in *The Second Time as Farce* are marked with an asterisk. Books reviewed are indicated in brackets).

'Achtung!', *New Review*, nos 39–40 (June–July 1977). (Martin Walker: *The National Front.*)
'*Fascism as a Mass Movement*, Mihaly Vajda', *Race and Class* (Autumn 1977).
'*The British Right*, ed. N. Nugent and R. King', *Race and Class* (Summer 1978).
'Culture Corporations', *Times Literary Supplement* (28 December 1980). (Michael Pye: *Moguls.*)
'Against the Mainstream', *Times Literary Supplement* (11 November 1981). (Richard Findlater, ed.: *At the Royal Court.*)
'By the Right', *New Statesman* (20 November 1981). (Paul Wilkinson: *The New Fascists.*)
'Classic Account', *New Statesman* (16 April 1982). (Stan Taylor: *The National Front in English Politics.*)
'The Good, Bard and Ugly', *Guardian* (21 May 1982). (Sally Beauman: *The Royal Shakespeare Company.*)
'Conservative Contradictions', *New Statesman* (10 June 1983). (Stuart Hall and Martin Jacques, eds: *The Politics of Thatcherism.*)
'Griffiths the Bear', *Listener* (5 April 1984). (Mike Poole and John Wyver: *Powerplays.*)
'Privatising the NHS', *Listener* (16 August 1984). (John Vaizey: *National Health.*)
'Shadow in the Sun', *New Statesman* (9 August 1985). (Antony Sher: *Year of the King.*)
'Re-entering Earth's Atmosphere', *New Statesman* (13 August 1985). (Michael Rustin: *For a Pluralistic Socialism.*)
'Divided They Fall', *New Statesman* (4 July 1986). (Mike Davies: *Prisoners of the American Dream.*)

'Twysided', *New Statesman* (22 August 1986). (Alan Chedzoy: *William Barnes.*)

*'Let Them Eat Dirt', *New Statesman* (26 September 1986). (Auberon Waugh: *Another Voice.*)

'It's All Done With Cameras', *New Statesman* (5 February 1988). (Garry Wills: *Reagan's America: Innocents at home.*)

'The Black Arts', *New Statesman and Society* (29 July 1988). (Kwesi Owusu, ed.: *Storms of the Heart*; Kwesi Owusu and Jacob Ross: *Behind the Masquerade.*)

'A painful case of déjà vu', *Guardian* (3 February 1989). (Raymond Williams: *Resources of Hope.*)

'The British Malaise', *New Statesman and Society* (10 February 1989). (Robert Brustein: *Who Needs Theatre: Dramatic Opinions.*)

'Ideology in the red', *Guardian* (3 May 1990). (David Selbourne: *Death of the Dark Hero*; Timothy Garton Ash: *We the People*; *Observer: Tearing Down The Curtain.*)

'The hooliganism Europe needs', *Independent on Sunday* (25 November 1990). (Vaclav Havel: *Disturbing the Peace.*)

'From the guff to the griff', *Guardian* (10 January 1991). (Francis King and George Matthews, eds: *About Turn: The Communist Party and the Outbreak of the Second World War.*)

'Whirlpools in the Danube of Thought', *Guardian* (14 March 1991). (Edward Behr: *Kiss the Hand You Cannot Bite: The Rise and Fall of the Ceauşescus*; John Sweeney: *The Life and Evil Times of Nicolae Ceauşescu.*)

'Apparatchat', *Literary Review* (August 1991). (Fedor Burlatsky: *Khrushchev and the First Russian Spring.*)

'The performance of a lifetime', *Independent on Sunday* (15 September 1991). (Michael Holroyd: *The Lure of Fantasy: The Life of George Bernard Shaw*, vol. 3.)

'Odd bedfellows', *Guardian* (28 September 1993). (Franco Bianchini and Michael Parkinson, eds: *Cultural Policy and Urban Regeneration: the West European experience.*)

'Crossing the mini-bar', *Independent on Sunday* (6 November 1994). (John Kampfner: *Inside Yeltsin's Russia.*)

iv. Conferences chaired by David Edgar at Birmingham University

'Regional Accents', 20–22 April 1990. (On regional theatre.)
'State of Play', 12–14 April 1991. (On new writing.)
'From Novel to Play', 30 November 1991. (On adaptations.)
'Beyond Words', 10–12 April 1992. (On the relationship of text to performance.)

'National Stages', 2–4 April 1993. (On the connection between theatre and nationalism.)

'All Passion Spent?', 22–24 April 1994. (On the crisis of content in British theatre.)

'Facing the Music', 7–9 April 1995. (On music and theatre in contemporary Britain.)

Tape recordings are available for some sessions.

v. Tape-recorded interviews with Susan Painter

Attenborough, Michael (7 November 1994).

Billington, Michael (19 July 1994).

Callow, Simon (23 January 1992).

Daniels, Ron (23 July 1991).

Edgar, David (16 January 1992; 21 February 1992; 15 September 1992; 25 May 1993; 24 November 1994).

Kavanaugh, Rachel (director of *Saigon Rose* at the Orange Tree Theatre, Richmond, March 1993; 29 March 1993).

McDiarmid, Ian (22 July 1991).

McGrath, John (29 May 1991).

Parr, Chris (2 June 1992).

Todd, Lily Susan (12 May 1991).

vi. Unrecorded telephone interview with Susan Painter

Jellicoe, Ann (7 June 1993).

vii. BBC interviews with David Edgar referred to in this book

Cushman, Robert, *Talking Theatre*, BBC Radio Four, broadcast 27 January 1988.

Kaleidoscope, BBC Radio Four, broadcast 2 September 1992.

The Late Show, BBC 2, broadcast 9 November 1994.

viii. Published interviews with David Edgar

(Listed in chronological order indicating interviews on specific plays, where appropriate, in brackets)

Dunn, Alison, 'The drawing board stage', *Guardian* (17 July 1973).

Grimley, Terry, 'Enter Stage Right', *Birmingham Post* (28 September 1976). (On *Destiny*.)

Grant, Steve, 'Through the Fire', *Time Out* (22–29 October 1976). (On *Destiny*.)

Watts, Janet, 'Right side up', *Guardian* (11 May 1977). (On *Destiny*.)

'Exit Fascism, Stage Right', *Leveller*, no. 6 (June 1977). (On *Destiny*.)

'Towards a Theatre of Dynamic Ambiguities', *Theatre Quarterly*, vol. 9, no. 33 (Spring 1979). This twenty-page interview (with Clive Barker and Simon Trussler) is the most comprehensive to date. It is reprinted in a shorter version in Simon Trussler, ed., *New Theatre Voices of the Seventies*, Methuen (1981).

McFerran, Ann, 'The Mad Woman of the Sixties', *Time Out* (12–18 January 1979). (On *Mary Barnes*.)

Grimley, Terry, 'Dickens of an Odd Play', *Birmingham Post* (6 June 1980). (On *Nickleby*.)

Radford, Tim, 'What the Dickens is going on stage', *Guardian* (14 June 1980). (On *Nickleby*.)

Asquith, Ros, 'A Dickens of a Play', *Time Out* (20–27 June 1980). (On *Nickleby*.)

Swain, Elizabeth, 'Interview with David Edgar', in Elizabeth Swain, *David Edgar: Playwright and Politician*, American University Studies Series 4, English Language and Literature, vol. 36, New York, Peter Lang (1986). (1981 interview of eleven pages on *Nickleby*.)

Fenwick, Henry, 'An Arresting History', *Radio Times* (21–27 February 1981). (On *The Jail Diary of Albie Sachs*.)

Berson, Misha, 'The Politics of a Playwright', Berkeley, California, *Threepenny Review*, no. 7 (Fall 1981).

Loynd, Ray, 'Playwright Edgar on *Barnes*', *Los Angeles Times* (7 December 1982). (On *Mary Barnes*.)

Beauman, Sally, 'David Edgar: Back to the Barricades', *Sunday Times Magazine* (16 October 1983). (On *Maydays*.)

Cunningham, John, 'Signals of distress', *Guardian* (17 October 1983). (On *Maydays*.)

Franey, Ros, 'Wrong politics, right world', *City Limits* (14–20 October 1983). (On *Maydays*.)

Simon, Francesca, 'The Urge to Protest', *New Society* (20 October 1983). (On *Maydays*.)

'Theatre in the 80s: An Interview with David Edgar', *Hard Times*, Berlin, no. 32 (Spring 1987).

Lawson, Mark, 'Hard Times for the Left', *Independent* (8 July 1987). (On *That Summer*.)

Martin, Mick, 'Selfishness versus Compassion', *Plays International* (October 1987).

Clifford, Judy, 'Character Deeply Dug', *The Times* (14 October 1987). (On *Entertaining Strangers*.)

Lawson, Mark, 'Left Alone', *Independent Magazine* (26 November 1988).

Armstrong, Murray,'The Cairo Commons', *Weekend Guardian* (27–28 May 1989). (On *Vote for Them.*)

McFerran, Ann, 'Relative Values', *Sunday Times Magazine* (25 June 1989).

Simmons, Michael, 'Tables Turned', *Guardian* (26 October 1990). (On *The Shape of the Table.*)

Clement, Martyn, 'Table Talk', *Plays and Players* (November 1990). (On *The Shape of the Table.*)

Nightingale, Benedict, 'Destined to take notes on the times', *The Times Saturday Review* (3 November 1990). (On *The Shape of the Table.*)

Truss, Lynne, 'He's talking about a revolution', *Independent on Sunday* (4 November 1990). (On *The Shape of the Table.*)

Grant, Steve, 'Red Alert', *Time Out* (7–14 November 1990). (On *The Shape of the Table.*)

Church, Michael, 'Altering egos for a perverted love story', *Guardian* (15 November 1991). (On *Dr Jekyll and Mr Hyde.*)

Lewis, Peter, 'A case of split personality with perpetual appeal', *Sunday Times* (17 November 1991). (On *Dr Jekyll and Mr Hyde.*)

Billen, Andrew, 'Will the real Dr Jekyll please step forward?', *Observer Magazine* (24 November 1991). (On *Dr Jekyll and Mr Hyde.*)

Grimley, Terry, 'Forget the Bard – send in the clowns', *Birmingham Post* (21 April 1994). (On the 1994 Birmingham Theatre Conference.)

'Metaphor for a new order', *Birmingham Post Weekend* (8 October 1994). (On *Pentecost.*)

Hanks, Robert, 'Speaking in tongues', *Independent* (26 October 1994). (On *Pentecost.*)

Lavender, Andy, 'New pastures green', *New Statesman* (21 October 1994). (On *Pentecost.*)

McGill, Stewart, 'Tongues of Fire', *Birmingham What's On* (6 October 1994). (On *Pentecost.*)

Sierz, Aleks, 'Stages of Struggle', *Red Pepper* 42 (November 1994). (On *Pentecost.*)

Grant, Steve, 'Writer's bloc', *Time Out* (31 May–7 June 1995). (On *Pentecost.*)

Secondary sources

Anonymous, *A Great British Success Story: An invitation to the nation to invest in the arts*, Arts Council of Great Britain (1985).

Ansorge, Peter, *Disrupting the Spectacle: Five years of Experimental and Fringe Theatre in Britain*, Pitman (1975).

Ash, Timothy Garton, *We the People: The Revolutions of '89: Witnessed in Warsaw, Budapest, Berlin and Prague*, Cambridge, Granta Books (1990).

Bakhtin, Mikhail, *Rabelais and his World* [first published in English in 1968], trans. Hélène Iswolsky, Bloomington, Indiana (1984).

Balzac, Honoré de, *Oeuvres complètes*, vol. 39, eds Marcel Bouteron and Henri Longnon, Paris: Louis Conard (1938).

Oeuvres complètes, vol.1, eds Marcel Bouteron and Henri Longnon, Paris: Louis Conard (1953).

La Comédie humaine, vol. 1, ed. Pierre-Georges Castex, Bibliothèque de la Pléiade, Paris: Gallimard (1976).

Barker, Clive, 'From Fringe to Alternative Theatre', *Zeitschrift für Anglistik und Amerikanistik*, vol. 26, no. 1 (1978).

'Alternative Theatre/Political Theatre' in Graham Holderness, ed., *The Politics of Theatre and Drama*, Macmillan (1992).

Barnes, Mary and Berke, Joseph, *Mary Barnes: Two Accounts of a Journey Through Madness* [first published by MacGibbon and Kee, 1971], Penguin (1973).

Beckerman, Bernard, *Theatrical Presentation: Performer, Audience and Act*, Routledge (1990).

Bentley, Eric, *The Theatre of Commitment*, Methuen (1968).

Bigsby, C.W.E., ed., *Contemporary English Drama*, Stratford-upon-Avon Studies 19, Edward Arnold (1981).

'The Politics of Anxiety: Contemporary Socialist Theatre in England', *Modern Drama*, vol. 24, no. 4 (December 1981).

Billington, Michael, 'Events following...', review of 'Events following the Closure of a Motorcycle Factory', *Guardian* (27 February 1976).

'A triumph of perversity', review of *Nickleby*, *Guardian* (23 June 1980).

'New maps of revolution', review of *Maydays*, *Guardian* (21 October 1983).

'Maydays manifesto', *Guardian* (28 October 1983).

'Stages we must go through', review of *The Second Time as Farce*, *Guardian* (14 April 1989).

'Split decision', review of *Dr Jekyll and Mr Hyde*, *Guardian* (29 November 1991).

'Call that a masterpiece? Critics list their pet hates', *Guardian* (24 December 1991).

'Thriving on the oxygen of protest', *Guardian* (7 May 1992).

'The playwrights who care in the community', *Guardian* (28 May 1992).

'First signs of the second-rate', *Guardian* (30 July 1992).

One Night Stands: A Critic's View of British Theatre from 1971 to 1991, Nick Hern Books (1993).

'The most significant sex change', *Guardian* (27 April 1994).

'One nation under a grave', review of *Pentecost*, *Guardian* (28 October 1994).

'Critical theatre', *Guardian* (28 December 1994).

193

Boal, Augusto, *Theatre of the Oppressed*, trans. Charles A. and Maria-Odilia Leal McBride, Pluto Press (1979).

Games for Actors and Non-Actors, trans. Adrian Jackson, Routledge (1992).

Boon, Richard, *Brenton the Playwright*, Methuen (1991).

Braun, Edward, *The Theatre of Meyerhold: Revolution on the Modern Stage*, Eyre Methuen (1979).

Bradby, David; James, Louis and Sharratt, Bernard, *Performance and Politics in Popular Drama: Aspects of popular entertainment in theatre, film and television 1800–1976*, Cambridge, Cambridge University Press (1980).

Brecht, Bertolt, *Brecht on Theatre*, ed. and trans. John Willett, Methuen (1964).

Bryer, David, 'Page turner, nice earner', *Guardian* (6 February 1992).

Bull, John, *New British Political Dramatists*, Macmillan Modern Dramatists Series, Macmillan (1984).

Stage Right: Crisis and Recovery in British Contemporary Mainstream Theatre, Macmillan (1994).

Byatt, A.S., *Possession: A Romance*, Chatto and Windus (1990).

Callow, Simon, *Being an Actor*, Methuen (1984).

Carr, E.H., *What is History?* [first published by Macmillan in 1961], second edition, ed. R.W. Davies [first published by Pelican Books in 1987], Penguin (1990).

Cave, Richard Allen, *New British Drama in Performance on the London Stage, 1970–1985*, Gerrards Cross, Colin Smythe (1987).

Chambers, Colin, *Other Spaces: New Theatre and the RSC*, Methuen Theatrefile, Eyre Methuen and TQ Publications (1980).

The Story of Unity Theatre, Lawrence and Wishart (1989).

Chambers, Colin and Prior, Mike, *Playwrights' Progress: Patterns of Postwar British Drama*, Oxford, Amber Lane Press (1987).

Coult, Tony and Kershaw, Baz, *Engineers of the Imagination: The Welfare State Handbook*, Methuen (1983).

Coveney, Michael, 'Words used as weapons', review of *Pentecost*, *Observer* (30 October 1994).

'Arts review of 1994: Theatre', *Observer* (18 December 1994).

Craig, Sandy, ed., *Dreams and Deconstructions: Alternative Theatre in Britain*, Ambergate, Derbyshire, Amber Lane Press (1980).

Curran, James (ed.) *The Future of the Left*, Cambridge, Polity (1984).

Curtis, Nick, 'Political turmoil', review of *Pentecost*, *Evening Standard* (27 October 1994).

Cushman, Robert, 'A Matter of Tyranny', review of *Maydays*, *Observer* (23 October 1983).

Davies, Andrew, *Other Theatres: the development of alternative and experimental theatre in Britain*, Macmillan (1987).

Dickens, Charles, *The Life and Adventures of Nicholas Nickleby* [first published in 1839], ed. Michael Slater, Penguin (1978).

Dunn, Tony, 'The Play of Politics', *Drama*, no. 2 (1985).

Edwardes, Jane, 'The Day of the Jekyll: Jekyll and Hyde at the RSC', *Time Out* (20–27 November 1991).

'Theatre: Preview', review of *Pentecost*, *Time Out* (2–9 November 1994).

'The best and worst of '94: Theatre', *Time Out* (14–21 December 1994.

Fisher, Mark and Owen, Ursula, eds, *Whose Cities?*, Penguin (1991).

Frye, Northrop, *Anatomy of Criticism*, Princeton, New Jersey, Princeton University Press [first published in 1957], Princeton paperback (1971).

Giddings, Robert (ed.), *The Changing World of Charles Dickens*, Vision (1983).

Goodman, Geoffrey, *The Miners' Strike*, Pluto Press (1985).

Goodman, Lizbeth, *Contemporary Feminist Theatres: To Each Her Own*, Routledge (1993).

Goodwin, John, ed., *Peter Hall's Diaries: The Story of a Dramatic Battle*, Hamish Hamilton (1983).

Goorney, Howard and MacColl, Ewan, eds, *Agit-Prop to Theatre Workshop: Political Playscripts 1930–50*, Manchester, Manchester University Press (1986).

Grant, Steve and Ali, Tariq, 'Old Radicals Never Die...', *Time Out* (13–19 October 1983). (On *Maydays*.)

Grimley, Terry, 'Mystery story with unrelenting tension', review of *Pentecost*, *Birmingham Post* (28 October 1994).

Hammond, Jonathan, 'A Potted History of the Fringe', *Theatre Quarterly*, vol. 3, no. 12 (1973).

Hanna, Gillian, *Monstrous Regiment: Four Plays and a Collective Celebration*, Nick Hern Books (1991).

Hare, David, *Writing Left-Handed*, Faber and Faber (1991).

Harrison, Tony, *The Mysteries*, Faber and Faber (1985).

Hay, Malcolm, 'David Edgar: Public Playwright', *Drama*, no. 151 (1984).

Hayman, Ronald, *British Theatre Since 1955: A Reassessment*, Oxford, Oxford University Press (1979).

Hewison, Robert, *Too Much: Art and Society in the Sixties 1960–75*, Methuen (1986).

Holderness, Graham, 'Schaustück and Lehrstück: Erwin Piscator and the Politics of Theatre' in Graham Holderness, ed., *The Politics of Theatre and Drama*, Macmillan (1992).

Innes, Christopher, *Modern British Drama 1890–1990*, Cambridge, Cambridge University Press (1992).

Itzin, Catherine, *Stages in the Revolution: Political Theatre in Britain Since 1968*, Eyre Methuen (1980).

Jellicoe, Ann, *Community Plays: How to put them on*, Methuen (1987).

Jenkins, Peter, 'National Theatre', *Guardian* (1 June 1977). (On *Destiny*.)
'How to play around with the politics of fantasy', *Guardian* (26 October 1983). (On *Maydays*.)

Jessop, Bob; Bonnett, Kevin; Bromley, Simon and Ling, Tom, *Thatcherism: A Tale of Two Nations*, Cambridge, Polity Press, in association with Oxford, Basil Blackwell (1988).

Keay, Douglas, 'Aids, Education and the Year 2,000!, *Woman's Own* (31 October 1987). (Interview with Margaret Thatcher.)

Kershaw, Baz, *The Politics of Performance: Radical Theatre as Cultural Intervention*, Routledge (1992).

Kushner, Tony, *Slavs! and Other Writings*, Nick Hern Books (1995).

Laing, R.D., *The Divided Self: An Existential Study in Sanity and Madness*, Pelican Books, Penguin (1965).

Laing, R.D. and Esterson, A., *Sanity, Madness and the Family: Families of Schizophrenics* [first published in 1964], Pelican Books, Penguin (1970).

Leach, Robert, *Vsevelod Meyerhold*, Directors in Perspective Series, Cambridge, Cambridge University Press (1989).

Levin, Bernard, 'The Truth about Dickens in Nine Joyous Hours', review of *Nickleby*, *The Times* (8 July 1980).

MacLennan, Elizabeth, *The Moon Belongs to Everyone: Making Theatre with 7:84*, Methuen (1990).

McGrath, John, 'The Theory and Practice of Political Theatre', *Theatre Quarterly*, vol. 9, no. 35 (1979).
The Cheviot, the Stag and the Black, Black Oil, Eyre Methuen (1981).
A Good Night Out. Popular Theatre: Audience, Class and Form, Methuen (1981).
The Bone Won't Break: On Theatre and Hope in Hard Times, Methuen (1990).

Marwick, Arthur, *British Society Since 1945*, Penguin (1982).

Mitchell, Tony, 'Popular Theatre and the Changing Perspective of the Eighties', *New Theatre Quarterly*, vol. 1, no. 4 (1985).

Morley, Sheridan, 'Politics in Action', *The Times* (19 October 1983). (Interview with John Shrapnel: *Maydays*.)

Nightingale, Benedict, 'History below the surface', review of *Pentecost*, *The Times* (28 October 1994).

Orwell, George, *Collected Essays*, Mercury Books, Heinemann (1961).

Osment, Philip, ed., *Gay Sweatshop: Four Plays and a Company*, Methuen (1989).

Page, Malcolm and Trussler, Simon, *File on Edgar*, Methuen (1991).

Paget, Derek, '*Oh What A Lovely War* and the broken tradition of Documentary Theatre', PhD thesis, Manchester University (1988).
True Stories?: Documentary drama on radio, screen and stage, Manchester and New York, Manchester University Press (1990).

196

Peter, John, 'Politics in the picture', review of *Pentecost*, *Sunday Times* (30 October 1994).

Piscator, Erwin, *The Political Theatre* [first published in German in 1929], ed. and trans. Hugh Rorrison, Eyre Methuen (1980).

Rabey, David Ian, 'Audience Engagement and Reflexive History in the Plays of David Edgar', *Critical Quarterly*, vol. 25, no. 3 (1983).
British and Irish Political Drama in the Twentieth Century: Implicating the Audience, Macmillan (1986).

Rees, Roland, *Fringe First: Pioneers of Fringe Theatre on Record*, Oberon (1992).

Reynolds, Peter, 'Community Theatre: Carnival or Camp?' in Graham Holderness, ed., *The Politics of Theatre and Drama*, Macmillan (1992).

Ritchie, Rob, ed., *The Joint Stock Book: The Making of a Theatre Collective*, Methuen (1987).

Rubin, Leon, *The Nicholas Nickleby Story: The Making of the Historic Royal Shakespeare Company Production*, Heinemann (1981).

Rutherford, Malcolm, 'Rambling through history', review of *Pentecost*, *Financial Times* (28 October 1994).

Sachs, Albie, *The Jail Diary of Albie Sachs*, Paladin (1990).
The Soft Vengeance of a Freedom Fighter, Paladin (1991).
'Preparing Ourselves for Freedom', *TDR*, no. 1, T129 (Spring 1991).

Samuel, Raphael; MacColl, Ewan and Cosgrove, Stuart, *Theatres of the Left 1880–1935: Workers' Theatre Movements in Britain and America*, Routledge and Kegan Paul (1985).

Schaffner, Raimund, *Politik und Drama bei David Edgar*, Die Blaue Eule, Essen (1988).

Seyd, Richard, 'The Theatre of Red Ladder', *New Edinburgh Review*, no. 30 (August 1975).

Sher, Antony, *The Year of the King*, Chatto and Windus (1985).

Sked, Alan and Cook, Chris, *Post-war Britain: A Political History*, Penguin (1979).

Spencer, Charles, 'Critics' Choice: Theatre', review of *Pentecost*, *Daily Telegraph* (5 November 1994).

Steinberg, Carol, 'Albie Sachs: Our Shakespearian Fool', *TDR*, no. 1, T129 (Spring 1991).

Stevenson, Robert Louis, *The Strange Case of Dr Jekyll and Mr Hyde and other stories*, ed. Jenni Calder, Penguin (1979).

Stoppard, Tom, *Arcadia*, Faber (1993).

Swain, Elizabeth, *David Edgar: Playwright and Politician*, American University Studies Series 4, English Language and Literature, vol. 36, New York, Peter Lang (1986).

Taylor, Paul, 'A masterwork in any language', review of *Pentecost*, *Independent* (28 October 1994).

Todd, Susan, ed., *Women and Theatre: Calling the Shots*, Faber and Faber (1984).

Trussler, Simon, ed., *New Theatre Voices of the Seventies*, Eyre Methuen (1981).

Wandor, Michelene, ed. and intro., *Strike While the Iron is Hot: Three plays on sexual politics*, The Journeyman Press (1980).
Look Back in Gender: Sexuality and the Family in post-war British drama, Methuen (1987).

Wardle, Irving, 'Back to ABC in the Tower of Babel', review of *Pentecost, Independent on Sunday* (30 October 1994).

Weintraub, Stanley, 'David Edgar', *British Dramatists since World War Two: Dictionary of Literary Biography*, vol. 13, ed. Stanley Weintraub, Detroit, Gale (1982).

Williams, Raymond, ed., *May Day Manifesto 1968*, Penguin (1968).

Yeats, W.B., *Essays and Introductions*, Macmillan (1961).

Zola, Émile, *Thérèse Raquin*, trans. and intro. Leonard Tancock, Penguin (1962).

Index

200